THE CITY WE MAKE TOGETHER

Humanities and Public Life

A Collaboration with the University of Iowa
Obermann Center for Advanced Studies

Teresa Mangum and Anne Valk,
series editors

The City We Make Together

City Council Meeting's Primer for Participation

MALLORY CATLETT AND AARON LANDSMAN

UNIVERSITY OF IOWA PRESS | IOWA CITY

University of Iowa Press, Iowa City 52242
Copyright © 2022 by the University of Iowa Press
uipress.uiowa.edu

ISBN 978-1-60938-827-0 (pbk)
ISBN 978-1-60938-828-7 (ebk)

Printed in the United States of America

Design by April Leidig

Printed on acid-free paper

Cataloging-in-Publication data is on file
with the Library of Congress.

To Dwayne Calizo

"With the end of empire, we are coming to an end of the epoch of rights. We have entered the epoch of responsibilities, which requires new, more socially-minded human beings and new, more participatory and place-based concepts of citizenship and democracy."

—Grace Lee Boggs, *The Next American Revolution*

Contents

PART III: INTERMISSION

PART IV: LOCAL ENDINGS

Foreword

Teresa Mangum and Anne Valk

If Americans learned anything about politics in the past decades, it's the importance of participating in local elections and local government. National politics can blind voters to the grueling work of state legislators, county supervisors, school board members, and innumerable other elected officials. Even the smallest communities rely on civic-minded leaders to stand as mayors and city councilors. At city council and local government meetings, every community resident has an opportunity to address local officials and express the values and priorities that they believe should determine matters ranging from zoning and economic development to policing, public health, and municipal spending. That's why in recent years, when most Americans were caught in the whiplash of national politics, Mallory Catlett and Aaron Landsman visited city councils across the country. In city council meetings they found a space of engagement where neighbors had to look one another in the eye as they wrestled with decisions that would impact their communities immediately, concretely, and very visibly. In the often exhausting and predictable yet quietly dramatic performance of city council business, Aaron and Mallory found hope for American democracy.

The City We Make Together: City Council Meeting's *Primer for Participation* is a fascinating account of Mallory and Aaron's engagement with city councilors and citizens as they all worked together to understand how, when, and why democracy works. The book opens by recounting how the pair developed a wise and generous collaborative process through a series of successes and near failures. Rooted in social and philosophical theories of performance, in ethnographic observation and interviews with officials and citizens, and in the actual work of cocreation, *The City We Make Together* teaches readers about local political processes and invites us to adapt this model to our own communities. If an actual local government meeting is a civic ritual that a community creates through a shared set of rules and agreements, the "show" *City Council Meeting* puts a rigorous artistic frame around it. That frame allows audiences to perform together, converting civic ritual into participatory art. The performance offers a rare, transparent experience of the spectacle and power encompassed within the often tedious ritual performance of local government. The model also demonstrates the capacity of participatory theatre to turn civics into engaging, experiential learning-by-doing. This experiment in civic theatre has now been performed in five cities and comes with curriculum designed for both high school and college classes.

The coauthors and cocreators bring unique talents, skills, and intellectual interests to this project. Mallory Catlett is an Obie Award–winning creator, director, and dramaturg and the coartistic director of Mabou Mines in New York City. She commonly uses theoretical and nontheatrical texts to expand what the theater can contain. She continues to draw inspiration from the limitations and possibilities of working with nonperformers and to use the task-based approach developed for *City Council Meeting* in both her teaching and performance-making. Getting people to participate in embodied collective research is key to how she generates collaborative works of performance and helps students to develop their own work. Aaron Landsman is a recent Guggenheim Fellow and Princeton Arts Fellow, and currently a PATHS Social Practice Artist-in-Residence at the Abrons Arts Center. As a visiting lecturer and Whitman Fellow at Princeton University, he has collaborated with scholars from African American studies, architecture, dance, history, literature, public policy, urban studies, and the visual arts. In both his teaching and arts practice, he continues to draw inspiration from the philosophy and social theory that shaped the *City Council Meeting* project, expanding and adapting the model to engage students in multidisciplinary performative explorations. He has used *City Council Meeting*'s tools and approaches to build a course for Princeton's Freshman Seminars program and to create participatory walking tours with students in theatre and history.

Catlett and Landsman's integration of methods from arts, humanities, and social science disciplines takes readers down one possible future path for the humanities. Like many artists today, they understand their work as aesthetically, culturally, and politically inspired cross-disciplinary research. *City Council Meeting* provides a brilliant example of a multidisciplinary practice in which the humanities are deeply entwined with the arts. The authors are committed to the understanding, interpretation, and reenvisioning of democracy rooted in collective research. In their process, cocreation allows a more just, generous, and equitable performance of civic participation.

One of the joys and conundrums of the Humanities and Public Life series is that we realize with each book that some of the most exciting work in "the humanities" is wildly *un*-disciplined. *The City We Make Together* has fascinating potential for entanglement with a host of disciplines. Together, the book and the authors' accompanying videos make this an immediately teachable project. Moreover, the method has the potential to transform students' and local communities' understanding of how education across disciplines can contribute to a healthy democracy. If you are teaching acting or playwriting, *City Council Meeting* offers your students a rare opportunity to create with nonactors and to explore performance as problem-solving. Scholars of performance studies will be especially interested in the opening chapters, elegant demonstrations of how to think through theories of social performance and then move those theories into experiential exploration. The book is also rich with possibilities for sociologists. Through careful ethnographic investigation, the authors capture the constraining power of social rituals and the opportunity to intervene in those social scripts through collective performance. For similar reasons, *The City We Make Together* has much to offer communications scholars and rhetoricians. Adventurous political scientists can animate the teaching of political processes and power dynamics and of civics more broadly, especially by collaborating with colleagues from theatre. And community organizations may find inspiration and discover ways to nurture collective decision-making and reinvigorate the civic participation required for a truly representative democracy.

And if you, like us—as coeditors of the series—long for evidence that democracy is still a priority and a practice across the United States, this book will be a great shot in the arm. It will reassure you that, despite the distant, polarized, seemingly impervious, and generally maddening state of national politics, people of good will are devoting time and energy, hearts and minds to democracy in their communities. Perhaps even more importantly, this book reminds each of us that in metaphoric and quite literal and visceral ways, each of us has a role to play. We firmly believe that this book and experiments you might adapt from it in collaboration with your own students, colleagues, community partners, students, and city councils can enliven your communities and, dare we hope, add a roomful of voices to the collective call for a more just world.

Acknowledgments

This book began as an article and a copy of the script published in *Theater* 43, no. 3 (2013). Thank you to editor Tom Sellar for seeing the work live and working with us on the article and the unruly text representation of the project. Lacy Johnson introduced us to the University of Iowa Press and the Humanities and Public Life series. Rachel Karp, our assistant director extraordinaire for the theatre work, also wrangled our book proposal, to great effect. Previously published authors in this series Anne Basting and Gabrielle Bendiner-Viani helped think through what the book might do. Thank you to the attentive and rigorous editing team that has included Annie Valk, Catherine Cocks, Teresa Mangum, Meredith Stabel, and Jacob Roosa. Morgan von Prelle Pecelli gave us detailed feedback on an early draft of our manuscript, which altered our course for the best. Sherry Kramer helped Aaron shape the book as dramaturgy, with great humor, detail, and clarity. Aaron would also like to thank Gregory Snyder at Baruch College for his mentorship and friendship over the years, and for specific inspiration on how to do ethnographic interviews.

City Council Meeting became a reality—conceptually, technically, visually, and sonically—thanks to our third collaborator, production designer Jim Findlay. His collaborative brilliance is in being able to see the essence of a work from many angles, before anyone else can, even the folks making it. Jim created a broadcast-quality video rig from scratch on a limited budget that accommodated with ease each space we worked, from a school gym to a courtroom to a 3,000-seat theatre. We could not have made the work without him.

Thank you, Paul Shambroom, for your inspiring photographic series *Meetings*, for your inquiry and interest in our work, and for being a great Pete Colt at our last performance.

In each city where we presented the show, a community emerged to make it a reality. From raising resources to helping us make inroads with different people and groups to spending time with us on the meeting and local endings, the following is a city-by-city list of folks to whom we are indebted.

Houston

DiverseWorks artistic director Sixto Wagan was the first presenter to support the work and a lead partner throughout the development process. His insights, his embrace of the project's unusual nature, and his advocacy to colleagues in Houston and other cities were cornerstones of the work's success. Additional thanks to DiverseWorks staff members Rachel Cook and Jennifer Garner, who supported the project on the ground. At Project Row Houses, curator Ryan Dennis helped build artistic and community ties throughout the process and opened the doors to the Eldorado Ballroom, site of one of our most successful shows anywhere. At the Mitchell Center, Karen Farber, Bree Edwards, and Nicole Romano helped ensure we had enough time in Houston to do the work well and helped bring the work to a diverse audience. The Mitchell Center also brought in David A. Brown and supported his travel to NYC and Tempe to take most of the fantastic photos you see in this book. Thank you to our Houston staffers: Autumn Knight, Assata Richards, John Harvey, Maria Cristina Jadick, Christa Forster, Carrie Schneider, and Maurice Duhon. Often they opened up new creative avenues and community relationships and learned the piece along with us. Thank you, Helene Schlumberger, David Feil, Nancy Douthey, Nicola Parente, Michiko McMahon, and John Pluecker, for production help and critique. Councilor Stephen Costello and Cinimin Howard both gave generously of their time for interviews and performed the work with grace. Kathryn McNeil helped us gain access to Councilor Costello, who jumped in to fill the Costello role in performance one night. Thank you to pastors and choirs at Fourth Ward's Rose of Sharon Church (Dr. Elmo Johnson, Michele Stanton, choir and band) and Iglesia Rios De Aceite (Pastor Hernan Castaño, Juan Gonzalez, choir and band). Thanks to the Project Row Houses after-school program, students, and teachers.

New York

HERE Arts Center's Kristin Marting and Kim Whitener, through the HARP program, worked tirelessly to help us connect to council members, funders, schools, and the public, and rolled with our many changes throughout the process. Thanks to El Museo del Barrio staff Gonzalo Casals, Kathleena Howie-Garcia, Meghan Lally, and Valentina Velez-Rocha and to LaGuardia Performing Arts Center staff Steven Hitt and Handan Ozbilgin. CUNY's

Prelude Festival presented the first work-in-progress of the project. Thank you, Frank Hentschker and cocurator Morgan von Prelle Pecelli. Thank you, John Lutterbie and SUNY Stony Brook. American Repertory Theater's Emerging America curator, Ari Barbanell, presented our first out-of-town tryout at that festival in 2011. Our NYC Working Group of artists included Mary Q. Archias, Hunter Canning, Frank Harts, James Himelsbach, Rachel Karp, Kevin Laibson, Barbara Lee, Arny Lippin, Clarinda Mac Low, Gina Stevensen, Victoria Vazquez, Elizabeth Zimmer, Kate Scelsa, Brian Rogers, April Mathis, Sayda Trujillo, Heather MacDonald, Salette Gressett, Suli Holum, Amy Jensen, and Hank Willenbrink. Special thanks also to Lisa D'Amour for early attendance and response. Social dramaturg Gavin Kroeber helped us frame and organize our work for the students. Our high school working group jumped into conversation and creativity with us for a year and made the ending playful, chaotic, and energetic: Alannah Bilal, John Catala, Chelsea High School; Emmet Dotan, Ella Geismar, Aphrodite Megaris, Mojique Tyler, Bard High School Early College in Queens; Alfany Caba, Dashley Nunez, Matthew Rivera, Alan Saenz, Middle College High School; Alcee Benjamin, Yonie Montes, Loren Salazar, International High School. Additional student performers included Max Cabra, Diandra Durand, and Xavier Pacheco. Thank you also to the following school liaisons: Valeri Thomson, Bard College High School, Queens; Rob Mitchell, Brian Rosenbloom, Erin Woodward, Chelsea Career and Technical Education High School; Linda Siegmund, Kim Tramontozzi, Middle College High School; Judith Sloan, International High School. Councilors Brad Lander, Gale Brewer, Helen Rosenthal, Melissa Mark-Viverito, and Jimmy Van Bramer participated bravely in the local ending. Additional local ending participants included educator/writer Julie Landsman and former Panel of Education Policy (PEP) board member Patrick Sullivan. Sullivan gave generously of his time in talking with us about his experience on the PEP board. Additional contributors to our NYC local ending were the Urban Assembly School of Music and Art principal Paul Thompson and writers/dramaturgs Kenn Watt and Hank Willenbrink.

Tempe

ASU Gammage was a lead partner along the way. Colleen Jennings-Roggensack and Michael Reed did so much for the work. Staff members Melissa Vuletich and Brittany Dale organized each visit meticulously. ASU faculty member

Linda Essig engaged with the project and with students throughout the project. Thanks to ASU Gammage tech staff Boyd Branch, Jessie Cabrera, and Emily Alvarez. Elizabeth Johnson and Gregory Sale coauthored our local ending and our community engagement and got the heart of the piece from day one. Our Tempe working group of staffers included Andrew Lopez, Jeremy Gillett, Keisha Locklear, Marcelino Quiñonez, Susan Amatouri, and Elizabeth Johnson. Thank you as well to Daniel Schugurensky, Shane Mueller, and Ben Watters. City council members Corey Johnson and Onnie Shekerjian recorded our orientation video with humility and grace. Thank you to all our participants in the local endings—to Nancy Hormann for her perspective on the small businesses and to Darci Niva, whose faith-based perspective, as well as her role working for the City of Tempe, was central to our work there. And finally, thank you to Heather Hernandez, aka Smilez, for her hard work and inspiration.

San Francisco

Thanks to the Z Space team, including Lisa Steindler, David Szlasa, and James Faerron. Erika Chong Shuch was a fundamental part of our production in San Francisco, hiring our local staffers, helping us build the ending, building trust with the local Bay Area arts community, and introducing us to Dwayne Calizo. Our SF working group included Dwayne Calizo, Claudia Anderson, Rob Avila, Awele, Jennifer Chien, and Sarah Curran. Guest performers included Oliver York, Jesse Bie, Carlye Pollack, Willa Gruver, Lindsay Ferrante, Merrill Gruver, and Michael Jeung. Thank you to Stuart Smith and Dave Earl. Councilor John Avalos recorded our video and sat for more than one interview.

Keene

At Keene State College, Sharon Fantl and Shannon Mayers were our two main points of contact; they understood right away how to use our project to strengthen ties between the college, town, and local government. Thanks to the staff of the Keene Public Library and Heberton Hall. Thank you to our Keene working group: Diana Duffy, Karen Purinton, Tanner Semmelrock, Anna Masters, Joanne Rhodes, Fiona Spiegler, and Jonathan Adams. Thanks also to the Waldorf School and Brian Kanouse at Keene State for hosting workshops.

Thank you to Councilor Carl Jacobs for your honesty and to Councilors Terry Clark and Emily Hague for participating. Brian Quigley was a helpful liaison to skateboarders and had deep insights on the value of alternative culture for kids. Our ending collaborators, skaters Colin Trombley and Greg Burroughs, were insightful, generous, and willing to board inside for us. Andy Bohannon— Keene's parks, recreation, and facilities director—was also helpful in mapping the various relationships and tensions in town.

City Council Meeting was made possible with funding by the New England Foundation for the Arts' National Theater Pilot, with lead funding from the Andrew W. Mellon Foundation. The project also received support from the MAP Fund. *City Council Meeting* was a National Performance Network (NPN) Creation Fund Project co-commissioned by DiverseWorks, in partnership with HERE, Z Space, and NPN. The Creation Fund is supported by the Doris Duke Charitable Foundation, the Ford Foundation, and the National Endowment for the Arts (a federal agency). This project is made possible in part by support from the NPN Community Fund. Support for the Community Fund comes from the Doris Duke Charitable Foundation, the National Endowment for the Arts, and MetLife Foundation. We'd also like to thank the J. M. Kaplan Fund for awarding *The City We Make Together* a Furthermore grant, which generously supports part of our promotional, photography, and publicity costs.

THE CITY WE MAKE TOGETHER

Prologue

INTRODUCING MR. PETE COLT

The process of making the performance *City Council Meeting* began when playwright and actor Aaron Landsman was in Portland, Oregon, to do a site visit with a theatre for a remount of the play *Open House*. He had been making work about cities for several years—as locations of specific kinds of intimacy, anonymity, and absence, as refuges, places for misfits to commune—but had not thought much about the structures or behaviors that define them. He had made work about specific issues, often presenting them in the kinds of places where people live their lives, like homes, offices, and bars, but had not given a lot of thought to how we perform power.

One afternoon, a theatre staff member took Aaron to city hall to meet with a commissioner (the Portland term for a city council member) named Nick Fish and talk with him about supporting *Open House*. At the end of their meeting Commissioner Fish suggested Aaron stick around for the public meeting, because it was going to be what he called "a hot one." Aaron thought to himself, *City government meetings are not hot* (which is true). As if reading his mind, Commissioner Fish said, "No, this one is about zoning." *Case in point*, Aaron thought. But he went because it seemed rude not to.

When he got to the chambers, he felt the theatricality of the setup. In this civic theatre, the most important players faced the audience from their literally elevated position of power at the dais; citizens and officials, some prepared, some not, came and faced the stage to speak to the council with their backs to the audience. Everyone's images were projected live on big monitors above the council. It looked a little like something by the legendary downtown theatre ensemble The Wooster Group and its director, Elizabeth LeCompte, an early innovator in the use of live and recorded video in performance.[1] Aaron couldn't believe he hadn't noticed this connection to theatre before. And then he remembered he hadn't been to a city council meeting before.

This became an interesting margin from which to observe: most people who come to local government meetings come because they are angry and need something. Aaron was there out of a curious obligation. That margin became a site of great possibility.

Also interesting was the fact that most people there seemed to have rehearsed. The room was packed, and many of those coming to speak brought testimony written carefully on index cards or in notebooks. Aaron asked a few of them what they were doing there. Some were speaking in public for the first time in their lives and were excited or nervous. Others had a specific ordinance they were supporting or contesting. They had *intent*, there were *stakes* to what they said and did. They had worked on how to most convincingly portray their point of view and their need in the two or three minutes the meeting would allow them for testimony. Just like actors and playwrights do for a play.

Soon after these realizations settled in, the council was called to order and things quickly got boring. The commission went through a cursory consent agenda, as well as numerous citizen testimonies. Speaker after speaker read their prepared testimonies almost without inflection, and city officials gave scripted reports on infrastructure proposals, which seemed a little like foregone conclusions. Was this democracy in action, or was everyone just going through the motions? The council members and staffers clearly knew the repertoire of the meeting agenda, had practiced it, and worked together to keep the proceedings moving forward. Even if they disagreed with each other, they kept up the appearance of teamwork throughout the meeting. Without a personal stake in the city of Portland, Aaron started to wonder when it would be OK to leave.

About twenty minutes in, the secretary called the name Pete Colt. A council member greeted him.

Here comes Mr. Colt. Mr. Colt, it's always a pleasure to have you with us. Uh, you know the rules, but for the record, please state your name, and you have two minutes.

Colt was dressed in a blazer, tie, and slacks. He looked about sixty years old, white, with glasses; trustworthy but just this side of normal. Everything he wore was a different shade of brown or beige. He brought a briefcase. The beginning of his speech, with his avuncular tone and manner, was clearly practiced, though he didn't read from a script. There was something slightly unsettling in how well he played his role. It was a little like *Mr. Smith Goes to Washington* meets the-guy-on-your-block-you-wave-to-but-cross-the-street-to-avoid.

He began:

Thank you. My name is Pete Colt. Uhm. I'm happy to see you up there, Commissioner Fish. And Commissioner Salzman, I want to apologize to you. Because I had lost faith in you when you were running the parks department and you were worried about the dogs that were infesting the park on 11th and 19th, and the feces. You said something that struck a chord with me and it made me say, 'Oh my god, he really is who he says he is,' and I'm gonna go to all the people I talk to and say, 'I was wrong, Commissioner Salzman really does care about our kids,' because you're right, we care more about our puppies and ponies than we do about our kids. So thank you and I'm sorry.

Aaron's impression of Colt—neighborhood wack job meets neighborhood hero—didn't change. Colt continued:

Now, I'm here to talk to you today because I live in the Kids Zone. The Kids Zone is everything within a quarter-mile walk of the Northwest Cultural District, and that includes Con-Edison Park on the river there. The Kids Zone is a zone where infants, toddlers, and youth come to play, work, learn, entertain, and entertain and live. I'd like to invite Mr. Paulson to come and move in there. Shirley Riley here is selling her home—

He gestured to a woman sitting near him.

—and I'd like to invite him to move in. It's a huge historic home. He'd have neighbors like little Carson, three years old. The reason he wouldn't want to live in our neighborhood is this and I'm sorry to say.

Here Colt opened his briefcase, put on a rubber glove, and dumped a bag of trash on the table: heroin works, used condoms, a dirty diaper, crack vials, and other refuse.

These are from the McDonald's on 18th Street, the Episcopal Learning Center, the Catholic girls' school right across the street from the children's symphonic choir. Those of you who know me from the neighborhood know that I pick up this stuff every day. I do not clean-up the vomit on Thirsty Thursdays. Although I do draw a line at bodily fluids—

A buzzer buzzed politely (this was Portland), indicating that his allotted two minutes were up, and the secretary said, "You're about at time." Colt thanked her and kept going.

The rector at Trinity Seminary and I agree that it gets tiring to pick up used condoms.

Another buzzer. Commissioner Fish, with whom Aaron had just met and who'd told him the meeting would be "a hot one," said from behind the dais:

Mr. Colt. Your time's up, but I have a more fundamental concern. What you've just put on that table is actually just considered hazardous material. And I don't know what you put there, what drugs are involved, but we now have a public health issue.

Colt didn't miss a beat. He turned with a flourish to face the crowd.

Thank you for agreeing with me. Thank you for making my point better than I ever could. Thank you for saying exactly what it is. The question is, how are we gonna help these kids?

At this point another council member had conferred with a security officer and announced that they were going to clear the room so they could disinfect, and everyone was hustled out of the chambers for a few minutes while a bailiff sprayed Lysol. Commissioner Fish got in a final rejoinder:

We appreciate your passion, but this was not at all well thought out.[2]

In fact, Colt's actions *were* well thought out. He costumed himself to win trust, understood the structures and expectations of the venue and event, and pierced those expectations just enough to call attention to his cause in a way that woke people up (in Aaron's case almost literally) to the immediacy of what was happening in the room. That's what great performances do, and what politics does too. Both use tools like dramaturgy—the way events are arranged in time and for what purpose—as well as staging and surprise to make their points. Aaron left feeling like he'd seen the best theatre that year.

His experience led to a lot of questions: Is a government meeting a performance of democracy or a real enactment? Or are they one and the same? How is democracy a messy and idealistic proposition that citizenry never can quite live up to? Should it be entertaining or dramatic? What do any of us bring into the room when we come to a council chamber—what preconceived notions, what cultural assumptions, what privileges or oppressions? What do art and bureaucracy have in common?

These questions, sparked by the performance of Pete Colt and the commissioners of Portland, Oregon, became the foundation of *City Council Meeting,* a production instigated by Aaron and created with director Mallory Catlett and designer Jim Findlay, which was developed and performed in five U.S. cities and is becoming a curriculum for high school and college students. The

project came about through research and experimentation and through challenges and developmental input from local participants in Houston, Tempe,
New York, San Francisco, and Keene. This approach allowed us—Aaron,
Mallory, and Jim—to frame the experience of participatory democracy and
speak to the value of curiosity for its own sake. We were aided by ethnographic
research, scholarship, and philosophical texts, and a deep engagement with
communities in the cities where we worked.

"No One Is Qualified"

Pete Colt understood how democracy is supposed to work and what his role
was in that arena—any of us can assume we can take part as equals.

"No one is qualified" is a phrase from French philosopher Jacques Rancière's
interpretation of Plato's reasoning that if democracy is really a government of
equals, then no one is better suited to lead than anyone else. Plato was not sure
this was a good thing.[3] Rancière's double-edged promise excited us and gave
us confidence as we made *City Council Meeting*. It offered a generous way to
frame the piece for an audience: What if we assume that no one in this room
is better than anyone else at doing this? What if no one is more qualified than
anyone else to read theory or make art or teach or learn?

As artists, this is exciting and terrifying. If no one is qualified, then, as the
progenitor of conceptual art Joseph Beuys says, everyone is an artist.[4] If no one
is any better suited to this than anyone else, then maybe the boring, chaotic,
formal process of negotiation and deliberation at a city council meeting is
actually idealistic. Maybe we don't need special skills to be in charge. Colt saw
how to work within that structure and push against it.

Plato's reasoning and Rancière's articulation of it helped us take risks in
our process. We often worked with school-aged children in the cities where
we presented the piece. If it's true that no one is more qualified to lead than
anyone else, and if all the other forms we've tried as a society (giving priority
to race, religion, gender, money, property, or family lineage) are flawed, maybe
children belong on the power side of the table too.

"No one is qualified" continues to be threatening and utopian by turns,
especially after the 2016 election. If no one is qualified, then so is everyone.
The principle of qualification becomes exclusionary. Perhaps Donald Trump's
victory was a victory of the no-more-qualified over the qualification that the
Democratic Party put forward. Hillary Clinton was touted as, among other

things, "the most qualified presidential candidate ever."[5] Her most common line of attack—"He's not qualified to lead"[6]—is a statement that is perhaps undemocratic at its core. If he is unqualified to lead, then citizens who support him might be seen as unqualified to choose for themselves. This whiff of exclusion and elitism certainly impassioned his voters. The silver lining, if there is one, is that in his lack of qualifications, Trump inspired record numbers of citizens to run for office themselves, with the 2018 midterm elections becoming a rebuke and often bringing in idealistic newcomers to the field, with massive numbers of voters turning out behind them. By turns these newcomers evince the constructive and destructive tensions embedded in Plato's interpretation of democracy: from Alexandria Ocasio-Cortez to Marjorie Taylor Greene, post-2016 U.S. politics is by turns harrowing and inspiring, depending on whom you ask.

Clinton's supporters weren't wrong about her, and clearly a theoretical conversation should never overshadow the darker forces of racism, misogyny, voter suppression, and other forms of bigotry that also contributed mightily to Trump's win. It is also possible to frame the election as a referendum on the Obama years, a fear of a Black planet. Both of this book's authors and our collaborators would have preferred another outcome in the election.

In retrospect, though, it might have been more effective for the Clinton campaign to focus on vision and issues more than on her qualifications offering inclusion in a sort of club of the qualified. I'm with her! She's qualified! Therefore, I am too! Therefore, if you're not with her, not only is your candidate not qualified, but maybe your own ability to choose is called into question. Maybe he's not qualified to lead and maybe you're not qualified to choose.

What does that say about how one of the major parties in America has come to view its adversaries on the democratic stage? And can local governments, then, with their messiness, their accessibility, even their tedium, be a place where Plato's qualification of no qualification still flies? Aaron's experience of Pete Colt speaking truth to power indicates it's possible, as do recent radical shifts in places like Minneapolis and Oakland around policing, race, and education.

How to Use This Book

The City We Make Together traces the evolution of our performance *City Council Meeting* and follows the through-line of the show. Each chapter refers to passages from the script, which is included as an appendix. You are welcome to read straight through or pick and choose chapters and sections that are most useful to you. We hope it is of value to pull apart this complex endeavor so that each component of the process and finished work can have its own resonance.

Part I: Orientation details how we arrived at many of our framing devices and structures. Part II: Meeting goes step by step through the heart of the piece. After that, the Part III: Intermission chapters discuss some of the nuts-and-bolts concerns of the production process, from how we conducted interviews, to how we built partnerships with venues and other organizations, to how much the work cost to create and tour. Finally, Part IV: Local Endings includes interviews with participants from each city where we presented the work. We have included a local ending script from Tempe, Arizona, and the others can be found online on the book's accompanying website. We hope you'll gain a sense of how the process unfolded, how it might be useful to you if you are working on something similar, and how our show may have felt to attendees and collaborators.

As artists who research rigorously from points of curiosity, we invite you to see and use the tool of theatre as a way to frame more layered issues, including the social structures that govern us implicitly and explicitly; the possibility of changing the power dynamics within our democracy; the opportunities and challenges of using ethnographic methods in scholarship and art; and the ethics of community collaboration—from raising resources, to compensating collaborators, to the impact of our work together.

We see several specific ways this book may be of use to practitioners, teachers, and scholars alike in theatre, performances studies, social practice, ethnography, and American studies.

For practicing artists and performance studies scholars, the book can offer ways to:

- script a participatory performance so that new audience members can walk in and do it via instructions, orientation, and play;
- tightly score an improvisation based on rules that an audience can follow;
- create an ambitious process within a community that allows many kinds of people to participate on their own terms, even as venues and funders tell you it's not possible or costs too much;
- conduct participant-observer interviews with new and longtime collaborators and create performance material with them in a way that coauthors trust;
- approach design concepts in a participatory performance;
- answer funder and venue questions about your work's impact in an authentic way;
- use community organizing strategies to build informed and well-invited audiences;
- consider the limits of what art-based interventions can do, can't do, and should or shouldn't take on.

For secondary and college educators and other cultural workers, we invite you to map our process alongside students, so that they can research their own communities; see intersections between performance, theory, and politics; and learn philosophies of democratic participation. In tandem with the book's accompanying website, you can adapt our performance structure to your classroom and community. Visit local meetings near you, interview players on your town's civic stages, take on some of the readings we did, and use what you learn to populate our structure with your own material.

We are sure there are ways to take elements of this book and put them into play that we haven't thought of yet. We welcome your engagement with the book and also with the ongoing process of our curriculum and research at citycouncilmeeting.org. Thank you for reading.

How We Got Here

INFLUENCES AND TRAVELS

After Pete Colt, Aaron went to local government meetings in many cities, transcribing specific moments and looking into the forms these meetings took in an attempt to find something unifying. He often piggybacked a visit to a council meeting with a teaching gig, a family visit, or a tour for one of his performance projects or plays. In the spring of 2009, the economy had recently tanked, and Barack Obama had taken office five months earlier. The tone of the national discourse was by turns harrowing and hopeful. The world seemed to be accelerating through a series of turning points.

As he attended meetings and met officials, Aaron deployed the ethnographic approach to interviews that he had learned from a longtime friend, Baruch College sociologist Gregory Snyder. For each interview, he told subjects he'd be writing up notes after the fact and would get permission from them before anything was made public or if anything needed attribution. Aaron had used this approach on prior projects and found it useful in building artistic material as well as a rapport with collaborators, especially new ones. Without the imposition of a notebook or a recording device, and with assurances that anything said could be changed later, he was able to build trust quickly with strangers and maintain it over the long collaborations the project necessitated.

In Bismarck, North Dakota, he met Commissioner Mike Seminary, a kind and forthcoming man who wore an American flag tie, shared very few of Aaron's progressive views, and spoke in-depth about his commitment to and joy in service. In Houston, Aaron saw what became a foundational meeting for our project in which church groups arrived en masse to oppose a council member's new drainage proposal. Sometimes the most theatrical moments came in response to the most innocuous or seemingly dry issues—ficus trees downtown, parking restrictions, small proclamations of exemplary behavior.

In San Antonio, a group of poised and brilliant Black and Latinx teenagers challenged the council not to leave their neighborhood behind in the city's new development projects. In Chicago, a fistfight broke out in the gallery between two supporters of the same piece of rent regulation; next to Aaron, an older woman activist narrated the proceedings for him and commented on each alderman's character ("He'd sell his own mother upriver." "He's an honest man, but spineless.") This wonderful acid-tongued and grandmotherly voice in Aaron's ear was like the meeting speaking directly to him as a viewer. The voices of the meeting itself became a significant part of our show.

His visits to meetings around the country and the performances contained within them led Aaron back to the work of 1950s Canadian sociologist Erving Goffman and his book *The Presentation of Self in Everyday Life*. Goffman wrote about how presenting oneself in a certain way, depending on one's demographic, was sacrosanct, political, a method of procuring or confirming status.[1] He also explicitly used the language of the theatre and dramaturgy to articulate his theories.

Watching Pete Colt dump the bag of trash, something clicked for Aaron about the way Colt deployed a costume (beige, formal, unthreatening), a set of behaviors (polite and humble), and demographic assumptions (harmless older white man). By looking "normal" but behaving unexpectedly, he brought attention to his cause and implied that the issue he was addressing affected average citizens.

Goffman's research offered a framework to view a council meeting as partly a performance, much like a job interview, a date, or a family dinner. That doesn't mean these events or the participants are inauthentic; Goffman's perspective may just challenge what we think authenticity is. His idea of impression management is the notion that we all engage in individual and team behaviors, putting forward the idea of ourselves that will be most effective in order to gain or keep authority.[2] This was a great window into the behavior of a local government meeting, at which councilors who may disagree with each other about a divisive issue will also dress, speak, and act in a way that maintains their own power.

Just like actors on a stage, everyone plays a role in a council meeting, has objectives, and deploys aspects of who they are in order to have those objectives met. More and more, Aaron could see how a local government meeting was a kind of tightly structured improvised performance that revealed tensions and values within a community, a scenario many of us can recognize and participate in or feel excluded from, depending on familiar cues.

Underlying much of our research are questions about what makes us visible to each other. How do we see each other differently based on how we behave and the preconceived ideas we bring to any situation? How does our position in the room affect our own behavior and the ways we are seen? How does disrupting who we think belongs in the seat of power change what seems possible to us, based on the access we've had to that same seat? Working with Goffman's research as a starting point, we could go beyond some of his simplifications around identity and perception while using his baseline propositions to help us think about our work.

When Mallory joined the process in 2010, these critical moments of observation and inspiration had taken place at meetings across the country over the past year, and Aaron had begun compiling transcripts. He also had two presenting and co-commissioning venues lined up, so the piece had a trajectory and a mission.

Mallory was coming off a string of big collaborative cross-disciplinary performances that ranged a lot in terms of style and content, which made her and Aaron able to be active and open in rehearsal together. Both liked working in nontheatrical spaces because they felt more open to the kind of exploration the pair wanted to do. As a director and dramaturg, Mallory's approach to language expanded the implications of working with transcripts. For her, language is *time recorded*, and her work investigates how this imposed ordering creates the procedures, histories, and memories that hold us captive.

At the time, Mallory was also questioning the primacy of representation in theatre and wanted to focus instead on the foundational idea of direct communication with the audience. *City Council Meeting* was an opportunity to make a performance reliant not on belief but on communication and understand how that might influence the form the performance would take, particularly given that the text was primarily verbatim city council transcripts.

Together, Mallory and Aaron read Robert Futrell's "PERFORMATIVE GOVERNANCE: Impression Management, Teamwork, and Conflict Containment in City Commission Proceedings," in which Futrell applied Goffman's framework to one city's local government meetings for a year. We saw how the rituals of behavior, script, and structure at a meeting contribute to an appearance of participation rather than its actual fact. Futrell's work also touched on the dramaturgy of meetings, which dovetailed with Mallory's interests and experience.

In our research we were looking for points of intersection between aesthetic and political action. We were drawn to Beuys, who posited that if everyone were an artist—politicians, lawyers, doctors, civil servants—social and political institutions might be more readily transformed through creativity.[3] We began to home in on the task of reframing a local government meeting as an object for contemplation, giving ourselves and the audience an opportunity to interact with it aesthetically as a way to examine first its form and then its modes of inclusion and exclusion.

We were also drawn to another avenue of Rancière's work in an essay on art called "The Emancipated Spectator," which situated our questions about democratic participation in relation to participatory live performance. Rancière's opening proposition is to challenge the opposition between viewing and acting —the age-old binary between passive and active viewing that goes back to Plato, who felt the theatre was "a bad thing: a scene of illusion and passivity that must be abolished in favor of what it prohibits—knowledge and action."[4]

When we reflected on our past experience with participatory theatre, this presumption of passivity seemed to be our problem. We didn't find viewing a performance—or, for that matter, seeing or hearing any kind of art—to be passive. Work that tried to "activate" us, where the artists tried to overcome the distance the artists themselves had created between their activity onstage and our "passivity," made us resentful. To us, the initial assumption (*You, viewer, are passive!*) instigates a physical and emotional manipulation (*Do this now! Feel this now!*). If we are not choosing to do something but instead responding to an artist's command, what is that activating? And isn't self-reflection, or engagement with a work of art, an active pursuit? Is it not active enough that we got ourselves to the venue, sat with the material, and made it mean something to us?

We looked back at our own experiences as viewers and found that much of the work that changed our own lives was what too often gets called passive. And the work that gets called immersive, interactive, or participatory tended to make us feel less connected to what was happening onstage because we weren't given room to engage with it on our own terms.

Rancière spoke to our experience and inclinations. The spectator "observes, selects, compares, interprets. She links what she sees to a host of other things that she has seen on other stages, in other kinds of places. . . . She participates in the performance by refashioning it in her own way."[5] Rancière helped us see that theatre was a lens through which to view the many modes of participation we encourage and facilitate.

City Council Meeting would let us make that lens more visible if our choices were not motivated by making the audience "more active." Especially when we worked with activists and politicians whose whole lives were deeply politically active and engaged, an assumption that anyone in the room with us was not active enough would have been a problem. Our working proposition became that we were all in this together—democracy and theatre-making alike.

Rancière also questions the theatre's use of interactivity as a strategy for creating community. Making people sit or sing together, stand in line, or fill out a survey does not create a collective body. He points to a different source of power: "What our performances—be they teaching or playing, speaking, writing, making art or looking at it—verify is not our participation in a power embodied in the community. It is the capacity of anonymous people, the capacity that makes everyone equal to everyone else. This capacity is exercised through irreducible distances; it is exercised by an unpredictable interplay of associations and dissociations."[6]

This interrelationship between anonymity and equality that Rancière articulates seemed to support Aaron's ongoing interest in the way public spaces define behavior and inclusion. As streetscapes and stores become homogenized in many locales, the misfit spaces tend to be public—parks, libraries, and council chambers. These are places where citizens can command time, space, and knowledge, even if just for a moment, without needing to command capital or conferred power of their own. At a council meeting, one has a direct line to people who seem to hold the strings, and all of us can honor the need for those voices to have an outlet. At the same time, these spaces are also governed by behavioral requirements that create a tension between freedom and restriction. You can come to the library, but you can't fall asleep or use the bathroom. You can testify at the council meeting, but only for two or three minutes, after you've waited your turn, and you have to abide by the norms or you'll be removed. Pete Colt was a misfit in the city and the government meeting gave him a space in which to use his marginal personality in the service of public good. But it also got the meeting shut down.

Colt made theatre out of a council meeting. Could we do that too?

For Mallory, Colt's deployment of procedural rhetoric, which often *prevents* action and inclusion, to shut down the meeting was a fascinating lesson in subversion and transgression. He had mastered the form and marshalled the language to effectively communicate the situation in his neighborhood.

For both of us, the theatre and politics offered an opportunity that coalesced in that moment and informed our whole project. It was an opportunity for citizens to be more eloquently themselves. We hope we've been able to do that too.

In some essential way, *City Council Meeting* is about replicating for an audience the pure experience of the Portland City Council meeting Aaron saw in 2009 by placing them inside of it. It works (when it does) by positing a local government meeting as a ready-made work of live performance.

What Is a City Council Meeting?

A city government meeting is where elected officials—alternately called councilors, commissioners, aldermen, or supervisors—interact with the elected mayor, the appointed city manager, and other civil servants to address issues brought up by citizens or initiated by the officials themselves. In nearly every city, in nearly every meeting, there is a dramaturgy, an order of events, that remains relatively consistent. Here, we've divided that order into acts, like you do with a play:

Act 1: Opening proclamations and citations—this is where the city gives awards to local heroes who have done or given something remarkable. The goal of this act is to show everyone assembled something positive about the city and its power structure and make the assembled citizenry or audience feel good about where they live. This act can imply that where we are is a good and orderly place, regardless of the tensions that may come up later.

Act 2: Often called the consent agenda, this part consists primarily of a procedural roll call on previously discussed agenda items. Though testimony from the public may be allowed, this act is generally a ritual, a formality.

Act 3: Often called the public hearing, this act includes discussions of agenda items on the table for future votes. This part can get heated between council members, and they will often bring citizens or voter groups in to speak on behalf of or against particular bills or ordinances. It's open conversation, but everyone has had a chance to prepare.

Act 4: Open agenda and citizen testimonies are combined here because their order alternates depending on the city. This is where citizens or officials can introduce new legislation or concerns; it's where things get really interesting, ranging from organized blocks of voters showing up in force to speak

Bismarck City Administration

June 17, 2010

Board of City Commissioners
Bismarck, ND

Dear Commissioners:

The Board of City Commissioners is scheduled to meet in regular session on June 22, 2010 at 5:15 PM in the Tom Baker Meeting Room, City County Office Building, 221 North 5th Street, Bismarck, North Dakota.

Invocation will be presented by a Chaplain from the Bismarck Police Department.

Future City Commission meetings are scheduled as follows:

July 13 & 27, 2010   August 10 & 24, 2010   September 14 & 28, 2010

MEETING OF THE BOARD OF CITY COMMISSIONERS

1.   Consider approval of minutes of the meeting on June 8, 2010.

2.   Canvass returns of the Bismarck Municipal Election held on June 8, 2010. (See attached information)

3.   Adjourn.

** OATH OF OFFICE ADMINISTERED BY CITY ATTORNEY TO COMMISSIONERS **

CALL MEETING OF THE BOARD OF CITY COMMISSIONERS TO ORDER

1.   Consider discussion of Commissioner portfolios

2.   Appoint Vice-Chair of City Commission

3.   CONSENT AGENDA

   A. Consider approval of expenditures

   B. Consider personnel actions. (See attached information)

   C. Consider application for tax abatement for (See attached information):
      • 2900 Ontario Lane #9 – Senior Citizen Homestead Credit – 2009
      • 2121 N Washington St #12 – Senior Citizen Homestead Credit - 2009

   D. Consider application for exemption of improvements and/or to commercial and residential properties. (See attached information)

Page 1 of the agenda from the Bismarck City Council meeting.
Photo by David A. Brown Photography / Houston, Texas.

about a particular issue to people concerned with space aliens having invaded their teeth.

In an actual meeting, the time frame for each of these acts can vary wildly, from zero minutes for act 4 (if no one shows up to speak, as at a meeting Aaron attended in Champaign, Illinois) to five hours or more (if everyone does, as we witnessed in Oakland, California, after Occupy Oakland had taken over one of the ports there). Cities may change up the order of events for specific reasons, but this basic framework holds true much of the time.

This structure serves several purposes. First, starting with the awards and proclamations section is a way to make citizens feel great about their city and their elected officials. Act 2, the consent agenda, is often full of bureaucratic codes ("Item 578.23B on your agenda, related to water and sewer pipelines"[1]) and can send people running for the hills, confuse them, or make it seem like everything has already been decided. This serves to thin the herd of citizens giving testimony. Making act 2 sort of impenetrable can help keep acts 3–4 from getting out of hand; cities can provide the semblance of access while taking the edge off the real thing.

Different factors offer different kinds of political agency for people in and outside of government, and these structures vary wildly, especially in large cities. In the smaller cities we visited—those with populations under a hundred thousand, like Champaign, Illinois, and Bismarck, North Dakota—you'll find more ready access to council members (even though, for instance, the former has council members and the latter supervisors). As Bismarck Supervisor Mike Seminary told Aaron, "They see me in line at the grocery store, or maybe we went to high school together. And because of that, I know—and they know—I have to respond to them."[2] Simply on the basis of population, cities like these might have a council member for every ten to twenty thousand citizens, while in Houston or Chicago the ratio might be triple that, or more.

In some cities the council has a lot of power, and in others very little. When the mayor has a lot of agency over the council, this is called a *strong mayor* system; when the council has more power, it's often referred to as a *weak mayor* system, in which the mayor is more of a city manager, an administrator more than a visionary.[3]

A seat on a council can be a point of visibility, a stepping-stone to higher office within the city or state, or a satisfying pursuit on its own for a citizen activist. New York City's council has little decision-making power but is a strong voice for constituents, while Minneapolis and Houston's councils are quite powerful on their own.[4] These different configurations of power can lead to real policy consequences. In 2020 in Minneapolis, the more progressive council had enough power to go over centrist Mayor Jacob Frey's head and voted to defund the police department.[5] Even though they were not able to follow through legislatively, they have prompted policy changes around how that city deals with and funds law enforcement. By contrast, New York City was not able to cut even 10 percent of the NYPD budget that same year, despite significant support on the council and popularly, since Mayor Bill de Blasio would not get behind that shift.[6]

Everyone we met who worked for the cities we visited expressed pride at their efforts to create more community buy-in to the process. Even if some of these efforts were misguided at best, a constant in local government that is conspicuously absent from the national stage is the desire for more people to have more of a voice. Even in a city as active and engaged as New York, a council district can be won by a tiny margin and turnout is often below 20 percent in local elections.[7]

Other, more affective things remained constant from city to city too. While it can surely be as corrupt, confusing, and exclusive as state- and national-level politics, at the local government level there was more room to hear from more kinds of people, and for points of view from the extreme to the sublime. This felt hopeful, a more responsive and accessible site of engagement.

When we found ourselves stuck in our creative process, we referred back to the way actual government meetings were structured, and to the ways Pete Colt re-authored that structure in Portland. This often led us to the next right decision. Early in development, we used actual council agendas to put our own excerpts into a cohesive order. Later, as we built out our staffer roles for the performance, we looked closely at their function within a government meeting and found they were great at calming tensions, asserting subtle power dynamics, and keeping things moving, all of which were strategies we deployed in our piece.

The script of our meeting basically followed the aforementioned structure and integrated text and other material from Bismarck, San Antonio, Houston, Tempe, Oakland, and Portland. In the following chapters, we go deeper into all three sections of *City Council Meeting* and into the research, readings, and experiences that informed our decisions around form and content. Which readings influenced us as we made specific parts of our piece? Why did we open with an orientation video? How did the meeting itself become not only a vessel within which we included audience members, but also a kind of character who spoke from the margins? How did each local ending differ; what worked and what didn't?

These chapters follow the outline of our script, with what we hope are exciting digressions that tease out some of the reasoning behind our decisions. There are also quotes from the script that act as signposts. They are meant to help you think about ways to approach your own community-engaged art-making, organizing, research, and scholarship. The act structure can also serve as a reference for those interested in the ways we use performance as a strategy to hold or upend power dynamics in many structures in our lives.

The Show

One of the first big decisions we made was that the audience should perform *City Council Meeting*. If the piece was first and foremost about civic participation, we wanted the form to lead us to a better understanding of why we do and do not participate.

A big part of our inquiry became what else time and language can do beyond telling stories through characters. Before *City Council Meeting*, neither of us had worked with bureaucratic language or taken apart social and political structures, but there seemed to be a pathway in these dense and loaded speeches and procedures.

We came up with three questions that guided us while making *City Council Meeting*:

- How could an audience run a performance together with no preparation?
- How could civic procedures—which we normally associate with boredom and anomie—draw our attention to the web of dramatic and interdependent relations and power dynamics?
- How could we make a piece of participatory theatre that we would enjoy, avoiding all of our experiences with that form in the past in which we were often asked to join the make-believe acts of a group of well-rehearsed actors without any of their preparation?

These questions helped us think about form, content, and context at the same time: If our show is about participation and democracy, how can the invitation into the space, the kinds of people who shepherd you through it, and the way the script is printed throw those issues into starker, more complex relief while still being legible to you if you just walked in off the street?

Once we put these questions at the center of our process, we were able to build the piece around them.

The Orientation: a four-minute video that asks audience members to make a choice about how to participate in the performance—as councilors, who act as council members and speak most of the text; as speakers, who get a piece of testimony; as supporters, who don't speak but receive instructions and take actions; or as bystanders, who simply watch as they would any performance.

The Meeting: a seventy-five-minute production, enacted by the audience with a group of trained staffers, both artists and nonartists. Comprised of local government meeting transcript excerpts edited together with some of Aaron's original writing, this section looks and feels a little like a poetic riff on a real local government meeting and follows the structure of most government meetings we saw.

The Local Ending: a fifteen-to-twenty-five-minute original performance created with and enacted by community members in each city where we presented the work. We often tried to get adversaries around a particular issue to cooperate on making this local ending with us.

By cutting and splicing together bits and pieces of meetings in several cities, our theatre work created an amalgam of the many places we visited—an archetypal local government meeting, or a city we made each night by performing it. We did this by figuring out what affects, situations, and structures might be common to most U.S. cities, even as language and form changed from place to place.

What We Made

What the three of us made was full of contradictions: a work derived in part from theory that spoke accessibly to artists and nonartists alike; a community-engaged performance that was simultaneously about boredom and empowerment; a rules-driven work that assumed we're all already capable of understanding and participating equally in our civic life.

Our agenda when we began was to create the show by following a thread of interest and the questions that arose from Pete Colt's appearance in Portland. Before Aaron attended that meeting, neither Mallory, Jim, nor he had been to one. Our associations with them had been those of most people: tedium, confusion, discomfort, an unseemly desperation, maybe even a kind of obsolescence. You only go if you want access to power, to get something done.

Maybe our lack of experience helped us clearly view local meetings as fodder for art more readily than if we'd been familiar going in. We were not qualified over anyone else to know what we were seeing. We were observing from the periphery and sometimes that allowed us to see things in a new way.

As we developed the project, we saw meetings in a dozen cities and talked to council members, mayors, city workers, and other citizens. We tried things that did not work, happened onto successful strategies, and did a lot of listening, arguing, and recalibrating.

We did not go in wanting to change people. We didn't have a message we wanted to spread about civic participation. The fact that our project ended up sometimes doing those things speaks to our combination of listening skills, stubbornness, and luck.

PART I

Orientation

The Orientation Video

We presented *City Council Meeting* in a range of spaces—from a working courtroom to a gallery, from a historic ballroom to a school gym, from a theatre to a former Masonic Hall—but the first thing the audience experiences is the same in each.

Once seated, they see an orientation video—often filmed with their local council members, students, or activists—that tells them about the choice they are going to make. The orientation video also sets the tone: playful, informational, and clear. A little bureaucratic and authoritative, like something you might see when you watch an orientation for jury duty in a big city. A little bit tongue in cheek. Kind of like the piece that follows.

The video begins:

In the Book of Laws, *the Greek philosopher Plato lists seven qualifications required for governing and for being ruled. The first four are based on what he calls "a natural difference"—the difference of birth. Parents over children, the old over the young, nobles over serfs, and masters over slaves. The fifth, Plato calls "the principle of principles," or the power of those with a superior nature, the strong over the weak.*

But for Plato, the only one really worth discussing is the sixth one: the power of "those who know over those who do not." So you have four categories based on hard facts: I was born before you, I was born richer than you, I own your land, I own you.

But these aren't as good as the two more theoretical pairs: natural superiority and the rule of science. I'm better than you, or I know more than you.

Boom. You'd think that was enough. But here's the thing: Plato lists a seventh category. It's something he refers to as "the drawing of lots" or "the qualification of no qualification." This is a form of government only a god could save: democracy.

So welcome to City Council Meeting, *where no one is qualified to be in charge. Or everyone is. God help us.*[1]

Part of the video was filmed locally in each city, with council members or activists. The remaining material was pre-recorded and included the essential choice each viewer could make.

You can be a councilor. Councilors sit at the council table and conduct the meeting. We have room for six councilors.

You can be a speaker. Speakers receive a piece of testimony that was given by someone at an actual city council meeting somewhere in the U.S. in the past three years. Speakers sit at the testimony table and speak directly to the councilors. If you want to be a speaker, we'll need your name, so we can call you up to give your testimony.

You can be a supporter. Supporters don't have to speak, but get simple instructions like stand up, applaud, answer your phone, or get up and leave the room for a few minutes, the kinds of activities that take place at any local government meeting.

You can be a bystander. Bystanders are people who just want to observe. If you're a bystander, we'll need you to exit the room until the meeting begins.

These are all roles that exist in any real city government meeting. They are all vital, including the bystander. Instead of starting with a presumption about who the audience is, *City Council Meeting* starts with a choice.

You can be as involved as you'd like.

The audience was asked how they wanted to be a part of the experience. We tried to put them at ease, focusing on clear communication with the audience through task- and text-based instructions rather than theatrical pressure to represent character and situation.

Given the political nature of the material, we were wary of the impulse we felt in other participatory pieces toward some kind of consensus, because that often slipped quickly into a need for everyone to buy into a particular ideology or story. That tendency left unchecked in a performance titled *City Council Meeting*, supposedly about democratic participation, could have been a big deterrent to viewers.

Although our intention was to disarm and to make material like Plato approachable, even as we poked fun at some foundational assumptions about the ways democracy operates in the U.S., our unorthodox approach was confusing for some people. Throughout the process, we were asked to instrumentalize the piece toward certain ends: community engagement, political awareness,

Frame from the orientation video showing the third choice of supporter.
Photo by Jim Findlay Photography / Houston, Texas.

education. We love all those things. We are pleased that people want to extract useful parts from this work of refraction and make it helpful.

But the tricky, potentially subversive, and hopefully enlightening thing about this piece of art is that, for us, it prioritizes revelation and reflection over achieving an end. We think the stories around the process of the piece, the anecdotes gleaned from informal conversations with mayors, staffers, and councilors, can sometimes be the most useful in helping people see that democracy, at its best, is really a governing of equals, of peers. We want both the way we got here and the show itself to raise questions more than answer them.

This was not always easy to understand or believe. At every turn, people wanted to know what our agenda was and what we wanted them to get out of it, what they could take home and repeat to someone. They wanted to know the value, using a definition of value they understood already but that might not apply to art, or at least not to *this* art. Perhaps in the context of fields like sociology or American studies our open-endedness can serve as an invitation for curiosity to guide research.

We were determined to let other people create the work's agenda. The viewer has to make it mean something; they have to coauthor the piece with us by being inside it, and then think about it, and then decide for themselves. When we call the piece "the city we make together by performing it," we mean it could not exist without the viewer, even the most seemingly passive one. Audience reflection makes the performance.

Our most satisfying feedback came from viewers who told us they talked about the production for hours afterward. In every city, individual viewers told us and our presenting partners that they could not stop talking about the piece. When we held formal postshow conversations, they were often exciting because they showed the many ways people responded to the piece. Following our final performances in Keene, Professor Brian Kanouse wrote, "the larger community was given the opportunity to engage questions about how Keene deals with its own public sphere, in addition to asking the questions of who gets to participate, be recognized, and able to effect change within this community."[2]

We were not driven to make our audiences more politically active. From our perspective, there was no passivity to overcome. People showed up. Their presence was proof enough of their activation. This simple perspective is how we overcame some of the problematic associations of three artists, specifically white artists, making community-engaged participatory performance in cities where we didn't live, often with collaborators and communities of color. We didn't arrive with assumptions about what our audience might lack.

When we got beyond a perceived opposition between active and passive viewers, our audience became a lot less monolithic. In fact, we stopped thinking of having one audience and realized that we were making a work with multiple publics, each with its own responses to the piece and to each other. In the four choices for how to participate in our show, as laid out in the orientation video, we created roles for several kinds of viewers. Or rather, we created a piece with four different audiences at once.

It is very hard to know how a work will affect a person. We wanted to show our audiences that what they choose has consequences; what they do with that choice is up to them. We all make choices that are political and have consequences all the time. If we can illuminate that, we've done our work.

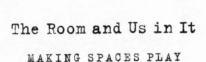

The Room and Us in It

MAKING SPACES PLAY

Right now, if you look around you, you'll see you're part of a group that has never done this before.

In our production, there is a "stage" with tables where the council members sit and an audience area where the speakers, supporters, and bystanders sit—like in any council meeting. Two large TV monitors face the audience area but are not viewable by the council members.

Spatially, each person is positioned as both a spectator and actor. For the speakers and supporters, the show is the council table and the TV monitors. For the councilors, the show is the audience: speakers, supporters, bystanders, cameras, and camera operators. For bystanders, the entire space is the stage and everyone else the actors. While our work differs significantly from that of Augusto Boal's Theatre of the Oppressed, his term *spect-actor*,[1] meaning "an audience member who is invited onstage to take part in the drama," works nicely.

We resisted any impulse toward spectacle in our design. Even though the technical setup of the show was considerable—five video cameras, two of them operated live by camera people, with TV-style video mixing and processing—there was nothing slick about the presentation. On purpose, most of the set could be put together with materials that most libraries, schools, church basements, or community centers already have—tables, chairs, lectern, and so on. We performed in many different spaces and always used what was already in the rooms where we worked. This helped reinforce the accessibility and inclusivity we wanted to convey, keep touring costs low, and highlight the way simple spatial gestures can create heightened power relationships. It also

Full table setup of *City Council Meeting* in the gymnatorium of
Chelsea Career and Technical Education High School, New York City.
Photo by David A. Brown Photography / Houston, Texas.

meant we could easily replicate the feel of the show in classrooms and school
auditoriums, where we often presented the work for school groups.

Making the Choice: The In-person Orientation

After the orientation video, our next ten minutes introduced viewers to staffers and gave each group specific information and rules to guide them through
the rest of the piece. First, the lead staffer, known as the city secretary, asked
bystanders to leave the room. She then asked for six volunteers to be councilors
and sent them toward the council table. Finally, another staffer gave out testimonies to viewers who wanted to be speakers and instruction cards to those
who wanted to be supporters.

Councilors were assigned a personal staffer, who gave them one-on-one
instructions.

Speakers gave their names to another staffer, who assigned them a piece of
testimony they might be called upon to give.

Supporters remained more anonymous. They were not required to talk to anyone. They just picked up an instruction card and returned to their seats.

Speaker and supporter orientations were short. Much of their ten minutes was spent watching the councilors being oriented, so they saw there was information that they were not privy to, which created its own kind of dramatic tension: *What do they know that I don't?*

Bystanders were asked to leave the room; they were not privy to any of the preparation. Their ten minutes were spent in the lobby, where they got a program. When they reentered the space, they knew by name the writer, director, and designer of the work; they were to have an experience akin to a traditional audience watching a play.

These differing orientations reinforced the choices participants in the audience had made so that they could reflect on them during the event. When it was all over, we wanted people to ask themselves what it meant that they had decided to move toward a power position, or away from one. How did their choices, or other people's choices, reflect any sense of entitlement or empowerment they may have come in with?

The in-person orientation created a sense of ordered chaos that helped us dramaturgically. There were choices to be made, lines to wait in, sign-up sheets to sign, and instructions and papers to receive. This sense of hubbub gave a clear indication that a level of looseness was OK, and it helped subsequent sections of the piece seem more ordered.

It also allowed us to run a meeting every night without the audience needing any special preparation. The idea was always to make everyone feel they could do this—a subtle, imaginative act we hoped would allow people to see their own civic life more creatively.

Finally, dividing and orienting the audience according to their own choices helped accommodate multiple modes of behavior and expectation in the space. Normally, theatre audiences are asked to conform to a certain standard, and this serves to unify perceived or actual differences among viewers. Everybody sits quietly, applauds at the end but doesn't make too much noise during the show, gets programs and reads them, follows the same rules.

But these rules are culture and period specific; they honor one set of behaviors. It's like if you're used to going to a Baptist church on Sunday, but someone takes you to an Orthodox synagogue: even if you have a good time and experience an epiphany or two, you might feel weird about yourself, like everyone knows the right way to behave except you. This cultural rift has sharp political implications, as MacArthur-winning playwright Dominique Morisseau elucidates in a description in *American Theatre* of an interaction with a white patron at a play. Her imperative for the field is "to say that, just like in church, you are welcome to come as you are in the theatre. Hoot and holler or sit quietly in reverence. Worship and engage however you do."[2]

At *City Council Meeting* we allowed many kinds of behaviors, with the traditional role of quiet audience member watching a show, which we called bystanders, being just one. Maybe if participants saw their own expectations about what theatre is as being within a range of possibilities, we could show them other differences and assumptions in a generous way too.

We designed the audience's ability to choose a role within the structure of our orientation in such a way as to create a shared agency among people who had chosen different paths, to establish Rancière's "irreducible distances" as well as mutual dependencies that put the real provocation of equality and democracy at the fore.

Meet the Staff

Our staffers were a local cohort of citizens whom we trained to guide the audience through the meeting. They functioned similarly to a staff in an actual city government, passing information to councilors, wrangling people for testimonies, and keeping the proceedings moving forward. The in-person orientation was when they got their time in the spotlight.

We developed the role of staffer by observing actual government meetings. In real city councils, we saw council members trying to keep up with a number of issues and procedures, including citizens coming to speak about particular issues or out of particular needs. All of them needed guidance. Staffers were the glue that held the meetings together. We were struck by how much agency they had to shape the feel and outcomes of local government.

We tried to make a sort of ideal amateur staff in each city. Most staffers were not trained actors. They were people who had an interest in the issues the project raised and who liked helping people figure something out. In the early development of the piece, we found that actors' natural and rightful need or training to be seen went against the actual role of support staff in real government meetings. These real staffers, whose job was often to help politicians stay (or seem) informed on issues, were great at being invisible.

In fact, a *City Council Meeting* staffer who was less skilled as a performer could often make audience participants feel more able to take on the challenge of being a councilor or speaker in our show. The unspoken communication that took place from staffer to councilor was, essentially, "If I can do this, you can too."

This runs counter to the way audience participation often works in theatre, where a trained performer, with weeks of rehearsal behind her, asks an audience member to "join" her in some way. For us, working with a Platonic notion

Staffers Susan Amatouri (*left*) and Jeremy Gillett (*right*) orient participants
at the start of the meeting on the ASU Gammage stage in Tempe, Arizona.
Photo by David A. Brown Photography / Houston, Texas.

of democracy—a ruling of equals, based on choice-making rather than innate
or given abilities and gifts—it was more important that audience members
recognized themselves in the staffers than see a player with specific expertise.
So our staff in each city usually consisted of people from diverse backgrounds
in terms of culture, age, gender, profession, and aesthetic.

FIND COUNCIL MEMBER NAMED SMITH.

INTRODUCE YOURSELF. GET HIS/HER NAME.

Thank you for agreeing to be a commissioner today.

We also found that staffers not from a theatre background had better questions as we developed the piece. They often got us out of our theatre-specific
speech habits when creating instructions for audience members to follow.

When we started developing *City Council Meeting*, we worked with a
smaller team of four staffers. Two would shepherd people into groups and
give them basic instructions in person, while the other two stood behind the
council table during the meeting in case something went wrong. Those four
were in charge of the whole orientation at first; there was no video yet. This
meant the orientation lasted a while and was often chaotic, and our work-in-
progress showings often got off to a late start. Because of the small number of
staffers on board, we also gave councilors the whole script; many would try

to read ahead rather than simply read the transcript in front of them, listen, and connect. After a particularly wonky work-in-progress showing at A.R.T.'s Emerging America festival, we decided to change things up.

Following that showing, in which the audience members who chose to be councilors took a lot of liberties with the script and amped up their performances, Jim offered a provocation: Could we get rid of the script entirely? He felt like we were giving the councilors too much to work with, and it was setting up the wrong expectation that the piece was more traditionally theatrical than we wanted. Wouldn't this preclude audience participation altogether? After a lot of back and forth, we began to get excited about all the different ways we could solve this problem and how the decision of when and how much information we gave the audience could influence their performance. The script could exist as spoken or written instructions, on note cards, or attached to the props and official documents.

Going forward, we added staffers so that each councilor was assigned one, and we gave councilors their scripts scene-by-scene instead of all at once. Having more staffers specifically assigned to individuals put the councilors at ease. When we gave them more support, we were allowing them to be present with the full range of possibility and action in the room. They were listening better, the goal of any good actor.

Giving the councilors less to go on but more help from staff made it clearer to the rest of the audience that what they were seeing was people like them engaged in the act of reading, trying to make sense of this official language for the first time. Watching them grapple with the text and listen to each other was more interesting than passing judgment on how good a performer each of them was. It gave a sense of a real local government meeting as a structured improvisation built around a strict set of rules.

The larger staff allowed us to work more locally too. The staffers became our connection to each community where we did the production, they made local viewers feel welcome, and we often relied on them for inside information about local characters, partners, and issues.

Another benefit to working with larger staffs was that it allowed us to create a more accurate semblance of an actual local government meeting through the additional activity onstage, along with Jim's live video design. In political meetings you often see staffers leaning in, whispering to elected officials, passing sheets of paper to them, and moving around behind them. With five people behind the councilors in our show, it started to look more like the real thing.

Jim's design also took advantage of the increased staff size. His video rig included two camera operators who shot the show in performance as well as three stationary cameras, and Jim called and mixed the different camera shots live, much the way cable news does. With five staffers and a secretary behind the councilors, we were able to choreograph a moment in which a viewer-as-councilor is shot in close-up by one of the camera operators, just as a staffer leans to whisper some information to them and just as another viewer-as-speaker is giving some damning testimony about that council member. In close-up, punctuated by sidelong glances and whispers, we created a subtle illusion of suspiciousness, highlighting the way media portrayals can influence our perception, whether intentionally or not.

When we expanded the staff, we also prioritized diversity, because we felt having a staff that represented the audience's cultural and age diversity would encourage people to volunteer for the more visible, participatory roles. We wanted the community of staffers to look like where we were.

In terms of our production model, a staff made up of local community members allowed us to travel from New York with fewer people. This meant more of our own resources, as well as those of the presenters we worked with, could stay local and pay local people. As we committed to paying ourselves decently for the expanded time we spent in each community, we paid our staff members for all rehearsal, development, and production time. We worked with presenters to determine as equitable a pay scale for them as we could. We needed our staffers to be thoughtful people who could engage conceptually with our project and process. They made the project better through their questions, critiques, and enthusiasm. And we relied on our local presenting partners to help find the ideal people.

Here are two examples of staffers who fit the bill ideally.

Arny: Everyone's New York City Uncle

Arny Lippin was one of Aaron's kung fu teachers and came to almost everything Aaron made. At the time we were making *City Council Meeting*, he was in his late 60s, a retired chemist with a bushy beard and a slightly absent-minded affect. He had been a part of some activist street theatre and puppet work in the '60s and '70s but was not formally trained as an actor.

At our first work-in-progress showing, we had not developed our orientation structure, so the beginning of the performance was a bit more chaotic

Staffers (right to left) Arny Lippin, Hunter Canning, Kevin Laibson, Mary Q. Archias, and Barbara Lee orient councilors in the gymnatorium of Chelsea Career and Technical Education High School, New York City. Photo by David A. Brown Photography / Houston, Texas.

than it ultimately became. Lippin signed up to be the mayor. Onstage, either because of nerves or eyesight, he could barely read his way out of a paper bag. Knowing this, we worried about how the audience would respond to having someone untrained at the head of the council table.

In fact, the effect was better than we could have planned. Viewers were on the edge of their seats as Lippin struggled through "Item 396–398, relating to trunk and sewer repair. Is anyone wishing to appear . . ."? They saw themselves in him. What would have been a disaster in a regular show was perfect for us. We watched the rupture between the real council meeting and what we were doing. The audience inserted themselves into the gap between the two because they saw that we were reframing a real-world political event as art, and when Lippin had finished, they cheered.

Lippin then began to work with us as a staffer and was instrumental in the development of the piece in New York. He was quick to ask questions (because he was often confused by what we were asking him to do), he was calm in stressful situations, and he responded as soon as a problem arose. He helped us clarify the language we used to talk to staffers and audience members. And his avuncular manner made him ideal for making audience members feel like they could get through the piece.

Once, when Lippin's instructional script said, "bring the audience stage left," he said, "What's stage left mean? You mean my left or her left?" He was demonstrating orienting an audience member from a position onstage, as if the audience member were facing him from a seat.

"Stage left is your left. The left from the stage."

"Well, that makes sense," Lippin said. "But how would I know that? It's not obvious."

He was right, of course—it's not necessarily an intuitive way to instruct someone where to move if they don't come from a theatre background. Even theatre people get confused by our own terminology: house left, stage left, audience left, upstage left, center left. At the end of a twelve-hour tech day, most of us are a little bit Arny Lippin.

This came up at a particularly important point in our process. We had been developing the work for two years through concurrent short workshops and residencies in Tempe, New York, and Houston; New York was a kind of central lab where we'd build ideas and strategies with a committed, rotating group of fifteen to twenty staffers and then take them to our local working groups in other cities. We were now about to move into production mode, first in Houston, then Tempe, then back in New York.

Because of budget constraints and our own availability, in Houston we'd be teaching the final version of the meeting to our staffers in eight three-hour rehearsals. This meant that the script was not just a document to memorize, as in a normal play; it was something to refer to even in performance, by people who had only a limited time with it beforehand. Some staffers would be coming straight from work to the show, where they would pick up the script and leap into orienting that night's audience.

This actually ended up as a positive for the project—we needed the whole event to feel accessible in a different way than one usually associates with that word. We *wanted* the staffers to be informal and read their instructions from scripts on clipboards at the top of the show, because it made participants feel that what we were asking of them was not going to be too hard or come from some specialized knowledge they may not possess. And it also reflected our research on democracy based on the citizen "who partakes in ruling and being ruled." This paradoxical form of action had to be modeled in the subtle communication between the audience making choices and staffers guiding their orientation.[1]

"If she can read instructions, I bet I could too, I'm gonna sign up for the council table."

Assata Richards: Voice of Houston

Because we had a great working relationship with our Houston presenters—DiverseWorks, Project Row Houses, and the University of Houston Mitchell Center—we did several research and process-based trips through which we assembled our staffers, researched local issues, and began building the piece. Houston has grown a truly engaged arts scene, much of which is rooted in the African American community. Venues like Project Row Houses have become a gold standard for spaces that are truly local, that both lead and respond to their communities. Their presence and our partnership made it easier for us to gauge when we were on the right track with our project there and whether resistance or confusion, we encountered was helpful, provocative in a good way, or just a result of our naivete.

Assata Richards came to one of our first orientation meetings for potential *City Council Meeting* staffers, set up by DiverseWorks, and she got up and left about halfway through. Later she became one of the most valuable individuals we worked with in any of the five cities where we made the piece.

At that first orientation meeting, as we described what we thought the process and work would be, Richards raised several issues of concern to her: Do people get to speak about issues that are important to them, in their community? No, we said, we tried that, and it wasn't what we wanted. *Why not?* she asked. We said we found that watching people wrestle with the voices and words of someone whose experience or identity was different than their own was more provocative to us. Richards said she understood what we were after, but it wasn't for her, and she left. We were saddened because we enjoyed being challenged in that way as it helped us articulate what we were after in the project.

In our discussions after that meeting, we realized the other problem with self-expression is that it can create a kind of cathartic experience for the audience, as if they'd actually spoken truth to power; they might be less rather than more likely to go to an actual government meeting. They might not feel the need. Instead, we wanted the performance to feel like a kind of embodied training so you knew what was happening and could act in the most empowered way when you got to the real thing.

A week later, Richards called back and said she wanted to take part, and she became part of our local cohort, which also included artists Carrie Schneider,

Autumn Knight, John Harvey, Maurice Duhon, Cristy Jadick, and Christa
Forster.

From day one Richards had questions and concerns about how we were
staging the piece. It turned out that she worked as an administrative aide at
the mayor's office, and she knew just how meetings were run. She helped us
figure out what kind of binders staffers should carry, how they should whisper
to councilors, and how agendas were set up. She encouraged us to organize the
staffer instructions in ways she thought made sense. She sometimes critiqued
our approach to the local ending.

Richards also gave us a vital introduction to the middle school in Houston's
Third Ward, the historically African American neighborhood where Project
Row Houses is situated. The students at the middle school then became part
of our most successful local ending in that city.

Richards is also a community pillar in Third Ward. She's an activist who
came of age as part of the Project Row Houses community. In addition to
raising a son there, she went on to get a graduate degree and a law degree and
has since created a groundbreaking program at the University of Houston.
Her participation in the project engendered trust from a lot of neighborhood
residents. We are proud that our process allowed for staffers like Richards to
weigh in, push back, and ultimately contribute to the project's success.

One of the most rewarding results of Richard's participation in Houston's
City Council Meeting came about several months after our shows there. In
February 2013 we got an email from her:

"I am entering the 2013 campaign for City Council as the representative for
District D. It is awesome in so many ways, and I deeply appreciate my experiences with *City Council Meeting*. I gained a lot from your work that definitely
contributed to my decision. Here's to civic engagement and local change. Take
care, Assata."[2]

Local leaders like Richards became crucial to the success of *City Council
Meeting* in each subsequent city. They helped us gain buy-in locally, opened
doors, and kept us honest. We learned that if we were open to critique, we
could grow together.

A New Way to Act

Anybody can do this. Anybody can do this. I don't know what I am doing.
There were many reasons why the usual confines of theatrical acting did not serve *City Council Meeting*. Some of these reasons were specific to each of us as artists, and some were about making the piece possible and illuminating our main themes and ideas.

Mallory often says that the moment she stops enjoying a performance is the moment she starts to question whether it's an accurate representation or not. At that point she is taken away from the story onstage and into questions of what is believable or not. For her, the "thrill of the fiction" is often a faster route to revelation. The range of human experience is so vast, how can any of us know but a tiny percentage of it? For her, something else is going on in this moment of comparison. The whole experience begins to suddenly rely upon the willing suspension of disbelief, and in protest she begins to compare her own fairly limited life experiences to those of the artists or characters. This is not to downplay the real concerns of people who have been historically and continually misrepresented or omitted, but to acknowledge the personal limitation of her own experience and a desire for art to reach beyond it.

For Aaron, the problem with naturalistic, representational theatre is simply that he wants to have two things honored at once: our ability to know something is not actually happening and our ability to get swept up in its spell. We think audiences are capable of holding a tension between these two states of belief at the same time.

Although *City Council Meeting* might have looked at times like a representational piece of documentary theatre, we didn't think our job was to convince the audience of its veracity. We just wanted to break an experience of democracy down into a series of tasks, using transcripts from actual meetings, and see if unrehearsed people could make it happen. To do this we knew from the start that we needed to focus on communication rather than representation.

From these principles, with these people and these words, we were trying to stage a conversation about participation: why it happens or doesn't, why we make the choices we do, how we perform power, and who gets to choose which roles.

Anybody Can Do This: Performing Tasks

THE SECRETARY WILL CALL YOU UP BY YOUR REAL NAME, BUT PLEASE USE THE PRINTED NAME WHEN GIVING THIS TESTIMONY.

During the in-person orientation, a staffer gave speakers a sheet of paper with this instruction. Like many instructions that make up *City Council Meeting*, it is both a practical and an aesthetic effort to position the audience and influence their performance. Embedded in this instruction is one way we dealt with the "acting" issue. Through a kind of bureaucratic diction and an emphasis on task, we asked viewers to trust that they were enough and did not need special skills to carry out their roles. That diction also mimics the language of actual governmental entities, which was important to us. Finally, the willingness of staffers like Arny Lippin and Assata Richards to be utterly themselves was the key to helping audience members trust themselves and the experience.

On a practical level, calling the audience up by their real names ensures they'll know their cue to testify. Theatrical rules about character were less important to us than simply communicating the tasks at hand. If we had insisted on testing the audiences' attention skills by calling them up by the original speaker's name, we would be testing whether they were good at representing and remembering a character, which was a misleading instruction. In a piece that was full of complexity, the communication had to be clear.

On a more subtle level, we did this because we wanted to create that "irreducible distance," to remind the audience of who they were right before they started to speak for someone else. We felt this distance was critical to a provocative performance. It's what we mean when we talk about being able to get caught up in the work's spell without having to suspend disbelief.

A key influence on our thinking about acting for *City Council Meeting* was Goffman's *The Performance of Self in Everyday Life,* which proposes we are always playing a role as determined by the space and the power dynamics

A boy in the speaker role at the Eldorado Ballroom
in Houston, Texas. Photo by Rachel Cook.

around us. This allowed us to see our audience as perfectly prepared. They had all the skills necessary, because they were human and necessarily performing themselves as situations dictated. We had nothing to teach them.

Our commitment to working with audience members as equals came from early failures. A common suggestion from talkbacks at our first work-in-progress showings was "You should really get actors to perform this. These characters and their concerns are so interesting, this audience can't really do a good job." We realized that if the audience felt this way, the whole premise of the piece was not working and we had to recalibrate what we asked of them. We decided on a new answer to this suggestion: "We did get actors, and you were awesome."

Performing Our Irreducible Distances

Rancière's idea from *The Emancipated Spectator* that "the irreducible distances" between anonymous people is what makes "everyone equal to everyone else" also played a critical role in refining our approach to acting. What we learned from watching the performance of racialized stereotypes, which occurred on occasion, was that participants—either by instinct or by assumption—

felt their job was to erase the distance between themselves and the person whose words they were speaking.

When a speaker seemed to struggle with how to say someone else's words, it was more compelling than when they thought their job was to become the person, to "feel their pain" and to act it. In city council testimonies, speakers first identify themselves, their background, and often their neighborhood, so it is hard to escape the sex, race, class, and ethnicity of the person whose words you're taking on. And because the audience self-selects their role in the meeting but not who they are going to speak for, chance dictates the intersection of both speakers' identities.

So when a thirty-year-old bearded white man from Williamsburg who carries all the outward signs of a "hipster gentrifier" has to say the words of a seventeen-year-old African American woman from the East Side of San Antonio who is testifying about disinvestment in her neighborhood, it's a tricky line to walk. For the self-aware, representing this perspective and taking responsibility for these words creates a beautiful tension.

We also saw the opposite: someone gets up thinking her job is to become the person on the paper, which leads her to perform her assumptions rather than just say the words as written. That irreducible distance between the speaker and the spoken for is taken over. This is the kind of performance that within the context of the piece is an example of "bad acting"—by which we mean a performance based upon assumptions rather than respect for the experience of another human being.

By identifying that we wanted to reveal that irreducible distance, we could make instructions and set tasks and rules that could nudge things in that direction. It is important to note here that, in our experience, the people most prone to performing stereotypes were white. Whether we were in a city that thought of itself as liberal or conservative, we noticed a kind of white entitlement to appropriate take hold in some participants. Those same people also seemed most oblivious to what they were doing, and then most undone if they realized they had gone too far.

We made clear to staffers across the board, those with acting training and those with none, that we were not interested in either them or the audience "becoming their characters." This emphasis on the irreducible distance—in this case the distance between the staffers, audience, and the actual council meetings we were enacting—addressed the social and political issues around representation and clearly conveyed our approach to a commonly asked question: Why don't you cast the audience in parts appropriate to them? Putting this issue on the table guided much of our discussions around how to instruct the audience, what to look for, and when and how to intercede if necessary. We were constantly making adjustments to the instructions and empowering the staffers to act upon their awareness of this issue.

Tasks and instructions were the central mechanisms that made all this possible. Whatever theories or ideas we held, whatever direction we wanted the work to move in, had to be translated into this mechanism. So there is a key relationship between the style of acting we were striving for and the task-based nature of the script. We wanted to make something that wouldn't work, that would fall apart, if real communication was not happening.

City Council Meeting is about strangers or anonymous people telling strangers to do something together. Step by step, one task, one instruction at a time.

What Not Acting Reveals

Our reliance on task and communication over representational acting allowed us to lay bare the way power operates in performance based simply on where you sit and what you say. As a council member in San Francisco said to Aaron during his research, and which a councilor says to the audience during *City Council Meeting*, "We put up a couple tables, put a few of us on one side, and the rest of us on the other, and boom! Power."[1]

For instance, we realized that the staffers could alter the experience of the councilors over time by changing and complicating the instructions and information as the meeting moved through each act. All these factors affected what people normally call acting, but none of them were about how well anyone played a character.

As we became more confident in our ability to communicate what it meant to act or participate in the meeting, we also had to accept the moments when some audience members took on full-blown racialized stereotypes of some of the testimonies. It was extremely uncomfortable for many of us and difficult to accept, but it had to be acknowledged; a rigorous set of rules led to resistance among some viewers, and they would not just act but act out. This also manifested itself as audience members sometimes going off script and improvising to get laughs. When this happened, we would address it with our staffers, with the venue, and among ourselves after the show and try to find ways to mitigate that potential for the future, even as we had to accept that the performance was not going to police behavior or shield us from the stereotypes we harbor and perform. In these moments where the overtaking of the irreducible distances occurred, we could see our discomfort with and the challenge of true equality.

At our most successful performances, the invitation we made allowed participants to consider the ways that certain kinds of conscious or unconscious behaviors are deemed appropriate or powerful, while others might subvert those standards. Further, some of those behaviors are traditionally associated with one race, gender, or cultural background. As white artists working in diverse settings and making a piece about how a democratic process is performed, it was important to expose some of these assumptions and revisit the work now, to see whether we made those assumptions clear enough.

We had to design *City Council Meeting* to allow that kind of acting out to be part of a spectrum of behaviors we were asking the audience to observe, judge, and reflect upon. That's a subtler form of communication than we often allow ourselves in theatre. And yet it's one of the form's greatest strengths— the unspoken communication made manifest, the subtle layers of presentation we don't often discuss. How a person says something has as much meaning as what they say. It's what Goffman describes as the difference between the *given* and the *given off* impressions we make on others through what we say and how we say it.[2]

For us, this was political. Ideally our piece exposed the performativity and limitations of a government meeting and exposed viewers' presuppositions within it. Could it also give us opportunities to see those limitations as openings through which we could alter the political fabric of our cities? Could enacting a government meeting as art allow us more freedom to change the structure of actual governmental processes? As several cities in recent years, from Portland, Maine, to Oakland and New York City, have begun integrating artists and creative processes directly into local governmental structures, the answer seems to be yes.[3]

As the project moved from city to city, the net effect of our clunky, paradoxical performance seems to have made the actual form of a government meeting less oppressive and more performative.

The Arrival of Jim Findlay

Early in the development process for *City Council Meeting* we became aware that we needed a collaborator who could design for us but also really play with and challenge the world we were trying to conjure.

The series of choices we devised for our orientation gave us a lot to consider. Within *City Council Meeting* there were at least four distinct performances that we had to accommodate once participants make their decisions. Councilors performed at the table onstage, supporters and speakers performed in the audience space for the councilors sitting at the table, and the bystanders had to be able to take in the whole arena of action. Each group created an audience for the other roles, which in turn created the performance. The show worked because spectator and performer converged through the giving and taking of power.

The unpredictable interplay among these forces—each viewer plotting her own way through the performance—is what gave the meeting its energy.[1] The variation possible within the performance was vast, night to night, show to show. Each city that performed it pushed the limits of our form. Throughout the development process and into the performances themselves, we were often catching up to our audience's ingenuity and playfulness.

The design needed to put a frame around the wildness. We asked Jim Findlay to come on board as a third collaborator because of his ability to hold the complexity of the structure we were trying to build and ask the simplest, most pointed questions to keep us moving forward.

As we were working on this book, Mallory and Aaron asked Jim to write a chapter on what he once referred to as *invisible design*—making choices as a designer that a viewer might not recognize right away, which is counter to the way a lot of scenic, sound, and lighting artists work. Often they, like writers,

directors, and actors on a production, are looking to put their visual stamp on
the space and event in some way. Jim's invisible design affected not only the
look of our project but the dramaturgy and text as well.

Jim responded to Aaron's request for a series of interviews: "Generally, I
hate looking backward. I don't like processing things. I feel like if you and
Mallory are writing this book and people are going to learn something, that's
great. I just don't want to do it. I do something and then I want to move on
to the next thing."[2]

But we twisted his arm and he agreed to a series of in-person and email
conversations, the results of which will filter through the book.

Here is some of our conversation:

Aaron: What is the first thing you remember about your entry into the
process?

Jim: I remember that there was this idea about making a theatre piece
into this sort of boring TV show, with the live feed and monitors and
subtitles, and that was fun to work on, but it didn't feel like designing.
Anyone could do that.

Aaron: I experienced this differently. I remember going into B&H Photo/
Video with you to look at live video-mixing hardware. We went into
this little room full of systems and consoles and things, and you immediately started speaking some foreign language of electronics to the guy
there. And what you came out with was a way to make a proprietary
system that used the kinds of video-mixing equipment and software
that churches and cable access TV use. You were able to solve the issue
of latency—when the video signal lags just behind the live action—
that's pervasive in live video feeds for performances and that would
have left our piece feeling less accurate.

Jim: I learned the first time we did that HERE work in progress, where
I tried to have us make this back wall that had a lot of character to it,
that this project didn't need my ideas. And then once I stopped having
ideas, I started responding to the space. The courtroom in Houston
was the place where that really gelled for me. There was enough there
that we didn't have to bring in any outside ideas or concepts. I hit a
point where all my ideas were wrong, or we didn't use them, and so I
was like, "I'm not going to contribute anything." And that is when I
became more of a third collaborator.

Left to right: designer Jim Findlay, director Mallory Catlett, and staffers Maria Cristina Jadick and Assata Richards prepare for the show in the Palm Center Courthouse in Houston, Texas. Photo by David A. Brown Photography / Houston, Texas.

Aaron: Has this impacted your work at all going forward?

Jim: Now when I'm working on a design project, I don't try to have ideas and I think this was the first time. I told a class of college students I was visiting that I think a designer's job is to create obstacles. I am now working with someone who was in that class, and she reminded me of that. I remember at the time thinking that no one heard me, but it was great to hear that a couple people really took that in.[3]

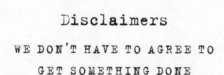

Disclaimers

WE DON'T HAVE TO AGREE TO
GET SOMETHING DONE

After we'd completed the orientation for all four groups of viewers, we invited bystanders back in from the lobby and everyone took their seats, with councilors in the front row.

At this point we felt *City Council Meeting* needed moments in which the piece itself could speak to the audience, where the scaffolding we'd built was rendered visible, where an authoritative voice could come through and keep them aware of the boundaries and possibilities within the show. These were check-in moments where we could kind of say, "Yes, this is still a weird show, but we know it, and you're on a path. Please trust us." We called these moments disclaimers, brief bits of playful or poetic text and action in which the piece's authors spoke directly to the audience.

The first disclaimer was the bridge between the orientation and the meeting to follow. This was a critical moment in *City Council Meeting*. We had to let the audience know that the relatively chaotic swirl of choice-making, instructions, and sign-up sheets we'd just put them through was going to resolve itself into something identifiable and rigorously crafted.

After everyone was seated, each councilor came to the front of the room, one at a time, and delivered a speech from a set of index cards. On the cards were printed text, and the councilors were instructed to speak the plain text and treat the bold, all-caps phrases as instructions to follow:

LOOK AT THE AUDIENCE.

People ask me how we're going to bring more people into the process. And every time I say the same thing. "You can't push a rope."

CLEAR YOUR THROAT.

You have to demonstrate that you really care. You have to get down and really listen to what causes pain for people. And then try to do something.

NOD SEVEN TIMES.

We don't have to agree to get something done.

SMILE.

Drawn from Aaron's interviews with real council members, other government officials, and activists, these speeches served several purposes: they created a transition from the orientation to the meeting, they showed the multiple audience perspectives that the choice-making of the orientation had created, and they galvanized the councilors into one body made up of individuals. They also made visible the way we instructed participants to read and respond to commands and drew attention to the silent physical realm of gestural communication.

Part of our goal was to give each viewer more than one sense of what was happening in the show: you're enacting a city council meeting; you're making choices of your own free will; you're being asked to complete specific tasks based on your choices and watching other people do things that stem from *their* choices. At no point did we want the experience to feel simple or seamless. We trusted that if we gave the audience several entry points to the work, and several concurrent things to focus on, they'd have the capacity to make sense of it themselves.

By watching a newly minted councilor respond to prompts, and by making those prompts legible, we felt like we could put viewers in two places at once— in the mind of the person they were watching and in their own reaction to what the councilors were doing. We feel like theatre often gets monolithic in its pronouncements and narratives, but life is always more than one thing at a time. So we tried to put each participant into her own conversation with the material, the rest of the audience, and the piece itself. The opening speeches helped show that density.

LOOK AT THE AUDIENCE. SMILE.

Hello. I thought it would be nice to be somebody else for a while. Thank you.

LOOK BEHIND YOU AT THE COUNCIL TABLE.

What brings us together? Very often something small or unnoteworthy. Like free Wi-Fi or a two-for-one.

NOD YOUR HEAD SEVEN TIMES.

My name is **SAY YOUR NAME** *and I approved this message.*

The language of the opening speeches as well as the disclaimers that appear later on video monitors or in one-on-one staffer speeches was often playful, riffing off the language of officialdom and bureaucracy. Since *City Council Meeting* is a strange enough piece, we hoped that a little levity might help audiences see the work as playful, even as we tried to ask real questions about big subjects.

PART II

Meeting

How the Meeting Works

AN OVERVIEW

Please call the roll...

Once all the participants who chose to be councilors performed their disclaimers and went to sit behind the table, the meeting part of *City Council Meeting* started. Lasting roughly seventy-five minutes, the meeting weaved together excerpts from five U.S. cities, along with procedures drawn from others, into a sequence of events that resembled a single city's government meeting. We wanted to give everyone the sense that we were creating a new city by performing these words together from the documents of actual ones.

Our meeting started in Bismarck with a kind of spectacle of a boring local government that featured the councilors reading prepared statements, staff members transitioning, and other officials doing their jobs, commemorating fellow citizens, and passing laws. As we entered San Antonio, Houston, Oakland, and Portland, speakers and supporters had an increasingly large presence. In real government meetings, the public has increased input later in the agenda, and this is where the tensions arise, where the impression that things are working gives way to real debate and inspired testimony. We wanted to allow these tensions, this shift in the dramaturgy of an actual government meeting, to be reflected in our performance.

We also set a specific dramaturgical arc to how the staffers gave instructions to councilors and speakers, as well as what they said. In the Bismarck section, only the mayor got a script and the staffers stood back, leaving the councilors to listen and vote yes on the consent agenda. As the meeting moved forward from one city to the next, the staffers began to give more personal instructions and scripted material. In Houston, the most overtly dramatic section,

Left to right: staffers Autumn Knight, Assata Richards, Carrie Schneider, Christa Forster, Maurice Duhon, and Maria Cristina Jadick feed information to participants at DiverseWorks in Houston, Texas. Photo by David A. Brown Photography / Houston, Texas.

the staffers gave their councilor backstory and the political history of each new speaker that came up.

From there, the meeting continued to build to a more theatrical realization, with more subtle ruptures and more complicated staging. A final disclaimer, delivered as a testimony Aaron wrote called "Audience Participation in the Theater," positioned us back in the room in a playful way. In the Oakland section, staffers helped audience members take over the proceedings, solve problems, and begin to speak for themselves.

Then, as things seemed to be getting out of hand, the meeting arrived at our one true representational moment. Instead of reading the name of an audience member, the city secretary called for Pete Colt to come up. An actor, the first person to perform without a script, reenacted the moment Aaron saw in 2009 that set the whole project in motion, ending with councilors' call to clear the room. Then there was an intermission before our local ending.

This arrangement of tasks, text, and actions over time allowed us to put a broad frame around what acting is, to extract it from traditional notions of emotion or psychology. For participants, the experience of being at the council table, delivering a testimony, or responding to instructions offered a kind of embodied learning. For educators, ethnographers, and other practitioners thinking about how we can teach and learn democracy, this approach might be a valuable tool.

Following are brief descriptions of each city—each scene or act—from which we excerpted text in the performance.

Act 1, Bismarck

CONNIE'S RETIREMENT SPEECH

And then I will ask, uh, the retiring commissioner to make a speech . . .
Bismarck, the first part of our performed meeting, was where Aaron realized that every local government meeting has some small moment of theatricality in it, even if it barely registers. One of his first research visits was to Bismarck, North Dakota. In a session that was meant to be mostly procedural and so was almost empty, he witnessed a retirement speech given by Connie Sprynczynatyk on the eve of her retirement from twenty years as a council member. Her speech and the exchange with the mayor that followed seemed a good way to locate us in our show.

SPRITZOMATIC (our shorthand for the actual council member's name before we looked it up): Uh, Mr. Mayor, I always wanted to be Miss America, but that, uh, wasn't in the cards. I was kinda OK being Queen of the City. But am I finally gonna get that crown?

MAYOR: Commissioner, this is pretty close. Uh, this is pretty close.
Bismarck was also a good opener for our show because it was both funny and boring, because it was *about* the boring nature of government meetings. There is a lot of talk of zoning and sewer lines. Sprynczynatyk retired and the new councilor was sworn in, so it was an opportunity for us to make a real transfer of power; we would cast one of our staffers as Sprynczynatyk, then swear in an audience member to take over.

For staging, we thought a lot about how to simultaneously model the action for the audience, set them at ease, and convey how the rules worked. Sprynczynatyk's speech is poignantly funny, so it helped to have this a little more rehearsed, to get everyone laughing.

I was given a lovely, uh, award from a coworker as I left to come to my last commission meeting. It was a Life Savers candy. He said, "Thanks for being a lifesaver for the city."

In every city, we chose to cast a male staffer in this role because it allowed us to clearly convey how the casting worked for everyone. We never asked the audience to put on any kind of affect for the race or gender of the person whom they were speaking for. We chose men to read Sprynczynatyk because it set an example for how this performance worked. If a man has to read for a woman, he simply reads the words on the page. No changes to pronouns need to be improvised. The best explanation was to do it. No set of instructions would be more effective.

Modeling was an important tool in the process, especially when the meeting began and the audience was still getting used to the invitation we were making to them and the rules of our piece. We had to determine what instructions could do effectively, and when they felt too complicated or confusing, we had to stage the idea, make it happen for everyone to see. In this instance we used a staffer, which had the added benefit of starting this important discussion with our working group in rehearsals. We never had resistance from the staffers once it was clear that taking a matter-of-fact task-based approach to playing Sprynczynatyk would be most beneficial to the rest of the audience as they navigated the performance for themselves. This was not any acting test. Being clear and letting people figure out for themselves how to reconcile the gap between the identity of Sprynczynatyk and the actor reading in for her was an essential first step in conveying what we were doing.

MAYOR: *You know, looking back I think that one of the most important things when I asked you was the Growth Management Plan. For those of you who aren't up to speed on that, it's our visionary plan to offer our community as a community that is orderly and organized. (*PAUSE*) Some of the more mundane things— she did the first solid waste task force. I think she was the, uh, self-proclaimed Sultana of Solid Waste. So let's be sure and get that down in the record, the, uh, Sultana of—*

SPRITZOMATIC: *Mr. President, you forget the Debutante of Debris.*

MAYOR: *Uh, excuse me, I'm sorry.*

SPRITZOMATIC: *The Guru of Garbage.*

MAYOR: *Ha ha, yeah.*

SPRITZOMATIC: *You know, the former mayor used to say, "If it smells, it's in Connie's portfolio."*

In our early showings we tried to have the staffer playing Sprynczynatyk

Secretary Victoria Vazquez swears in a new participant councilor at the
LaGuardia Performing Arts Center, Queens, New York. Photo by David A. Brown
Photography / Houston, Texas.

memorize this text, but that gave the impression to the audience that performing was something actors do and prepare for. If the staffer just read from
a script, it modeled what everyone else up there was doing.

After her speech and conversation with the mayor, Sprynczynatyk retired and a new councilor from the audience was sworn in to complete the
council table, now entirely made up of audience members. The staffer who
played Sprynczynatyk would soon take over the individual staffer role for her
replacement.

The swearing in was also a unique moment in the piece because it was the
first time that two members of the audience, with minimal help from the secretary (who was also a staffer), spoke to each other face-to-face. Reading from
a set of index cards, the mayor recited the oath of office; the new councilor
listened and repeated the lines, left hand on the Bible and right hand raised.

This taking of the oath captured what we thought was best about the
project. It was poignant even in its fiction to imagine someone in the audience taking on this new responsibility. It had an out-on-a-limb feeling—two
fairly unprepared audience members essentially playing a scene together. It

was often humorous because there was inevitably a part of the oath that was difficult to remember, so they would hit that snag and solve that problem in real time—though if they got really lost, the secretary was there to help. In a tiny way, they would go "off-script." And then everyone in the audience would applaud this generous act and welcome the new councilor.

CITY ATTORNEY: *I further swear*

COUNCILOR: *I further swear*

CITY ATTORNEY: *that I am under no direct or indirect obligation*

COUNCILOR: *that I am under no direct or indirect obligation*

CITY ATTORNEY: *to elect or appoint any person, to any office position or employment,*

COUNCILOR: *to elect or appoint any person, to any office position or employment,*

CITY ATTORNEY: *under the city government.*

COUNCILOR: *under the city government.*

CITY ATTORNEY: *Congratulations.*

One of the things we learned from this swearing in was that sometimes the piece needs to break. These breaks, these moments when someone asks for something to be repeated again, or when the mayor just shows the new councilor the cue card—remind the audience that this has never happened before. What they are seeing is unique and no one is fully prepared.

We learned that mostly people want things to work, to follow the script to the point that *City Council Meeting* could start to look like a play even under these circumstances. You could feel a certain comfort in the audience that everything was under control—there was a writer and a director in charge. This had to be disrupted occasionally to remind everyone what was really going on here. This movement from the rehearsed Sprynczynatyk staffer to the swearing in of an audience member as councilor shows the ebb and flow of modeling and instruction toward improvisation and breakage that was critical to holding the attention of the audience.

Disclaimer: The Meeting Itself Wonders

There were only three people in the audience at the beginning of this meeting. Who are those three?

This disclaimer appeared on the monitors at the beginning of the section excerpted from Bismarck. It allowed audience members to create the feeling

of the Bismarck meeting Aaron attended and asked them to choose collec-
tively who would embody the three citizens who came to the actual meeting.
Because the monitors were not visible to the council table, this moment also
created a sense that while they might be in the power position, the councilors
weren't getting a complete picture of what the speakers, supporters, and bystanders were being told to do. There was power on both sides of the table now.

This moment comes right after Sprynczynatyk's speech and the swearing
in of a new council member, which was itself a subtle turning point. After the
new councilor took her or his seat, the video monitors said:

PLEASE STAND.

ALL BUT THREE OF YOU PLEASE GO TO THE BACK OF THE ROOM.

At this point the audience had to decide, generally awkwardly and in si-
lence, who would remain to fulfill the role of the three citizens at the meeting.
A combination of observation, self-selection, and acquiescence played out at
each performance, slightly different each time. Sometimes it was quick and
sometimes it took a few minutes. Usually people surveyed the room to see that
they were all engaged in the same project, or to clarify what the instruction
meant.

From the back of the room, the audience witnessed a city council meeting
in which decisions were being made but only three people showed up. As they
watched, the following disclaimer rolled across the video:

*Be ready to be bored. Be ready to watch a kind of irrelevant, antsy unfolding
around you that wonders if it's even worth it. This room breathes and thinks of
itself as it goes.*

THE MEETING ITSELF WONDERS.

Are you even here? Or are you just represented?

At some performances, small local dynamics or tensions from the actual
city in which the show was happening would play out. In Keene, two friends
playfully argued over who would be part of the three people left and who
would join the crowd in the back. People waved to each other, shook their
heads, chatted. In San Francisco, Z Space's risers were loud and clunky, so
the movement to the back of the room was unignorably loud. The important
thing was that the audience was in control of this action, even though it came
about because of our own assertion of the production's authority.

This interplay—a reminder that no one here was really in charge or had
done this together before—was a key facet of the piece, and one to which we
referred several times in the meeting. Periodic reminders of our relationship to

The audience stands at the back of the room to recreate the empty space
of the Bismarck meeting with only three people in the audience, which also
shows the vast size of the ASU Gammage space in Tempe, Arizona.
Photo by David A. Brown Photography / Houston, Texas.

and dependence on each other to enact what we were proposing helped drive
home the message that we were all choosing our roles.

In a way, this never-been-done-before aspect of our show is true about all
theatre, something we wanted to highlight. Even in the most traditionally
acted, tightly scripted and cued play, it's still a new performance for a new
audience each night. This day hasn't happened before, and the performance
should always be new.

Having these reminders come as objective-seeming statements on a video
screen rather than as a more subjective or emotional appeal did something
subtle. It poked gentle fun at the nature of an authoritative voice within a
democratic process even as it asserted the power of the piece to create rules
and boundaries. And by giving viewers just enough information to get the task
done, it allowed them a small moment of empowerment together.

Act 2, San Antonio

PROPS, PAPERWORK, TESTIMONY

You've just sat through a two-hour presentation on the city's annual budget.
This was the video disclaimer that moved us into the San Antonio section of the meeting. Using the overhead monitors, we jumped in time and space into another city. The shift to San Antonio was made more pronounced because the audience had been standing at the back of the room for the end of the Bismarck section, thanks to the prior disclaimer that asked them to leave only three people. The instructions to sit and then the act of switching cities became physicalized. If the disclaimers were timed just right, the two-hour budget presentation became an inside joke for the audience to enjoy.

The San Antonio section was the first time we used speaker testimony and was an example of how actual government meetings allow for public testimony, even though the budget was a fait accompli: a semblance of giving voice without giving power. The movement from city to city within the meeting was something only identified for the seated audience due to the placement of the video monitors concealed from the council table. There were small clues—one staffer changed the council member nameplates, while another staffer passed out the actual budget from the San Antonio meeting Aaron had attended. As the speakers gave public comment, council members could peruse that document. All the documents at the council table were taken from the actual meetings we saw, with the city names themselves redacted. The budget allowed the councilors to experience something the rest of the audience did not, while changing the nameplates of the councilors allowed the rest of the audience to experience something the councilors did not. Our goal was to point to distinctions each group made via their choices about how to participate.

Empty council table set for the start of the meeting in the Eldorado Ballroom,
Houston, Texas. Photo by David A. Brown Photography / Houston, Texas.

The use of primary documents was key to the experience of the council
members. It grounded the action at the table in the daily workings of that civic
body. It filled out this picture of authority while also underscoring the mundane complexity of this position. Until *City Council Meeting*, we had never
looked at ordinances for sewer trunk lines, but the maps and schematics from
Bismarck were even more confusing than we could have imagined. So there
is a funny irony in the documents giving a sense of authority *and* increasing
confusion, which lends credence to that observation we often have when politicians seem not to really understand the information they are given; it might
be easy to let your political or ideological views take precedence over really
understanding the nuts and bolts of engineering and how it actually affects
people. If you simply believe taxes shouldn't be raised to solve these problems,
you don't have to actually try to understand the information and documents
that give you your power and authority. So the councilors, in a subtle way,
experienced this confusion and had to put on a good face. Councilors often
perused the documents, a task that created an appearance. The fact that the
documents were all real kept them awake to that experience.

In our performance made from transcripts, we included all the different surfaces on which the written word showed up. Props were an opportunity to communicate something to participants, either through text or the literal weight and visual life of the object. In the Bismarck section we had a service award for Connie Sprynczynatyk made at a local trophy store, and the mayor had to read it to her. The city's annual financial statements functioned to show audience members that councilors had access to information that viewers had only heard about in a disclaimer.

The paperwork and props were important design elements in the sense that they carried metaphoric weight on a set that was mostly very functional. By design, most of the set could be put together with materials that most libraries, schools, church basements, or community centers already have. We performed it in many different spaces and always used what was native to the rooms we worked in. With a simple container, we could surprise viewers with the complexity of the civic content. Our background in touring theatre pieces was useful as this approach gave us flexibility and was economical. Our local partners didn't have to pay for a truck and cartage or a big crew to set up. We had one rolling suitcase for all the paperwork and props, with the exception of those budgets, which we had to mail in advance.

Slapping these heavy budgets loudly on the council table at the top of the San Antonio section was a way to signal to everyone that the meeting was taking an in-depth turn. This section also raised the stakes for the speakers, and the props and design set a more charged stage for the young people's testimonies that we used. All of a sudden speakers were asked to perform politically loaded text from teenagers in disinvested neighborhoods, asking the council to reconsider proposed (and generally forgone) budget cuts.

My name is Tequondria Taylor and I'm seventeen years old. Thank you for allowing me to speak to you in regard to my concerns in my community, the East Side. Most kids on the East Side have been caught up in crimes and gangs and has no way out. I come here today to present to you that I have lived on the East Side most of my life and there have been many blessings from these streets. I don't want to be classified as a bad Black child from the East Side. Here today, my voice may be—may be one of the many you will remember. I'm not leaving here today without a positive outlook on what we have presented to you. I ask you today to create more opportunities for my youth . . . for my youth community; save my brothers and sisters from these crimes and gangs. Hear me out.

After the jokey, folksy tone of Bismarck, these testimonies offered a chance for viewers to think about their own differences, from each other and from the person whose words were being read, as well as the responsibility to relay another real person's words into the room. It also provided a slightly more activated speaker performance for the councilors to watch. In San Antonio, the room became more dynamic, with all four participant choices putting together a larger picture. The picture itself was more complicated in terms of whom our system serves, whose voices are included in the democracy we play out in council chambers, and how people must perform themselves in specific ways in order to be seen and heard.

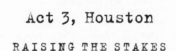

Act 3, Houston

RAISING THE STAKES

I think there's a real belief on their part that this is a desperate situation and not just a, a money issue or a tax issue. That, that we have a very serious, serious, um, concern here. And I listened to them. Because they know what they're talking about.

In the Houston section of *City Council Meeting*, the dramatic action began to get more intense. As staffers fed information and backstory to councilors, testimonies became more heated, and this changed the perception and experience of the councilors. The testimonies included longer back-and-forths and more dynamic exchanges. Coming after San Antonio, in which the young people's testimonies often attuned viewers to the fact that the texts they were reading were the words of real people with serious concerns, the Houston passages continued to build in dramatic tension. These exchanges were part of a meeting Aaron saw in 2011, at which megachurches attempted to thwart Councilor Stephen Costello's infrastructure proposal to keep the city from flooding when it rained. This was five years before Hurricane Harvey did just that.

At the meeting Aaron attended, church groups came en masse, and several pastors spoke in soaring, biblically inspired rhetoric:

There's definitely a cloud that exists. That cloud affects all of you and affects our city. Because we want the issues before us, agree or disagree, to be resolved in a way that everything was done properly and right.

The congregants stood silently in unison in a show of solidarity. Aaron happened to be sitting next to several of these congregants and was surprised when they stood up. What was remarkable was that the pastors, all eloquent speakers, did a great job of making Costello seem crooked. For his part, almost

Three participant councilors listen to the testimony of speaker participants in the San Antonio section of the meeting in the Palm Center Courthouse in Houston, Texas. Photo by David A. Brown Photography / Houston, Texas.

pugilistic in his willingness to argue back, Costello added to a sort of criminal allure. This exchange became a key part of our script.

The Houston section was also a great chance to take full advantage of the supporter role in *City Council Meeting*.

SUPPORTER CARD

Actions to do during the meeting:

  1) Stand in solidarity when Pastor Steve Riggle speaks his testimony.

  2) If anyone smiles, smile with them.

  3) What small thing do you do when you are having trouble concentrating or find something boring? Do that. At least once.

If you have a cell phone:

  Please leave your cell phone on. If it rings during the meeting, please go to the back of the room to take the call. Answer it by saying, "I'm in a meeting." Quietly finish the call, then return to your seat.

If you have a smartphone, you can have a Twitter conversation with the meeting: #citycouncilmtg or @citycouncilmtg.

Our goal was to create a sort of hive of activity—staffers passed councilors individual speeches to read while whispering quick asides, the live cameras filmed councilors more closely, and the room grew more energized with supporters and speakers more activated.

We also changed the way we used live video in this section, filming the councilors more in close-up, switching among camera shots more quickly, using chyron titles with the councilors' individual names, and choreographing the staffers more tightly. This let us create a sense of suspicion, doubt, or support toward any one councilor we chose. When a testimony seemed to imply Councilor Costello was on the take—

. . . but he did receive the contract. It's $1.7 million. Uh, he was then appointed to chair of the, uh, drainage committee.

—we zeroed in on the audience member playing Costello, seated behind the table, so that the camera seemed to amplify the suspicion. We manipulated the media and choreography of the meeting subtly to show how even nonverbal cues influence what we think about what we're seeing and how what we see is rendered so differently depending on whether it's live or on-screen. As theatre makers interested in Goffman's concept of impression management, this felt vital to the piece.[1]

At the heart of the Houston conflict was the fact that the city's infrastructure was not equipped to deal with rising sea levels or increased rain. Councilor Costello's plan was not as much about taxing public and nonprofit entities, as his opponents suggested, as it was about saving the city from constant flooding. After the San Antonio testimonies that alerted the audience to issues of difference within a city more generally, Houston allowed us to focus on one pressing issue and tease out the inherent complexity and theatricality of it. The section ends with a council member saying to the church constituency:

When I had the opportunity to talk to a group of engineers, they told me that they weren't concerned about the future. They said they were really scared that we were all gonna be

under water

in no time.

For the first time, we not only gave a councilor a dynamic piece of text to say but also broke up the lines so they'd say the words with extra emphasis. One of the things that became clear in this section was that watching someone read a powerful piece of text without any real rehearsal gave off the same effect as watching someone choose words carefully so that their importance comes through. Without asking anyone to "act" in the traditional sense, without making them feel like they had to have a special set of skills to pull off this reading, we were able to get strong performances out of our councilors.

The Houston scene built on the drama of the preceding testimonies from

San Antonio, revealing how large, divisive issues—climate change, police violence, gentrification—were often addressed in local government meetings, and often in a more direct way than they could be at a national level. Houston is where everyone could see the whole structure we'd created in motion at once and where the issues themselves became more complex than before. The machinations of the artwork mirrored the political engines that were revving faster and louder, all at once.

The scene also allowed us to create seeming allegiances and divisions within the audience, with some privy to more background knowledge about a specific councilor or speaker than others. The Houston section was where the voice of the meeting itself became a little like a Greek chorus, offering warnings at one moment and empathic portraits at another, putting everyone in the position of having to decide for themselves who seemed most trustworthy.

Act 4, Open Testimony

TEMPE, OAKLAND, AND PORTLAND, WITH A
DETOUR TO AUDIENCE PARTICIPATION

From Houston we moved into open testimony, which built toward what felt to some like chaos and to others like direct democracy. For this section we included speeches from Tempe, Oakland, and Portland, moving from issue to issue and city to city more quickly. We added elements of active participation to both give a sense of what actual meetings feel like at times and to build momentum. This was also the section of the piece where our authorial voices came out more clearly, in the only testimony Aaron wrote from scratch, called Audience Participation. In addition to building toward a climactic ending for the meeting, act 4 was a way to plant seeds for the local endings we made in each city, about which we go into detail in following chapters.

Tempe: The Brand of Downtown

We began this section with a testimony from the first meeting we attended in Tempe, which became pivotal to our local ending in that city. A woman from the Downtown Tempe Community, Nancy Hormann, spoke after a very detailed presentation by engineers about ways the city could address the expensive upkeep of ficus trees along the main drag of Mill Avenue by replacing them with a more climate-appropriate kind of tree.

And we would like to continue that brand and see if there's a way that we can work with all of you to complete the "leafiness" of downtown with our ficus trees.

After the catastrophic and biblical floods of the Houston section, this slightly quaint and funny testimony offered a brief respite. It also showed how appearances and aesthetics, in this case the appearance of a climatically unsustainable tree downtown, are deployed by city officials and the public to thwart

Left to right: staffers Elizabeth Zimmer, Clarinda Mac Low, Hunter Canning, Frank Harts, Gina Stevensen, and Victoria Vazquez watch as a speaker with the Audience Participation testimony takes over from the mayor at the LaGuardia Performing Arts Center, Queens, New York. Photo by David A. Brown Photography / Houston, Texas.

more viable alternatives. This might be one of the risks of democracy Plato warned against. We learned later that talking a lot about ficus trees allowed Tempe residents not to talk about the increased population of homeless people in town, which we discuss in our later Tempe chapter.

AUDIENCE PARTICIPATION: MAYBE I DON'T LIKE YOU

Following Tempe, our next speaker testimony was Audience Participation. In a sense, this was as close as the piece got to more traditional participatory theatre, in which an audience member is asked to jump into a structure and perform as a member of a cast might. This testimony also kept our authorship of the piece more visible and active, which we hoped would set up the local endings we created in each city.

Our next speaker is [_____], speaking on audience participation in live performance.

We handed out Audience Participation with all the other speaker testimonies. The distinction, however, was that Aaron wrote this testimony, and the speaker who got it also received a little extra orientation so they'd feel comfortable with their tasks. The text was designed to allow someone in the audience to usurp the power of the mayor.

This speaker was called up toward the end of the meeting, allowing the person time to sit with and prepare what to say and do. By this time, authority had been established. The mayor and the other council members had become pretty believable in their roles; the open testimony section made them feel they could simply sit back and listen. We wanted to introduce a new and potentially subversive possibility to our proceedings.

Instead of speaking from the podium, this speaker's instruction was to walk up and stand behind the existing mayor, put a hand on the mayor's shoulder, and say:

I am the new mayor. This is not me saying this.

They'd then whisper to the mayor that they could go take their seat in the audience.

This is something that doesn't happen at a city council meeting—a calm yet undiplomatic usurpation of power. In part, we wanted to demonstrate a possibility that exists more readily in an artistic context than a political one.

In effect, the Audience Participation testimony became a live disclaimer that surfaced as testimony to reveal a subtextual layer of the show. The meeting talked back to viewers, encouraging everyone in the room to ask questions that might even undermine our power as artists and the made-up power of the mayor and councilors.

After taking the mayor's chair, the audience participation speaker continued:

Maybe I don't like you. Maybe when your opinions come up in conversation with other people, I disparage them. I don't enjoy honoring your feelings or beliefs. My tolerance of you is tested daily. Most of the time, I dismiss you in my thoughts. Let me get a show of hands.

*Who thinks we can all agree on something? **PAUSE.***

*Who thinks it doesn't matter? **PAUSE.***

*Who doesn't know? **PAUSE.***

I don't know either.

Absorbing and acknowledging the fact that judgement is inherent in any meeting was key to our atmosphere of inclusion. Actual city council meetings are spaces that you must share with people you don't like or agree with, people who are often tedious and maybe waste your time. There are points at the start of the performance designed to slow or even bore the audience, to induce this feeling and consciousness of judgement. By acknowledging and making space for our differences, we can take steps toward including each other in the conversation. People have different jobs, different roles, different opinions. In the meeting, you have to sit with those things and negotiate them.

Formally, Audience Participation is a big speech that, for the first time, required an audience member to put things in their own words:

EXPLAIN TO THE AUDIENCE IN YOUR OWN WORDS THAT YOU DON'T KNOW WHERE TO START. PAUSE.

During this speech the staffers pass around index cards and pencils to everyone in the audience and the speaker asks them to write on them:

Write something you think no one here will agree with. Or that you care so much about you can't stand it. About yourself, or about God, or about drainage, or ficus trees. Or something more important. Write down the opinion you think no one will think is OK.

They are instructed not to put their names on it, but:

Make sure it's readable. And someone will say it for the record. That's how we're a community.

We wanted to make and show how we could be a community in disagreement, in difference, consenting to do something together, inspired by Rancière's embrace of democracy as "the capacity of anonymous people, the capacity that makes everyone equal to everyone else."[1] This had become a key concept for us throughout our process.

Audience Participation was always an exciting moment for us because it allowed a particular speaker, an audience member who likely arrived just like everyone else, to create something of her own within a tightly regimented performance of power. At each performance, that speaker took a unique approach. One might sound very reasonable and kind when they did the text, while another took a lot of pleasure in the power grab.

At the end of the Audience Participation, we gave the audience a minute to write on their cards before staffers collected them. We wove a reading of these cards into the beginning of the local ending of each city where we performed.

In our first and last performances in Houston, something unanticipated happened with Audience Participation. In the first showing, the Audience Participation speaker was a young Latinx singer from a local megachurch whose choir sang after the intermission in the ending. It was a powerful moment to see her take over the meeting and set up the local ending in a magical way. In our last Houston performance, a young girl who we worked with on the local ending asked us directly if she could read that testimony. She said she wanted to take over the room and say a thing that everyone might have been thinking but wouldn't admit. Of course, we obliged her sense of purpose and agency.

In both instances this came up organically, either by chance or request, but as we moved forward, sometimes we gave this testimony to a participant from the local ending—high school kids from New York City, a skater from New Hampshire—as it felt like a way to introduce a character who would reappear later.

Oakland: Bobby Valentine

Hello, my name is Bobby Valentine.
PAUSE. LOOK AT CAMERA.
We, and by we I mean the humanity on this earth right now, are mired in an infinitude of deeply seeded illusions about the nature of reality. And these illusions are based on fear.
PAUSE. LOOK AT CAMERA.

On our first visit to San Francisco, with our presenter Z Space in November 2011, there was no city council meeting scheduled. It was the height of the Occupy movement, however, and Oakland was an epicenter. Protesters were taking over the steps of city hall in a major encampment. Mallory had been a frequent visitor to Zuccotti Park in New York and knew there had already been a major confrontation with the police and calls for then mayor Jean Quan's resignation. There had just been a big peaceful march at the port—a handful of protesters vandalized a building and started a fire downtown, and over one hundred people were arrested.[2]

We had just missed the Oakland City Council meeting that dealt with the fallout of the march, so we watched it together online. The chambers were packed. The police gave a rundown with a PowerPoint of the damage incurred, after which hundreds of people lined up to give their sides of the story. Unlike other open testimonies we had seen, there were so many people who wanted to speak that the city secretary called them up in groups of three to five. People got so animated, enraged, or enthusiastic that they sometimes had to be led outside by security.

The multiple conflicts and passions in play made it riveting and productive for us in many ways. First, the tension between what we call peaceful protest and what we call destruction of property meant that there was not one unified front among the citizens testifying, even those who participated in the action. Second, we saw a protestor identify council members who had marched but who now sat silently behind the council table. This porous and dynamic arrangement of rhetoric and power complicated our research in a great way.

When Bobby Valentine came up and addressed the mic, we were captivated. He spoke without notes and in oddly complete paragraphs broken by blank stares into the eyes of the council members. He had Jesus-length hair and a tunic. He was at once easy to write off and totally credible as he spoke to the councilors seated safely on their side of the table.

There is a wave of love and peace and understanding and compassion that is raging, sweeping through our souls. You can act in fear. You can think in fear. You can speak in fear. Or you can act and think and speak in love and compassion.

This was a testimony that encapsulated all our favorite qualities—a misfit speaking truth to power, a character easily written off that our performance could honor. In purely theatrical terms, it was great writing too, and we were excited to see it read in public by a lot of different people over the course of the production.

We eagerly anticipated Bobby Valentine each night. A lot of times it was a middle-aged woman. We don't recall a time when it was read with any sort of disdain or irony.

We chose a series of testimonies from this contentious Oakland meeting because they offered a great example of an audience taking over, revealing and complicating the dramaturgy of a government meeting and amping up the conflict within our piece after the theatricality of Houston and the provocation of Audience Participation.

Similar to the way we worked with councilors in the Houston section when we gave them text about epic floods and corruption, no acting was required of the speaker to be convincing as Valentine. Simply by reading the words, his eccentricity and possibility shone. The real Valentine challenged the norms of how to behave at proceedings like these. If our audience member had played eccentric, they might have lost us; by simply and clearly repeating the words, they were more accurate to how the actual Valentine looked and sounded and carried an authority in the room.

We talked about our show as "a city we make together by performing it," an amalgam made up of several cities' lives. We started in North Dakota in a room where only three people showed up, and by the time the piece hit

Speakers, supporters, and bystanders in the Oakland open
testimony section of the meeting at ASU Gammage, Tempe, Arizona.
Photo by David A. Brown Photography / Houston, Texas.

Oakland, there were hundreds. The mayor had at some point left the meeting,
and people were getting aggressive. Valentine's mention of fear was an important reminder of an often-real dynamic between those who rule and the public.

In the Oakland section, we worked to build a sense of chaos. The staffers
got the audience to stand up and form long lines to the back of the house, as
if they were about to offer their own testimonies. In the front was a group of
three speakers, and Valentine was the first. They were all complete characters
with outspoken opinions on what had happened at Occupy and how the police handled it.

Right after Valentine, a woman named Sadiyah pointed out that the police
presentation omitted peaceful aspects of the protests that included even some
of the council members themselves. Her words seem as poignant as ever now
and highlight the way multiple points of view, often conflicting, share space
within a performance of civic engagement.

*Um, lastly, I appreciate your taking the time to show a few things that were
wrong with yesterday and the last two weeks while taking no time to lift-up the*

things that were wonderful about the march. Where were the pictures of the baby brigades? Where were the pictures of the community and the family that got started at eight o'clock in the morning and went 'til dusk? Where were those pictures? Where are the pictures of the families that are foreclosed by the banks that you took so much of your city—so much of your PowerPoint—to show us? Where are the pictures, lastly, of you all? Many of you know and need to get on the correct side of all of this. Many of you were out there yesterday. Where were your pictures standing with us?

Finally we heard from Max Alstead, a protester just released from jail who still didn't have his wallet and who laid out why he felt violence could not be tolerated or negotiated with as it endangered the lives of peaceful protestors. While specific to the time and place of Oakland in 2011, this testimony also highlights tensions that continue within protest movements.

What I cannot support is the idea that we can use conversation to deal with the violence that we saw last night. There were people there, there were people there waving claw hammers at people who tried to put out fires. And there were people there among the movement who were saying that vandalism is not violence, and those people are wrong.

Behind the speakers was a line of audience members, all of whom had other Oakland testimonies in their hand and had been instructed to stand by staffers. Some of these speakers had spent the whole performance in anticipation of this moment, not knowing when they would be called on to speak. Twenty-six distinct Oakland testimonies were distributed to the audience. As the meeting unfolded, the information on each of their pages was revealed in its larger context. This created allegiances among audience members, and as the piece progressed those allegiances became larger and louder. This also mirrors what happens at an actual government meeting when the proceedings run out of their allotted time.

This accumulation of unspoken alliances was reinforced by the supporters, who were grouped to stand in support of different speakers. In San Antonio, supporters were told to stand for the kids from the summer youth program; in Houston, for the megachurch pastor; in Oakland, for the protesters.

By the time we performed the show in San Francisco in July 2014, the Occupy movement had largely gone underground, but the audience members, many of whom were from Oakland, brought their memories to it. They embraced this section of the piece with a sense of ownership we had not seen in other cities. This often happened when we performed material from the city we were in, reinforcing our proposition from the orientation video that the words they were hearing and saying had actually been spoken by someone in a local government meeting. In this case, maybe that person was a neighbor or someone they knew.

In the aftermath of the uprisings in many U.S. cities and towns around racial justice and reckoning, we want to point out that our and the movement's understanding of what we call violence is more nuanced than before. Like the actions that took place in the wake of George Floyd's murder in Minneapolis, the Oakland black bloc contingent that started fires and smashed windows was largely nonviolent toward people. While our sympathies include people at the Oakland council meeting who were calling out those actions as counterproductive, we do want to acknowledge the difference between breaking windows and killing people.

Portland: Sheila Harton, Breakage

Item 396 is, uh, Sheila Harton, testifying on illegal secret testing on citizens. Ms. Harton?

At a work-in-progress performance at HERE in New York City, an accident happened between audience members. The person reading Audience Participation read the instructions so quickly that it was hard for other viewers to hear or know what to do. At a certain point, another audience member yelled out, "Could you repeat that, please?!" And they did. Everyone seemed to implicitly take in that what had happened was within the possible framework of *City Council Meeting* but had not been planned.

This led us to insert several moments in which the piece seems to break so that the audience can be reminded that their particular group is doing this together for the first time and they are dependent on each other to correct mistakes until it works.

The immediacy and sense of release that was created when an audience had to overcome the "mistakes" was palpable and extremely valuable in galvanizing the performance. It first happened during the swearing in's repeat-after-me sections. When the Audience Participation speaker asks for the audience's help to pass out cards and pencils, they are instructed to say in their own words, "I am going to have to stand here until you do this. I really need your help." This echoed the moment earlier in the piece when the mayor has to say "today's date" at the starting of the meeting. It wasn't printed on the page, which meant we got to watch them try to remember what day it was (who hasn't had to do that?). Fill in the blanks. Or how the audience applauded when a kid sitting at the council table heroically got to the end of some bureaucratic language. These moments of relief, humor, and forgiveness were pivotal. At a certain point we realized we needed to engineer moments like these throughout the meeting and hand it over briefly over to the audience.

The Sheila Harton breakage happened right before the climactic entrance of Pete Colt. As in the actual meeting in Portland, a woman was called up to speak who was not there. Aaron had distinctly remembered this moment from that day in Portland because she had signed up to speak to the council about "illegal secret testing on citizens." One could only imagine what this would be about, and it was made more comic by the fact that she didn't seem to be in attendance.

In the show, the moment came right after the staffers had gotten the audience seated after the chaos of Oakland meeting. We changed cities from Oakland to Portland, and as the councilors and secretary were settling everyone down, the absence of Harton seemed appropriate and funny. To us. But in work-in-progress showings, this moment never quite landed. We realized that the chaos of Oakland made everyone very attentive to what was happening but also disoriented them enough that quick gestures and asides could easily get lost. So we introduced a more punctuated break.

Ms. Harton?

PAUSE, 5 SECONDS.

Does anyone have a piece of paper with the name Sheila Harton written on it? Testifying on the illegal secret testing of citizens?

STAFFERS IN THE AUDIENCE LOOK AROUND FOR THE SPEAKER, ASKING, *"Miss Harton?"*

STAFFER 1 FEEDS COUNCILOR SALZMAN THE FOLLOWING LINE: *Apparently not here today.*

In highlighting this moment of breakage, we staged the thing we never wanted to have actually happen: the moment we called a name and no one responded. We had worked to make contingencies for this as we created the piece; for critical testimonies we always had one staffer in the audience who could jump in with a copy and hand it to someone to read. But it never happened. It turned out that rather than things falling apart because audience members wouldn't hold up their end of the agreement, the audience's natural impulse to cooperate and follow the rules actually needed to be pointedly disrupted as a reminder that we were all here, encountering each other this way for the first time. Sheila Harton's absence was an opportunity to translate a mishap from a city council meeting into that reminder.

Pete Colt

Following the brief, intentional rupture of Sheila Harton's missing speaker, the actor playing Pete Colt was called up from the audience. He was called by his character name, dressed like the actual Colt. He spoke memorized text, worked with props, and proceeded to disrupt the proceedings by dumping trash in front of the council.

No one in the audience was prepared for this, and it often produced a hush, a serious attention that allowed us to clear the room for intermission and prepare for the local ending. As dramaturgy, this allowed the theatricality of a seemingly non- or antitheatrical piece to build up enough that people would want to come back and see part two, the local ending.

We often worked with someone who both fit the type of the actual Colt and had some local significance to the project itself, either politically or artistically: in Houston, local poet and playwright John Harvey filled the role; in Tempe, it was social practice artist and ASU professor Gregory Sale, who also worked with us on the local ending; in New York, it was award-winning stage actor James Himelsbach, a regular in both Mallory's and Aaron's work; in San Francisco, it was local activist Robert Ernst; and in Keene, Paul Shambroom, the photographer whose work initially inspired the project, came to perform with us, bringing the work full circle in a way.

We also handled how we used video differently in this section. At the moment when our performer playing Colt reached for his bag to dump it on the counter, the live video changed to archival council footage of the real Colt dumping actual garbage. This footage also captured Portland City Council members interacting with Colt.

This turn in the video created a mismatch between the performer and the man on the video, between the council members in Portland and those

James Himelsbach performing Pete Colt in the gymnatorium of
Chelsea Career and Technical Education High School, New York City.
Photo by David A. Brown Photography / Houston, Texas.

audience members sitting at the council table of the performance. At the same
time, this was the first moment we had rehearsed in the traditional sense, the
first time a prepared actor came up and played a role. We wanted to remind
people that they were in a performance and that the thing they were seeing
represented had really happened. We wanted them to be in two places at once.

The decision to change the rules of the video in this way seemed theatrically necessary as well. To create this climactic interruption that was going to
clear the room, we needed surprise, to shift the perspective. We also wanted
to assure the audience that this theatrical moment wasn't a fiction we created
for effect.

This propulsive ending moment to the meeting in *City Council Meeting*
helped bring together some of the main themes we wanted to bring out in the
piece. It continued to challenge each audience member's capacity to consider
whose side they were on and think about how we perform ourselves, whether

we are in power or speaking to it. Pete Colt's small, polite transgression was a moment of democratic and theatrical action that also nicely wrapped up the meeting of our piece with a sense of expectation. And by clearing the space, the audience physically experienced the moment as Aaron had, and they went into intermission with something to discuss.

PART III

Intermission

Organizing at Home and on the Road

The following two chapters act as a bridge between the meeting part of *City Council Meeting* and the local endings, which we describe in detail later. We also touch on how we used interviews as a creative tool, organized our audiences using community organizer approaches and tactics, and funded and produced the work. For us, it is important to discuss how the work became financially possible. There are many ideas of what producing a successful artwork costs, and we want to offer some clarity in our case.

Although the subjects in this section may be most legible to theatre artists, we hope they will also serve to inform practitioners and teachers in the humanities who want to do something similar or take on a version of the work with a school, as we are beginning to do. We feel that theatre-making offers a unique way to unite a body of research undertaken by a class or cohort through a collaboratively created live event.

In the fifteen to twenty minutes of *City Council Meeting* between the meeting and local ending we made in each city, we needed to do three things: reset the space so that it no longer fulfilled the expectations of government-meeting-as-theatre; get local cohorts and the performance space ready for what would come after intermission, our local creative encounter between political adversaries; and give the audience a chance to download and parse what they had just experienced, which was strange and often charged.

Because this was a lot to accomplish, we usually took our time and served snacks, making sure everyone in the room was comfortable and ready. This is in marked contrast to the normally rushed feeling backstage during a typical theatre intermission.

Organizing the Audience

One of our goals in having a truly diverse audience was to allow different kinds of people to witness each other through the lens of the piece. Throughout the creative process, we felt that if we did the right kind of organizing to get a mix of people into the room, viewers and collaborators would be comfortable enough to figure out the piece together, even if that meant sharing the experience with people they didn't normally come across. If that person sees a moment as funny, but it makes me angry, what can we learn about how our shared language might diverge depending on where we come from or how we relate to the person speaking? Could these questions provoke a sense of introspection among participants?

This notion of the audience's role is something UK performance ensemble Forced Entertainment talks about eloquently—reframing the role of the viewer in a subtle and thorough way. In *Certain Fragments: Contemporary Performance and Forced Entertainment*, Tim Etchells writes, "We are watching the people before us, not representing something but going through something. They lay their bodies on the line ... and we are transformed—not audience to a spectacle but witnesses to an event."[1]

Thanks to our New York City creative advisor, Gavin Kroeber (a producer and artist who had worked on the seminal conceptual project *Waiting for Godot in New Orleans* in 2006), we called our approach toward viewers "organizing the audience." Kroeber gave us spreadsheets and other tools that community organizers use for manifesting political actions. In other cities we also benefited from our presenting partners' long history of deep work among diverse local communities.

Often, we found simple approaches worked best. In each city we tried to employ a group of staffers with enough demographic diversity to represent that city as much as possible. We had local figures—council members, activists, or artists—record the orientation video. And we did a lot of visits in each city to churches, schools, business leaders, and government entities.

Community-Engaged Touring

In experimental theatre and dance, there are often two outcomes that funders, artists, and venues alike prioritize around new works: touring and community engagement. On some level these two outcomes can be at odds with each other, given the scarcity of resources available to the field through the traditional means of grants, commissions, and fees.

Touring as it's usually conceived of is necessarily efficient—a company of artists arrives in a town, sets up, performs, tears down, and moves on, usually within a week from start to finish. Community engagement (a kind of vague catchall that tends to mean prioritizing work with local residents who may not be part of the usual art-going audience, as well as prioritizing cultural, gender, and age diversity) needs time to be done meaningfully. Many funders and presenters want both the efficiency of the traditional touring model and deep community engagement at once because they are undercapitalized and seek ways to piggyback one priority on the back of another. In this resource-strapped model, community engagement can mean cramming a workshop between technical rehearsals or giving a single talk to a group of students who come by the theatre at lunch. When resources are scarce, community engagement can sometimes mean a kind of enhanced audience development.

It is rare to have the funding to both tour and engage with communities, as we did for *City Council Meeting*. Once we got into developing the work, we found that touring in the traditional framework might end up feeling cursory and exploitative in the places we were working, so we had to find a new way to travel as well as more resources to support that.

We had locked in venues in three cities by early 2011, when we were getting deep into our development process—Houston's DiverseWorks and UH Mitchell Center, New York's HERE Arts Center, and Tempe's ASU Gammage. These venues understood the differences and possible overlaps between touring and community engagement and helped us put significant resources toward both.

In Houston, Aaron had a long working relationship with the artistic director of DiverseWorks, Sixto Wagan, and with Project Row Houses, having made a project there in 2005 and visited several times since to teach workshops. In Tempe, ASU Gammage came on board through an introduction by Wagan, who saw a connection between our project and their history of multiyear collaborations, some of which, like Pat Graney's *Keeping the Faith*, were so successful they were taken up locally and had a life beyond the originating artist's residency.[2] The lead support of a three-year HERE Artist Residency in New York also helped DiverseWorks and Gammage commit.

In addition to a genuine desire to get behind the art itself, *City Council Meeting* met an organizational priority or goal for all of these anchor partners.

DiverseWorks was looking for ways to do more collaborations with the UH Mitchell Center and Row Houses; Gammage saw our process and our piece as a way to solidify growing relationships with local community members and elected officials; and HERE was driven to support work by mid-career multi-disciplinary artists through multi-year commitments. Venues that came in with this kind of enlightened self-interest were more likely to be enthusiastic about the massive amount of work required on their end to bring the project to fruition.

With our lead partners in each place, we raised enough money to spend more time building the process and the work specifically for each city than an experimental live performance can usually afford. This is also thanks to significant early support from the Jerome Foundation, the National Performance Network (NPN) Creation Fund, and other local foundations and donors in Houston and Tempe.

The Value of Work-in-Progress Showings

Because audiences performed this piece, we had to do a lot of fully produced work-in-progress showings to get it right. We learned from each developmental showing—at HERE in New York, in Boston, and even in our early performances in Houston and Tempe—usually from something unexpected going wrong or some obvious gap in our thinking.

As we developed the show through a weekend of performances at the Emerging America festival at A.R.T. in Cambridge in early 2011, two things happened that pointed the way toward a final form.

At that point we still hadn't made the orientation video, we were only working with three staffers, and the audience on our first night was larger than expected, so it took much longer to get the piece through orientation than we'd hoped. We ended up with a crowd of people outside the theatre struggling to hear one person with a clipboard explain the relatively complicated rules of the piece. It had started going off the rails before it even began.

Then, even though we'd been delayed, there were latecomers, who added to the confusion but also showed us where the piece was working. At one point, a guy peeked into the venue. Audience members were reading about drainage to a council full of other closely listening audience members. Everyone looked pretty serious, like they were doing their jobs. The man walked up to Aaron, a little shyly, and asked, "Is this a council meeting?" Aaron said, "No, it's a theatre piece." He looked relieved and took a seat.

The next night, in the middle of a particularly long pause between testimonies, another audience member shouted out "What the hell!" to no one in particular. Nevertheless, the meeting persisted.

These two instances showed us that what we were making was on the line between art and not art, really good and really bad. And that was where we wanted the work to live. By really good, we mean the audience felt like it was witnessing an event (a real government meeting), and by really bad we mean embodying and revealing something about civic procedure, boredom, and anomie in a compelling way (rather than simply being a boring or confusing event).

We often say our favorite kind of theatre can accommodate multiple responses, so even though we don't want everyone to wonder what the hell is going on, we don't mind if it pushes that envelope a little as long as there are clues participants can grab on to if they want. And sometimes the thrall we hope they feel about the virtuosity of a production, an actor, a script, or a design concept can get in the way of the real transfer of questions and meaning. We make work where you can see the seams and make your own decisions.

This might be counter to the aims of more traditional research, where the goal is to make a hypothesis, test it, and reveal a distinct conclusion. With our artistic research, the possibilities must include varying responses from viewers and multiple ways of seeing the same moment performed.

Paying for Time

We cannot overstate how unlikely it was and how fortunate we were to receive the funding we did for *City Council Meeting*. It's a strange, complicated piece, both an invitation to participate and a critique of the way participation is normally practiced in city government, as well as an embrace of the folly and genuine good intentions that define local politics. Because of the early support of our partner venues and the larger grants that came in later from New England Foundation for the Arts' (NEFA) National Theater Project, the MAP Fund, and NPN's Forth Fund, we were able to pay ourselves to work long enough on developing the piece so it could both travel city to city and remain engaged with local communities. We could balance the demands of developing and producing the piece in three cities at once. For much of the process, Aaron drew a monthly stipend to act as creative producer. This meant that interactions with a presenter or community partner in one city carried over into the creative process and put all the parties in conversation with each other throughout development and production. Finally, the funds we raised on our own and with presenting partners allowed us to competitively pay local staffers, artists, and local ending collaborators in each city to take part in the work. Our travel model—fewer of us coming from New York to work longer with local participants—meant that resources stayed or went local rather than only going to the artists from out of town.

In the end, the budget to develop and present *City Council Meeting* in five cities was just over $260,000, including artists' fees, many of our technical and promotional expenses, travel, and research. On top of that, the presenters we worked with in most cities paid for their in-house administrative expenses and often covered our housing, travel, and per diem. So all told, the actual cost of making this work, start to finish, was likely around $350,000. While Houston,

New York City, and Tempe each took significantly more resources because we were developing the work for two to three years there, our final two cities of San Francisco and Keene came in at a total cost of $28,000–$35,000.

Because of the way the project was funded—through a combination of project grants, development funding, presenters' fees and commissions, and individual contributions—the cash income and expenses varied from city to city. For instance, our housing was sometimes covered by the presenter and at other times paid up front as part of our tour fee depending on the agreement we had. Grants from organizations like the National Performance Network and National Theater Project put money in the hands of both artists and venue partners, with an expected match from the venue; allocation of resources was something we negotiated specifically in each city. A detailed budget breakdown is available at citycouncilmeeting.org, as is a development and production timeline.

We are of course thankful beyond measure for the exceptional funding we received. We also feel like U.S. arts funding is often implicitly centered around a kind of efficiency model in which artists and nonprofits, especially small ones whose work is entwined within marginalized communities, are asked to do immense amounts of work and produce transformative results for little or no money. And while exceptional, our funding was not extravagant. Aaron, Mallory, and Jim were paid $1,100 plus expenses per week on the road (without benefits); Aaron took $1,000 a month as creative producer; and no arts administrator working at any of our venues was making a particularly high salary.

We feel the arts, like any other part of the public sector in America, would do better with a lot more money available so that more significant and long-term collaborations like ours could be created by artists from across spectrums of income, geography, race, gender identity, and culture. If every project that sought to make meaningful relationships in communities had the kind of funding we did, there would be more works like *City Council Meeting* created and exchanged, by a more diverse range of artists, with greater impact. In light of movements within the performing arts like Creating New Futures and We See You, White American Theater, we also feel any increase in resources should be put in the hands of the artists and companies making the work instead of the gatekeepers and bureaucracies administering the funds.

We developed the work in Houston for a total of eleven weeks and spent roughly the same amount of time in Tempe. In New York, we had fifteen weeks with our working group, including two fully produced work-in-progress performances. Because of this relatively luxurious amount of time in two cities outside our own, we were able to come up with a way for the show to be locally engaged and on tour simultaneously. For San Francisco and Keene, we winnowed the number of weeks we needed to develop the piece to six. We did two or three early visits of two to seven days each. We worked with our presenting partner to meet staffers and other collaborators; met local figures in elected politics, activism, and the arts; and saw at least one council meeting. Because the venues had a way to use our piece as a vehicle for achieving some other organizational goal, the partnership was strong even in these last two cities.

In all five cities, when we returned for the production residency, we spent three weeks finishing the local ending and training staffers to run the meeting. By training a local working group to run the meeting in each city, we could travel with just the three lead collaborators and a stage manager rather than a whole company of performers, which would have proven cost-prohibitive to most presenters.

Our work together was both synchronous and asynchronous, particularly in the later stages of the process. As the project evolved there was more trust in our abilities to work in many places at once, requiring us to cover more ground. Mallory's process allowed her to teach the meeting to a group of staffers in seven or eight rehearsals. We'd start by having them read through the whole meeting script as if they were both audience and staffers, so they could get a sense of what participants might go through in performance. Then we restaged each section, integrating guests as test-case viewers, so that by the end of the rehearsals the staff would have had a chance to run the meeting on their own, without us.

Meanwhile, Aaron would interview community members participating in the local ending, Jim looked at spaces and design possibilities, and the three of us would end the day talking through the ideas and material we'd accumulated. Working this way meant we could each follow our own interests without the project losing cohesion.

Together, we'd also use those production residency weeks—both in rehearsal and outside of it—to find out more about the local issues we were exploring for the local ending and about larger cultural dynamics specific to the city. We drew on the staffers informally to fill out our cursory understanding of a city. While Mallory was training the staffers to run the meeting, Aaron would finalize interviews with collaborators for the local ending and start working on the script. Jim worked simultaneously as production designer for the ending and production manager/run crew for rehearsals. This made for a busy final residency, but it also helped make the production into a kind of community celebration when it worked. And it allowed for informal or accidental transfers of information and collective buy-in from staffers and community members.

Over the course of developing and presenting the work from 2010 to 2014, we turned down several invitations to travel with the work to theatres that were less invested in what the work could do for them, as well as us. Again, while all the spaces and cities we spoke with had the intention to engage with communities in a deep and meaningful way, the time and money resources that would have allowed them to follow through were not always available.

We also chose not to follow at least one possible engagement for the project because of how it might have impacted the city where we hoped to work. We had several conversations and site visits about a potential culminating performance in Detroit in 2015 through connections Aaron had made teaching workshops there regularly. Through the multidisciplinary artist Invincible/ill Weaver, the organization Allied Media Projects, and activists who worked alongside philosopher Grace Lee Boggs, we had become excited about the way that Detroit was constantly creating innovative means of hyper-local governing simply in order to get their basic needs met, contrary to the way the city was portrayed as having failed. Through the city's bankruptcy, there were self-created civic bodies in exile—water boards, school boards, and library boards—that continued to meet even after they'd been disbanded by the state.

Our thought had been to turn over the local ending to various small groups of citizens, who could then use our project to bring awareness to each other and perhaps fight the encroachment of capital that was threatening to undermine their homes and their work. But by that time, we had run through all the funding we had available.

We decided not to continue with the project there, despite enthusiastic invitations locally, because we would not be able to bring appropriate resources to a place already impoverished. Our work would run the risk of being an extractive rather than mutually supportive and aggrandizing endeavor. In subsequent years, we watched other arts organizations and projects carry out well-intended work designed to celebrate vital and rigorous art and organizing in Detroit but that instead mostly contributed to arts-led gentrification at the expense of local residents.[1] For us it was important to recognize when available funding might have had a deleterious effect on a community, as well as on our own finances.

Participant-Observer Interviews

When we figured out the basic premise for the second part of *City Council Meeting*—a short performance created in collaboration with local political adversaries—we decided to use a participant-observer interview technique Aaron had deployed on earlier projects. This technique involves building trust over time, having several conversations with interview subjects (often in places where they feel at home), and giving them the option to go back and change the text you make together.

Working this way helped avoid what Jim Findlay calls "parachuting in to do community engagement"—arriving in a city, spending the minimum time required to get interviews with key people, recording those interviews, leaving, and then making a piece in which we use those subjects' words. With this work, we felt it was important to be as vigilant as possible in understanding power dynamics, structural inequalities, and our roles in them. We feel that acknowledging those dynamics and structures can bring awareness of new possibilities and that the work doesn't need to be *about* change for a process to embody its possibility.

Ethnographic Process

Aaron learned his approach from Baruch College sociologist Gregory Snyder, whose technique involves no recording devices or note-taking during interviews. Aaron and "Professor Greggy" worked at the same restaurant after college; as Snyder developed his methodology, Aaron was an early reader of his first book, *Graffiti Lives*. Aaron later tried out the methodology on his own projects.

Snyder works with members of subcultures, most recently graffiti writers and skateboarders. He talks to them in spaces where they are comfortable—bars, hangouts, a skate site—then a day or two later writes down everything he remembers from the conversation, fashioning a sort of ethnographic monologue. He then shows his subjects a draft and they have another conversation to ensure that the voice and information feels right to both parties.[1]

As theatre makers, we find this method valuable for a number of reasons. First, it allows people to be at least partly on their own terms when talking to an outsider. It acknowledges the power differential between subject and interviewer while putting both on a more equal footing. It helps people feel at ease and less on the spot (especially helpful for us when talking to politicians and activists) and can help bring out the performative nature of interviews. Finally, without a recording or notes, we remembered the most important things people said, and we were subconsciously arranging and grouping things in creative ways before we started writing them down. Put simply: your mind is more creative than your recorder.

Being beholden to a subject with whom we were developing a relationship, rather than a recording of that person from a single point in time, led us to make surprising and dynamic choices together with our work. It also helped us avoid what Snyder, quoting sociologist Norman Denzin, describes as "unidirectional claims that argue definitively that *this* is how *they* are," instead allowing our own subjectivity and identity to be recognized, along with the power dynamics at play between artist-researcher and subject.[2]

In San Francisco, as Aaron and singer Dwayne Calizo talked about the changes San Francisco was going through, it became clear we were really talking about a loss of innocence, a kind of cultural aging process. To embody this, we put Calizo's text in third person and decided to have a teenage boy perform it, rather than Calizo himself.

Snyder developed his technique in part as a provocation to some prevailing methods in sociology. He felt that most sociologists assume a kind of safe, distanced "neutrality" from their subjects, which he found suspect. How can you make an intervention into a subculture, assume any neutrality, and at the same time get close? If you add race, gender, and class to this equation, it is dangerous to believe your point of view is neutral.[3]

We want to offer that same provocation to our field.

Imagine you're a white, relatively middle class, gender-normative theatre artist and you're making a project with someone who's trans, queer, and home-less. How can that relationship not be on some level exploitative? Even if you offer them coauthorship credit and a fine rate of pay, for instance, it will still be your work. You'll be able to take advantage of it through career building, publications (like this one), and other means of financial and social capital with which the art world often trades.

Very often the people we worked with on *City Council Meeting*'s local end-ings did not have access to resources we did. Even though many theatre artists feel pressed for money and time, many of us still carry privilege with us when an institution brings us in, opens doors, confers expert status upon us, and allows us to make intellectual property using other peoples' words, voices, images, and experiences.

The technique we use necessitates a deeper connection than *arrive, in-terview, leave*—the journalistic or artistic equivalent of a one-night stand—because we later have to come back and show you what we wrote. You're going to have to approve our authorship (or not approve it) before the material gets onstage. Very often our subjects in *City Council Meeting* performed their own words, which meant approval (or not) could make or break a show. We like that high-wire act; it makes for more adventurous art while keeping us on the spot as authors in a way that seems ethically appropriate.

Is it possible to do the kind of work we did exploitatively? Of course. Es-pecially in a field in which there is no Institutional Review Board[4] governing how research is conducted, funded, or used.

We advocate that you recognize you're coming into a situation that, whether painful or celebratory for your subjects and collaborators, may not be your own. You're using a relationship with someone's firsthand experience or beliefs to make art. It's good to be respectful of that, to see your positional-ity at the outset. And as Mallory and Aaron have gotten more deeply involved in traditional scholarly research, we realized that there is no set of standards to which artists are held responsible in our work—thus, artists working this way have to hold themselves accountable in terms of their integrity and be transparent about their failures.

Our Ethnographic Process

This is Aaron's adaptation of Snyder's participant-observer interview tech-nique, which Snyder uses in *Graffiti Lives* and subsequent writings.

If you've ever worked as an actor, musician, or dancer, you can think of an interview as a kind of rehearsal or performance—it will involve preparation and technique, which you will then forget on purpose so that the moment itself is freed up. This is also helpful if you're interviewing someone you know well in a different context. Make the interview special and unique so that you can charge up the air around it.

Step 1. Get to know your subject. This can take a day, a week, several visits over the course of a year or two, or longer. The value of getting to know your subjects prior to interviewing them is that the interview will draw on everything you share. You'll be attentive to their cadence, nuance, feints, and rhetorical style; you'll be watching for significant eye contact (as a device to gain your sympathy or as a moment of real courage and connection, among other possibilities); and you'll draw on previous conversations and make reference to them.

Step 2. Leave enough time. We've had great interviews that have lasted as little as ten minutes. We've had interviews that we thought would last ten minutes but went on for an hour. More often than not, if you leave enough time, you'll get more and better material. Even if your interview subject only has a few minutes (twenty to thirty minutes should be a minimum), you want to leave a little time at the end in case you want to continue the conversation beyond its allotted time.

Step 3. Arrive with questions you don't know the answers to. Journalists and lawyers often need to get confirmation of simple facts. We're doing something different. If you don't know the answer, your subject may not either, and answers that are not certain are more theatrically and philosophically interesting. You can always fact-check and follow up later.

Step 4. Make clear agreements in writing. Before you start, be sure your subjects know they can revisit what you write about them later, and that they have the right to request you not use something that comes up in conversation. We never had a problem with this during *City Council Meeting*, probably because we established trust with subjects. This helps subjects understand that you're not simply taking what they say and leaving, and that the interview is a step in a process.

Step 5. Try to memorize your most important questions. This way you don't need to go back to a list of questions every time you want to ask something.

Step 6. Take a couple of minutes before the interview to clear your mind. You want to listen and check in on whatever emotional baggage you're bringing in from your day. You want to be gracious, generous, and clear. If you need to warm up by swimming, doing yoga, or going for a run to focus, make time for that.

Step 7. Start by reiterating the basics you've agreed on about interview length and opportunities to make changes later. We always tell people that we may lobby to keep something they're unsure about, but they can ultimately decide.

Step 8. Monitor your enthusiasm. Many of us have an empathic tendency to nod, murmur, or otherwise affirm what's being said. This is OK, especially if you have a very shy or nervous subject on your hands, but make sure it's a choice and not a reflex. Practice with friends to see what it's like to ask them a question and then remain neutral while they talk. What does it mean to simply listen? How does that differ by culture and gender? Just asking these questions of yourself can make you more mindful. In the interview, someone who is used to telling stories to elicit a certain kind of response may get flustered if you're a little more restrained. That's not always a bad thing, because it gets them out of their comfort zone. You might also be able to listen better if you're not able to perform your usual sympathetic response. You might more accurately hear what's being said and how. You may get off your own center when you can't make someone struggling to articulate themselves feel good, and being a little off center is a great place from which honest conversation can spring.

Step 9. Let there be silences if there need to be. An awkward pause is a human pause, a break in our daily rehearsed dialogues, and those pauses often lead to honest reflection and spontaneous, real interaction.

Step 10. Allow yourself to veer away from what you think you want to get from this interview: follow-up questions and new lines of inquiry you didn't expect are all wonderful. Go where the energy is.

Step 11. Unless you have to, don't write down notes right away. Later that day or the next, write down everything you remember. The salient topics or opinions will likely come up first. It's good to stick with it for a little longer than you think you need to, because ideas that may have seemed unimportant in conversation will help you make connections later. If you're dealing with a particularly long conversation—more than an hour—you can break up sheets of paper by fifteen-minute increments and just focus on one at a time, recalling as much detail as possible within each short block.

Step 12. Write up the script. Trust your instincts for what's most interesting, not just what fulfills a certain argument. This is when working from memory can become creative—you may want to make notes or sketches of material to add once you go back to your interview subject or list questions in the margin you want to ask of either the audience or the subject. Try to write down nonverbal expressions—tone, habits, repetitions—that make the person you talked to truly themselves.

Step 13. Take what you've written back to the subject. Find out what they are excited by, what they think you got right or wrong, and what steps you can take together to move it forward. If you've built trust with them, your subjects will likely be excited and want to make the work better with you. Your vulnerability here is key—the fact that they have some agency in this process means you are on more equal footing.

Yes, this is a thirteen-step process, and yes, it's complicated—a lot to consider and not for everyone. But it works for us because it acknowledges power differentials and asks both interviewer and subject to be vulnerable and collaborate. Ideally, that's why we're all in this together.

It's also important to say that not all subjects are right for this approach. There's nothing keeping you from deploying a combination of interview approaches. Some artists really want to record things, for instance. Some subjects might too. There may be other interviews you get on a moment's notice and have to take notes during so that you don't lose the fine points. It's all OK. This method works for us most of the time.

An Aside on the Value of Boring Research

Around the time we were making *City Council Meeting*, Aaron asked a journalist friend how his research process worked. He explained that journalism is often more boring than people realize. "You go and can't find a source," he explained, "then you go back, and someone talks to you, but the story is not the right one. You can't verify what someone is saying. You wait around. And then, maybe two weeks later, you go back and a little door opens. And then it closes and you have to go back, until you finally piece it together."[5]

This validated something we had noticed while making our show. Sometimes our process is boring or leads to dead ends, and for very understandable reasons—budgetary constraints, time constraints, presenter and audience and artist expectations—artists don't always leave time for those detours and dead ends. For us, those obstacles are part of what makes a project succeed.

In Tempe, for instance, we spent two or three afternoons in the back room of Tumbleweed, an organization for the homeless, listening to stories of potential local collaborators. Most of these stories did not feel right, and then we met Smilez, who became a pillar of the project for us.

Similarly, in Houston, we sat in on numerous church services, local meetings, and other activities where there was no *material* benefit to our production, but we were able to learn something—either affectively or concretely—about the overlapping cultures of the city and the people in it.

We invite artists working on socially or community-engaged art projects, as well as student and faculty researchers doing community-based learning or service-learning projects, to insist on the time it takes to listen enough to get bored, to go past the useful material into the unexpected. For those of us who travel to make work like this, losing yourself enough to get past the initial spark of discovery means you're probably doing the work.

Questions for Schematic Theatre

As we worked on *City Council Meeting*, we came up with a list of questions that we think are helpful for theatre practitioners and teachers to consider when making their own new works. We also hope this can be of use to humanities research; how can you question not only the content or form of the research but also the context and history within which your work resides? This list is a beginning. There are more questions that might be specific to one or another discipline or situation. We hope these serve as a starting point.

- What sort of rooms or spaces should this performance (or class or interview) be held in?
- What role does the space have in this particular city, town, or neighborhood?
- What kinds of performances already take place here: meetings, book groups, plays, conferences, sales pitches, love affairs?
- How does our role as insiders or outsiders in this community impact how the work might be received, and how can we include community members or text to reflect that?
- How do we account in our process for differences in geography, ethnicity, race, gender identity, or other markers of power and privilege?
- What role does language play in this work? Is there anything about language that we want to show more clearly? How do we do that?
- Who should perform this piece? Should they be skilled in performance techniques? How will their level of skill impact audience members who may be asked to join the performance (or may want to whether or not they are asked)?

- How do we make the script most usable by the people we think should perform? Is there theatre jargon in there that we could do without? Is there another way to say "upstage left"?
- How does communication function in our performance? Can people really listen to each other? How can we rehearse and enact listening rather than simply representing it?
- What are we assuming, and can we make our assumptions plain so they can be improved upon by our artist and nonartist collaborators?
- What commonly assumed rules about seeing performances (or conducting field research or teaching a course) might impact how people experience what we are doing? Do we need to address those rules, break them, or honor them? All of the above?
- How much money do we have, what are our priorities, and can we avoid exploiting professional art workers and nonprofessional participants alike?
- How long will all this take to do right, really? Does it have to fit into the semester or annual constraints of presenting seasons and academic years?
- What other work already does or has done what we want to do?

PART IV

Local Endings

Narrators and Translators

In this final section of the book we'll go through each city's specific development process and local ending. We close with conversations with our partners,
looking back over six years later, and an update on the political issue taken up
in each local ending.

The local ending and our approach to it came about after in-progress showings of the meeting in New York City and Boston let us sense the expectations
of the audience after the first half, where the meeting ends abruptly with Pete
Colt and viewers are asked to clear the room. What would we bring the audience back into? How does a piece that ends on such a natural high point
continue? Were we going to choose a side? Offer a political position?

In the following chapters we describe our process for making each local
ending, with reflections from key participants in each community where we
presented the piece. These included curatorial and administrative staff from
venues where we worked, the staffers and other collaborators in local cohorts,
and students from New York City's working group. We wanted to look back at
how the piece had impacted them, personally or in the context of their venue
or city, but on their terms, rather than a funder's or our own.

At times, the piece's impact could still be felt in how an organization
thought about community collaborations or in the way an individual's work
evolved; at others we had to jog someone's memory about what had happened in the piece. Both kinds of feedback were useful for us. We knew, for
example, that Assata Richards, our staffer in Houston, had run for the actual
city council, placing third in a field of nine candidates, and was now working
on neighborhood issues at the University of Houston. By contrast, one of our
favorite high school working group members from New York City, Alannah
Bilal, whose insights were pivotal for us in making the piece, had to be reminded who we were before she began to recall the experience of working on

the project. We wanted to see impact in a more personal way, as well as within the culture of the organizations with which we worked, and learn from it.

Finally, we look at where the issues we focused on stand in each city at the time of this writing. This is a way to point out that the raw material of our local endings was local political issues and subjects that in many cases continue to evolve, with real-world consequences, victories, and defeats. Returning to look at this process now has been an attempt to know how much one work of art can hold in terms of philosophical questions, ethical engagement with community members, and viable experience for viewers to enjoy and take part in.

By giving *City Council Meeting* a local ending specific to each city, we were able to ask how culture could respond to politics without us making assumptions about each place before we visited. We challenged ourselves, as three white artists from New York often traveling to smaller cities and working with non-white collaborators, not to impose our version of community engagement.

Although we were not trying to hide our political leanings, we felt that revealing them in the end would be banal and predictable: news flash, artists are lefties. After sitting through the meeting's rules-driven provocations, we wanted to make something sublime and surprising—a little theatre magic that let audiences see themselves and their city in new ways. How would art deal with the civic tensions the meeting embodied and revealed? We framed local political life through the lens of an artistic gesture.

At first, we thought the local endings would include bold gestures: office paper dropping from the lighting grid like snowflakes, heavy lighting and video design that would appear unexpectedly and overwhelm viewers with its beauty. But as we thought through what the piece was asking and demanding, we felt those kinds of ideas would end up capitulating to a desire for spectacle, an easy wow factor, which we were less interested in than the piece's ability to reframe local politics as art. Even though some of our endings did involve big aesthetic gestures, we made sure they came from an issue that came up locally and from conversations specific to that city.

We often ran up against expectations from our collaborators and presenting partners about what we wanted the project to accomplish, as well as deeper questions and assumptions about what art is supposed to do. Arts funders often want us to talk about how we impact the communities where we work using metrics more appropriate to service delivery than cultural production—how many people came, how old they were, of what gender or cultural identity, from which zip codes. In evaluating work, presenters and theatre companies alike often combine these kinds of numbers with somewhat grandiose rhetoric about the ability of culture to create community.

But we were working with communities already very much created, with their own histories, aesthetics, and ongoing, vital dialogues. In developing these local endings, we were able to articulate that our agenda was to put a frame around the act and structures of civic participation and democracy, so that the ongoing work our collaborators were doing—as politicians, activists, educators, and artists—might be seen differently. We didn't have a message to deliver or exploit; we had a medium to reflect some of the messages a city was already speaking to itself. We were participant-observers, navigating our own connections and histories while hopefully centering each community's unique tensions within our framework.

Rancière's *Emancipated Spectator*, which had been revelatory for us in thinking about acting and building the meeting, was helpful here too, as we brainstormed possibilities for local endings.

We were more interested in the fact that our piece doesn't necessarily build unity among audience members but allows a space for that disunity to flourish, what Rancière refers to as "the irreducible distances" between anonymous people that make "everyone equal to everyone else." This potential theatre could be "a new scene of equality," an "emancipated community of narrators and translators."[1] On the most successful nights of *City Council Meeting*, we felt we created moments in which people could see themselves as both distinct and part of an event that included many individuals participating on their own terms.

After traveling and doing site visits in Houston and Tempe, we also decided that we should honor our subjective experience as outsiders looking inward. We wanted to walk a fine line between knowing a place like a resident and apprehending it with fresh eyes and ears, championing both local knowledge and our own idiosyncratic take. To do this, we decided to use the first meeting we observed in each city as the jumping-off point for the local ending there. Having already gone to meetings in several cities, we found that there was always some small theatrical moment with resonance beyond whatever issue was being discussed or debated. Forcing ourselves to stay with what we saw and extrapolate from that would give us a chance to go deep, to build on something real, to find resonance under a procedural surface.

This got us into arguments with some local residents and collaborators.

They questioned the randomness of our decision to go with what we saw first. Why choose issues that seemed mundane or uninteresting, like drainage in Houston, ficus trees in Tempe, or skateboarders in Keene? Why not use the platform we'd created to speak directly to hot-button issues like gentrification and homelessness?

Our response was that to go straight to the pressure point and push on it would be to pretend we had authority over a place where we'd just arrived as guests. We also found that seemingly mundane issues were often entry points to more problematic, intractable subjects. Drainage became a way to talk about or avoid talking about climate change and the separation of church and state; ficus trees were what Tempe talked about instead of dealing with home-lessness; skateboarders were easier to address than chronic underemployment and a crumbling social safety net. By starting with the surface, coming in from outside, we could get people to make something together without blowing up tensions in a gratuitous way. This is not so different from an ethnographer using an interactive device through which subjects can perform themselves by engaging in a specific, identity-based activity, rather than simply talking about an issue. By acknowledging our role as visitors with limited time to spend in a place, we let local cohorts and collaborators feel ownership over the ending section of *City Council Meeting* while also trusting us to lead from a point of curiosity.

Once we decided to work from what we saw and to create some kind of local response to the meeting, we made a set of ground rules. We would invite people on either side of a specific local issue to perform together in the cre-ation of explicitly aesthetic experience. This let us improvise and adapt rather than feel like we had to define what we were doing before all the participants involved could weigh in.

In each city we ended up with a radically different ending.

In Houston, we paired Councilor Steven Costello with church choirs and middle school kids, the constituents on the opposing side of his push for in-frastructure changes to the city.

In Tempe, we involved a young woman who had recently gotten a home after years living on the streets; the head of the Downtown Tempe Commu-nity, a pro-business group; a city worker who took care of the ficus trees; and a woman who served the homeless on behalf of the city.

In New York, our hometown, we spent a year meeting with a diverse group of students from four high schools about the issues of standardized testing and mayoral control of the school board, and we invited council members and education experts to be a part of the ending each night.

In San Francisco, we partnered with local choreographer Erika Chong Shuch and her company to make a piece about gentrification and the death of the city's counterculture, as personified by an HIV-positive opera singer, single room occupancy resident, music teacher, and pillar of the queer, punk performance community, Dwayne Calizo.

In Keene, we worked with two local skateboarders and two council members to address tensions between the town and the local college, and between the city and its skaters.

If the meeting asked audiences to step into someone else's shoes, someone likely from another place or a different background, the local ending flipped the script. Now they got to watch local residents make art out of their own struggles and debates, their specific place and time.

For us, making the local endings drew on a different set of skills. Aaron used his ethnographic approach to interview local ending collaborators and collaborate on text. Mallory and Jim drew from their broad palette of compositional and dramaturgical tools as director and designer.

In each city we made threads between the meeting and local ending so that the ending didn't come completely out of the blue but rather completed the audience's experience. Often, after we began to develop the ending, we cast our ending performers as staffers so that the figures the audience encountered at the beginning led them through the whole experience. We sometimes used the same chairs, tables, or monitors in the local ending as we did in the meeting, just in a new configuration. The index cards that audience members filled out during the audience participation section of the meeting were recited by staffers as people came back to the newly configured space after intermission.

While we began conceptualizing the local endings in early visits to each place, we often didn't make the material until the final stage of the process, concurrent with staff rehearsals. This created a productive feedback loop in which local staffers could help us pick apart what we were making as we made it and separate good ideas from less good ones. On any given day, we would often spend part of our time working on the meeting and part of it working on the local ending so that the two had a relationship simply through proximity and time.

Each local ending came with its challenges: collaborators that were hard to reach, sensitive issues that would shift and change overnight, a general suspicion or confusion about what we were up to. Sometimes we didn't know either. In this work, Aaron, Mallory, and Jim often worked on asynchronously, following different leads and tangents. On a good day, we were open to problem-solving and listening rather than making snap decisions or assumptions.

Houston

ELDORADO BALLROOM

---

*Engineers have a habit of questioning faith. We see things in black and white—
you do this, you don't do that. But now I'm on the council. And this is a performance. And everything is shades of gray.*

City Council Meeting's first official public performances were in Houston,
Texas, a coproduction of DiverseWorks, Project Row Houses, and the UH
Mitchell Center. Because it was our opening city, we were flying a little bit
blind in terms of how to make the ending. Throughout the process we relied
heavily on our presenting partners and our working group to ensure we were
doing honest work and bringing in a diverse audience.

Aaron had worked with DiverseWorks and Row Houses on a previous collaboration—his 2005 NPN-funded play, *What You've Done*—and had some
sense of how each institution worked. He and DiverseWorks artistic director
Sixto Wagan had also worked together on a professional development program for local artists. Wagan opened the door to working with the Mitchell
Center through its director, Karen Farber, and also helped make great invitations to possible working group members. Because we were able to pull together resources and get to Houston for several visits, Aaron and Mallory were
able to spend a combined total of about seventeen weeks in the city over two
and a half years.

Without necessarily knowing it at the time, we used Houston to solidify
parts of our process for making the ending that would carry through all four
subsequent cities. Aaron saw the electrically charged council session that
yielded the text for the Houston section of the meeting on one of his first
visits. There, a council member named Stephen Costello was being vilified
by local churches and defended by local activists for his new drainage plan.

In addition to the material we used for the meeting, we also found that there was something lively and surprising about a council chamber when adversaries were in the room together. Aaron was surrounded by a diverse, committed, and dynamic set of performances, unexpectedly riveting and discomforting.

If we could get these adversaries to cooperate in any way as part of our project, it would be a worthy pursuit. We felt like just getting them in the room would be enough of a challenge, and that, perhaps counterintuitively, that challenge would relieve us of the need to come down on one side or the other with what we created. The simple act of having people collaborate on a creative gesture would embody something about the nature of politics and participation that we found compelling. The context and form would be as important as the content.

We found that taking on a seemingly impossible challenge like this kept us moving forward with ambition, curiosity, and humility. If we were going to get Councilor Costello in the room alongside representatives from the churches that publicly excoriated him, we'd have to ask a lot of questions, listen well, and make ourselves vulnerable. It would have been more expedient, perhaps, to just work with people who felt as we did: that his drainage proposal was sound; that churches, especially megachurches like the ones who showed up en masse to protest Costello, were more interested in protecting their financial and political power than in helping the community. But that would not have embodied what we were discovering about how the democratic process, or an artistic treatment of the material, functions differently than simply making a statement on one side or another.

The idea of an impossible challenge—something that is too big to work or just seems like a really bad idea—is a thread connecting this project to other new theatre work in New York around this time. Companies like Elevator Repair Service (ERS), where Aaron was an ensemble member for several years, and artists like Young Jean Lee often start by provoking themselves to make something that seems unlikely to work, "tasks we assign ourselves that are impossible to complete."[1] Or, as our colleague playwright Lee says, "What's the worst possible play I could write?"[2] ERS members have often talked about how that kind of challenge helps keep the company honest—if we're doing something that probably won't work, we have to work extra hard if we're even going to have a chance. That kind of risk informed our idea for the ending of *City Council Meeting*.

We first got access to Costello via his publicist, Kathryn McNeil, who was a friend of the UH Mitchell Center's director, Karen Farber. On an early visit, Aaron and Farber were discussing the council meeting he'd just seen and Aaron expressed some curiosity about Costello, whose calm, pugnacious affect he'd been interested in as the churches tried to make him look bad. Farber texted McNeil, who agreed to meet us for lunch that same week. This was a great introduction to how much Houston, like many cities, worked through personal connections. If you wanted to get someone, you just asked who knew her, and eventually you'd find someone to bring you together. Surely this was true of other places where we made the piece, but nowhere more so than Houston, where politics and culture seem to overlap in a series of concentric circles of small town–like connections.

At lunch, Aaron pitched McNeil the project, and she became an early ally of ours, agreeing to lobby for Costello to perform with us and submit to a series of interviews. Through McNeil, Costello became the cornerstone of our ending—with his name attached, we could convince church representatives to at least talk to us and perhaps join the work.

During subsequent residency visits to Houston between late 2010 and the production in October/November 2012, we interviewed Costello a number of times and worked hard to get buy-in from his more skeptical staff members. We canvassed local churches that had publicly signed onto the efforts to have Costello's drainage proposal defeated. We learned that the churches' interest was financial: Costello's proposed drainage fee would be assessed on nonporous land, meaning paved areas owned by businesses and homes. The churches owned a lot of parking lots, so they'd be paying hefty fees. We learned that one of Costello's strategies to finance massive infrastructure projects was to bypass traditional city bonds and tie the projects to a fee, which led the churches to fight back on the grounds that it was a thinly disguised tax.[3]

What this arcana meant in the theatre of local government meetings was that church pastors claimed the city was trying to open the door to taxing the church, while Costello and his allies could argue that what was being asked of the congregations was akin to paying their electric bills. Although not super splashy on the surface, it led to highly dramatic rhetoric about the separation of church and state, the corruption of government, and the duty of all of us to pay for the services we use from the city. This is something we saw on council room stages throughout the country: different actors making something mundane into something grandiose (i.e., drainage is actually about church-state separation or our constitutional rights) in order to motivate supporters.

One of the most telling moments about how tightly the circle of power operated in the city was when Aaron and Costello were discussing the work of a lobbying entity for the churches that had made the campaign against Costello both public and personal. When Aaron mentioned he wanted to talk to a church lobbyist whose name had come up at the council meeting, Costello took out his phone, called him, and asked him to meet with Aaron. After hanging up, Costello said, "Yeah, that's how it works. We tell each other to be ready, or that we are coming to the next meeting, or that we are speaking on a certain show. We give each other a chance to respond."[4] This helped us understand that the meeting is a forum at which to prepare arguments for the public audience. There were no surprise attacks. Costello and the lobbyist David Welch, of the Houston Area Pastor Council, were coauthoring the play.

Time and time again, the local democratic process and competition proved valuable to our artmaking. Every actor on the political stage needs venues to connect with and convince possible supporters—having a captive audience each night of a hundred potential or actual constituents they might not otherwise get to meet was valuable. Even with social and traditional media playing an increasing role in politics, getting together with people in a room is vital for local elected officials, not to mention theatre artists. Once the churches heard Costello would be part of our show, a number of them at least gave us time for interviews, and some agreed to be a part of the work. Interestingly, though the main instigator of the campaign against the drainage plan was a white-run megachurch with a lot of resources (and a lot to lose), they did not end up participating in the performances. Instead, the churches of color were able and committed partners.

Mallory, Aaron, and Jim visited services at several megachurches, a diverse ethnography in and of itself, and often met with pastors. It's worth mentioning that while all our presenting partners were profoundly helpful and supportive in Houston, the fact that we were seeking to work with white megachurches and other Baptist congregations was unsettling for a couple of them. The churches have a long history of anti-LGBTQIA+ lobbying and points of view, including vilifying Houston's first lesbian mayor, Annise Parker, who was in office while we were working there.[5] For DiverseWorks artistic director Sixto Wagan, our blurring of the lines separating church and art, our desire to have adversaries in the room, was something he supported completely in concept but felt personally uncomfortable with. We recognized that we had an easier time approaching these church constituencies because we were straight and white, and from out of town. Wagan gave us the space to build the work, and even when his own values were challenged, he went as far as he could to make connections and conversations happen. He just didn't go to church with us.

While we were visiting Houston, our activities also included:

- classroom visits in public and private high schools;
- several weeks' work with Honors College students at UH (a primarily commuter-based student body);
- church services—everything from Black Baptist storefronts to megachurches in the suburbs, as well as meetings with pastors, priests, and congregants across the city;
- visits with arts organizations;
- informational sessions through Row Houses, DiverseWorks, and other partners;
- interviews with small local press outlets;
- street fairs, food fairs, music events, and theatre;
- informational meetings with civil engineers;
- meetings with staffers and council members;
- and, of course, visits to council meetings themselves.

What all this activity meant was that we were up on many of the local issues facing Houston, from excessive flooding after rainstorms, to the lack of zoning in the city, to the political power wielded by churches, developers, and tenant organizations. And by being up on the issues, we could speak knowledgeably (for outsiders) with many of the players and potential players, which made it easier for them to feel respected and buy into what we were doing. It also allowed us to create backup plans if our pursuit of the church choirs was not entirely successful.

During almost every site visit, Aaron and Costello met for coffee or breakfast and talked about drainage, the city of Houston, engineering, and the battle with the churches, which now also included the school district (which similarly oversaw a lot of parking lots and didn't want to have to pay fees). Costello had enjoyed a career as a civil engineer and council member (and lightning rod) in Houston politics. He is your prototypical "self-made" man— wealthy, accomplished, and utterly confident in himself. He'd been chosen by a group of engineers to run for council because he was the most charismatic of the bunch. As he put it, "being the most charismatic of a group of engineers is a low bar."[6]

Ethnographic interviews were paramount in the work with Costello. As we got closer to him, he began to open up. At one point, Aaron asked him why he'd gone into politics when his private practice was going so well; he asked Costello if it was faith, a sense of mission, or something like that. Both Aaron and Mallory were genuinely curious about this, since there was no imperative for him to help fix the city in the ways he'd proposed, especially given the amount of oppositional scrutiny to which he'd been subject.

When Aaron asked him about this, he laughed, which was a bit rare for him, and said, "You ask a lot of questions I don't know the answer to." And then he genuinely considered it. And he still didn't know.[7]

So on one hand, it was a dead end. But a minute or two later he started talking more personally about his evolution—from an overweight, two-pack-a-day smoker and workaholic who didn't even know what a marathon was to a competitive triathlete who lost one hundred pounds and moved toward public service. What he didn't know was disarming to him; what he did with his life made great stories that humanized him onstage.

You ever hear about "running a dog to death"? You can get a golden retriever to play fetch with you until it drops dead. You can do that if it loves you that much. You can get your own body to do that too. I had started running already, but not a lot, and then one day I saw these people go by with numbers on them. Running. And I asked somebody, "What's that?" And they said, "That's the Houston Marathon." And I said, "What's that?" I didn't know what a marathon was. And so I went and bought a book about it. And I thought, I can do that. And I did.

We took on the ambitious challenge of presenting the piece in three different Houston locations, with three sets of ending collaborators. Each night, a different church or school group performed—alongside Costello for two nights and McNeil (filling in for him because of a last-minute conflict) on the third. We worked with Iglesia Rios De Aceite, a suburban megachurch, on the first night, the middle school kids from an afterschool program on the second, and the Fourth Ward's Rose of Sharon Church on the third. For the churches, we met two or three times with the music directors and pastors to explain that their choirs would perform music of their choice, alternating songs with text drawn from Aaron's interviews with Costello.

The integration of the church choirs brought up a couple of aesthetic and political challenges that, while difficult, were instructive in honing our approach to subsequent local endings. While we were able to visit and speak with a diverse range of churches, and while we worked the political levers decently well, *City Council Meeting* was still unusual enough that we had a hard time getting some congregations to commit to being part of the show. In the end, though some of the white megachurches gave us interviews or invited us to services, none of them agreed to perform. The two groups we did have were congregations of color.

We chose choirs because we wanted the churches to feel like they were contributing artistically, putting something forward that was vital to their ministry and a source of pride, just as we wanted Costello's monologue to reflect something personal and poetic about his life and choices. The fact that the choirs were people of color and Costello was white added a problematic layer to that. We ran the danger of the people of color providing soulful music while centering the transformative journey of a white man, which was not the kind of theatre magic we wanted to make. If the choirs had been white, it would have had different meaning. While we weren't able to entirely escape this dynamic visually, we made sure the choirs were able to participate in the meeting as they wanted, and Mallory staged the ending each night as a conversation about power between music and speech so that everyone could play a more central role.

At Project Row Houses, in their historic African American ballroom, the Eldorado, we performed with the school kids. Here we were able to navigate the power dynamic more successfully because we chose to have Aaron write an interlocking monologue for one of the kids that put her and her friends on equal footing with the councilor. Our failure to get a white megachurch to participate led us to find another solution and to make the most of our relationship with Project Row Houses.

The choice to write for Cinimin Howard made all the difference. It meant we had to put more work into understanding her and her perspective, which gave her and the Row Houses community more buy-in and deepened our own investment in our work. With the choirs, we had made choices that allowed them to participate easily. We put in effort by visiting their churches, which probably had a greater impact on us than it did on them.

We were very fortunate to have a lot of support from the Row Houses community. Project Row Houses started in 1993 with the purchase of a series of row houses in the Third Ward. Cofounded by James Bettison, Bert Long Jr., Jesse Lott, Rick Lowe, Floyd Newsum, Bert Samples, and George Smith, the organization provides both art and community spaces in this historic African

American neighborhood. As the organization has grown, it has become a kind of cultural steward and political voice for the neighborhood, spawning low-income rental housing, creating a community development corporation, and taking over the Eldorado Ballroom, which had fallen into disrepair. Prior to closing in the 1970s, the Eldorado had been an important locus of Black culture in Houston, hosting artists like Duke Ellington, B. B. King, and Della Reese, among others.[8]

Now a beacon for truly local, truly powerful arts organizations across the country, Row Houses has built so much trust within the community that working with them is a special experience, one that affords artists like us (white, nonlocal) a meaningful sense of collaboration built on the premise of listening and mutual respect.

Assata Richards and Autumn Knight, two of our Houston staffers, were instrumental in successfully building an inclusive Third Ward audience. At a certain point during our process, both women suggested we do a demonstration of the project for sixth and seventh grade students at their neighborhood middle school; we were planning a workshop for high schoolers with another staffer, Christa Forrester, who worked at an elite prep school in the suburbs.

At the advice of Richards and Knight, we decided to speak to the students at an after-school activity session and workshop in the Eldorado Ballroom. Richards organized a bus for the students, and we set up our tables, mics, and a monitor at the Eldorado.

What we discovered was that for middle school students, a chance to sit at the council table or maybe even in the mayor's chair was a powerful moment. Perhaps they gained an enhanced sense of what was possible for them. Perhaps they just enjoyed playing like they were in charge of each other. They immediately understood in a very sophisticated way how the structure of the room and the rules governing it created power. They loved making fun of each other as they read the very bureaucratic testimonies, and they related strongly to some of the more emotional ones. In short, we had a blast.

This afternoon workshop with the students took all of three hours, including prep time. It fit nicely into our creative process, helped our staffers get more accustomed to the project, and helped us see the work animated by a new audience in development. We did not have to do anything extra, except perhaps reframe what the project itself could be and for whom. Mallory revealed herself to be an excellent shepherd of rowdy middle school kids, and the teachers seemed to feel everyone was being respected.

What these three hours did for the project can almost not be measured. On a simple level, the students told their families about the project, and their affect must have demonstrated the care and respect we took with them. Because of this, their families came to the Eldorado show, along with some of the DiverseWorks audience and some friends of ours from out of town, making it one of the most successful performances of the work ever.

Even more fundamentally, the experience with the middle school taught us that school kids could relate to the project, which helped us build the ending in New York City, and that simply asking people to come understand what we were doing before the official performance would make everyone feel welcomed more readily, especially those who might not already be comfortable with the ritual of going to the theatre.

The students became part of the ending at the Eldorado. Because the schools were on the same side of the infrastructure and drainage issue our ending addressed, we were able to work with these students the same way we worked with the church choirs for the other shows.

Because the students were part of it, they brought their families, friends, and neighbors. Because Richards and Knight vouched for us, the energy going in was curious and welcoming. The show was packed and felt like a neighborhood celebration.

Not only was the experience helpful for us, but it also allowed Costello to venture to a part of the city he did not normally visit, which he did with great enthusiasm, and share his perspective on what helping to run Houston was like; it also allowed Cinimin Howard, a twelve-year-old girl, to sit with her friends, face-to-face with a council member, and talk about her concerns for her neighborhood and the city.

Part of what is going to make me a good leader is that I'm naturally nosy. I just nose into something. Nose, nose, nose, you know? And I find out a lot. What somebody's doing, what they are getting into. Sometimes I just look at somebody and think about what they are thinking about.

One of our worries about the Eldorado Ballroom show in Houston was that the piece might come off as condescending, like a lecture about the importance of civic engagement to a community that already worked hard at both participating in official structures and protesting on the streets, as well as forming their own organizing bodies. Did a neighborhood this learned need to be told that local government is both awkward and hopeful, a performance of power that can be harnessed for the sake of empathy and persuasion?

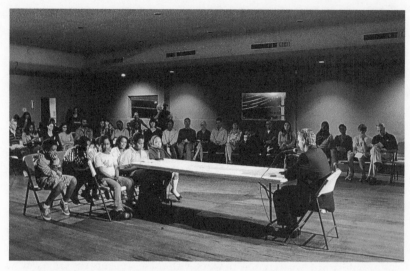

A group of middle school students, led by Cinimin Howard, in conversation with
City Councilor Steve Costello in the Eldorado Ballroom, Houston, Texas.
Photo by Rachel Cook.

COSTELLO (to the room): Is education a quick and easy process?
ALL KIDS: No.
COSTELLO: Neither is government.
ALL KIDS: OK.
COSTELLO: The soul is complicated. The city is complicated. There are so many
directions people want to go in and we can't all agree. We can't.

HOWARD: Democracy is supposed to mean that you don't have to be born pow-
erful to be in power. You don't have to know more. You just have to convince
people. So how are we doing? Are we living up to that?

It turned out that what was satisfying to the Row Houses community was
that we reframed what they did as something creative. "You turned what we
already do as politics into art," a man at the show said. "I didn't think of us
that way before."[9]

Sixto Wagan and Assata Richards

Sixto Wagan was the artistic director of DiverseWorks when we made *City
Council Meeting*, and he now directs Houston's BIPOC Arts Network Fund,

which focuses on grant funding, advocacy, and community building activities. Much of our conversation with Wagan centered on the interplay between organizational and individual relationships. A strong working relationship is one that can be informal because it comes out of an intentional practice. We spoke about expertise and the difference between *shared* and *given* permission.

DiverseWorks signed onto the *City Council Meeting* because "it was an extension of [their] commitment to community engaged practice," but Wagan felt the work presented opportunities that were not fully realized. As the relationship with Project Row Houses was already strong and there were natural affinities, *City Council Meeting* was able to strengthen that relationship. But in the case of the church choirs, those relationships were not developed after the show. Wagan expressed regret that someone from his staff was not more involved in our communications with the choirs.

We also spoke about *City Council Meeting* as a socially engaged project with a very specific culminating event, which added to its power but demanded that it be as aesthetically rigorous in performance as it was in its process of community engagement. As Wagan put it, "How does a singular event catalyze or continue a series of relationships that are building?"

Wagan described how the marketing of the piece presented challenges to the way DiverseWorks normally represented its season of events. In Houston, we made posters that looked so much like announcements for an actual city council meeting that we feared it might deter some potential audience members because they didn't know why they should attend this mock local government meeting. As Wagan said, "There are echoes of the civic process itself. If it's not directly affecting you, then why are you coming to see it?"

If *City Council Meeting* succeeded as a performance to reveal the "capacity of anonymous people that makes everyone equal to everyone else, exercised through irreducible distances," how do these distances get in the way of the desirable sensation of a positive community impact? And does that sensation mask another possibility—the possibility to recognize differences even as we work together?

Another question the show raised in Houston and everywhere else was whether our interest in making a performance about civic participation fit into the framework of community-engaged art that people were accustomed to. How different are these two ideas?

For Wagan, this brought up questions of continuity for artists and organizations alike, as many of us think in two- or three-year timelines: "How do we think of this work as in connection to the next work? What way are we building intentional connections between these projects?" And can making a project like *City Council Meeting* for multiple formats—a theatre work, a book, a curriculum—help build new appetites and possibilities for artistic works in the future?

We also spoke with Assata Richards, who now teaches a class on art and community engagement at the University of Houston. Richards's current focus is on work that shifts power around economics, with a passion for accelerating cooperatively owned businesses started by Black women.[10]

Richards noted that there is "a need to understand how you do work that is participatory and engaged." Particularly, she asked what children brought to the process and how they opened up the project to a wider audience of people. "These were children from the neighborhood. They were connected to these systems. Children and schools have a rootedness to community in a very particular way." We spoke about how engagement, participation, and a willingness to talk to a broad range of people lead us to a plan B that included the students in our performance at Project Row Houses, which was much more successful than our plan A because it was responding to the facts on the ground.[11] This would become a recurring theme in future local endings, and our experience in Houston with Richards made us more able to listen and adapt.

Drainage in Houston

Eight years after our performances, Houston residents ranked flooding as the most important problem facing the city and its neighborhoods.[12] The initial proposition that Steven Costello initiated and pushed through the city council was later held up in the courts, revoted on, and passed in 2018, an example of how long a democratic process can take to complete.[13] There is still controversy over the proper allocation of the drainage fees the city collects, which became an issue in the mayoral candidacy and 2020 reelection of Sylvester Turner.[14] But there seems to be no debate over whether the city needs the fee. In fact, in 2019 the State of Texas amended its constitution to include a Flood Infrastructure Fund Amendment to deal with the effects of climate change.[15]

Tempe

SMILEZ

Sometimes my boyfriend and I plug in our phones and put them next to each other all night. So it's like we sleep together on the phone.

At times while making *City Council Meeting*, we dealt with ethical dilemmas arising from our work with community members; these feel like common points of concern for many socially engaged artworks. We're defining *community members* here as individuals who lived in the city where we were working and did not necessarily consider themselves artists. Like many who enter a creative process with privilege, some decisions and relationships tested us and our community collaborators.

In Tempe, one working relationship brought us to a line between our work with a local community member and the potential for exploiting both her and our local artist collaborators' good graces. We at least dipped a toe on the other side of what's OK, depending on whom you talk to. The line came up when we worked with a young woman named Smilez who had been homeless in Phoenix and Tempe and who worked on the local ending with us at Arizona State University (ASU) Gammage. We also added two collaborating artists who lived in the Phoenix metro area, which added another layer of complexity and possibility to our work there.

On our first visit, we went to a council meeting as our normal introduction to each new city. By now, we had begun the process in Houston and New York and seen meetings in several more cities. Having lucked out with Houston's highly theatrical drainage-related meeting that Aaron attended, we tested out this method in Tempe. While almost all the meetings we saw had at least one moment of innate theatricality, our first meeting in Tempe was kind of a dud. The biggest issue on the table was ficus trees.

These trees, we learned, are not native to the desert environment. Nonetheless, when Tempe, Arizona, decided to rebrand itself in the 1980s as a way to lure businesses, residents, and tourism, they planted rows of ficus trees along each side of Mill Avenue, the main drag and the beating heart of the city's consumer commerce. They also made a lake, which has become a sought-after site for triathlons and other sponsored events. In order to keep the ficus trees alive, there are special irrigation systems under the sidewalks; several trees would die every five to ten years and have to be replaced. All told, the cost to the city was thousands of dollars per tree.

So the meeting was about whether it would make sense to continue replacing the trees. First we saw a very thoughtful presentation by two landscape architects who'd been contracted by the city to look at alternatives. They showed how the Chinese pistache tree looked a lot like the ficus but would stand up to the dry heat of Tempe and be more cost effective—though the leaves would fall off in the winter, while the ficus kept their leaves all year. They ran the numbers on each type of tree. Someone on the council brought up the fact that the ficus trees were repositories for starlings, which left copious droppings on people's cars when they parked on Mill. There was a brief moment when good sense seemed to prevail. And then a citizen weighed in.

Her name was Nancy Hormann:

I am not a resident, but my heart belongs to downtown. And I am here representing the board of directors of the Downtown Community. And I wanted to talk about the Mill Avenue landscape.

And today I wanted to make sure that the council knows that the DTC[1] voted unanimously to support keeping ficus trees on Mill Avenue. Um, over three years ago we presented a report showing if ficus trees had been maintained properly, that they [are] a good alternative for down here.

And we feel that, like the Mill, like the bridge, our ficus trees are a brand of downtown. And we would like to continue that brand and see if there's a way that we can work with all of you to complete the "leafiness" of downtown with our ficus trees.

The rest of the citizens weighing in were business owners on Mill Avenue or simply citizens concerned about the city's branding and appeal to tourists and triathletes. They clearly had the ear of several council members too. The measure to replace the ficus trees with something more sustainable was defeated. It was kind of like, "Yeah, thanks for that well-researched scientific presentation, but we like the ficus."

On one hand, this fit a pattern we saw in other cities: a representative of a group of constituents gathered supporters together in numbers that would impress the council and get the vote they wanted. On the other hand, the ficus tree issue seemed like a dead end, and we left feeling a little stymied. How could this relate to more pressing issues, even metaphorically? At the previous cities' meetings, there had been moments when the heart of a city seemed to reveal itself, even if only briefly. Tempe's obsession with ficus trees was confusing to us, since what we saw on Mill Avenue seemed like a fairly typical commercial main strip, so we were surprised by passion and strong feelings about it. It was interesting, however, to see how aesthetics were instrumentalized for political ends.

It's worth mentioning the freedom we were given by our partners at ASU Gammage to follow our impulses and really do our work, as well as the difference between Gammage and the other venues with which we were working in New York and Houston. Where the prior cities' partners were smaller, grassroots organizations, often focused entirely on alternative or experimental work, Gammage was an economic powerhouse in Tempe: they operate a three-thousand-seat auditorium where they are the leading southwestern presenter for Broadway road shows.[2] If *Lion King* or *Hamilton* go anywhere in the southwestern U.S., they go to Gammage, often selling out weeks at a time, year after year. This gave them clout, standing, and an obligation to the city. Gammage patrons eat at local restaurants, patronize local businesses, and stay at local hotels, often coming in for the day from as far away as Albuquerque and other regional cities. Their executive director, Colleen Jennings-Roggensack, and associate director, Michael Reed, were committee members of the DTC, had the ear of the city council, and were responsible for a lot of business activity on Mill Avenue and beyond.

So Gammage was on some level part of the "brand" of downtown that Nancy Hormann had talked about. We worked there with a sense that even as they gave us freedom to do what we wanted with our project and resourced us generously to do it through multiple site visits and a great production budget, we wanted to be sensitive to their place in the city. Fortunately for us, Gammage had a history of long-term community engagement and collaboration with artists from outside of town, as well as a desire to build an appetite among its audience for experimentation and engagement through their years-long Beyond series.

The day after the council meeting about the ficus trees, we walked around town and noticed a lot of homeless kids and young adults begging for change or just hanging out. If you live in New York, San Francisco, or a few other metro areas, you'll recognize them: tattoos, a denim vest over a black T-shirt, piercings, dirt-scrubbed faces, and a high degree of engagement with the people they ask from. They don't let you off the hook. They can be a pain in the ass.

Sometimes they made comments at people passing by that bordered on harassment. Sometimes they created what for business owners was an eyesore, but for us was an interesting window into a silenced part of the discussion Tempe was having with itself about its identity as a city.

No one had talked about homeless kids at the council meeting we'd just seen, but we noticed them hanging out under the ficus trees for shade. Was that why some people wanted to change what kind of tree was there? Were the starlings people talked about as a nuisance a sort of inadvertent metaphor? Could we make them one? When we caught Jim Findlay up on what we were thinking, he asked if we could have a forest of ficus trees onstage.

As we went deeper into Tempe's political culture—attending meetings and conversing with city hall staff, Gammage staff, council members, and other members of the more accepted community—we found that these young people also symbolized a certain set of predicaments for the city, and we decided to pursue some of these individuals as collaborators. On future visits we began to do research around our hunch that there was something to be found in the relationship between the ficus trees on Mill Avenue and homeless young people. We found out that people in Tempe saw themselves as more liberal than their neighbors in Phoenix to the west and Chandler to the east. In terms of their approach to homelessness, this was at least partly true—the official policy toward these young people was a kinder, gentler approach than Phoenix had. At the same time, Tempe didn't want to seem *too* generous toward its unhoused population for fear of everyone flocking to them for services that, in the middle of an economic slump, they couldn't afford.

When we met with staffers from city hall, they'd ask us about the project— Tempe is small enough and Gammage is connected enough that we had a lot of access to councilors and staffers there, and they all got to know the project. We'd tell them we were going to do our ending about ficus trees, and they'd roll their eyes. "Oh god," they'd say, "everyone has an opinion about the ficus."

We'd say, "Yeah, but no one is talking about the homeless people hanging out under them."

"Because no one knows what to do about them, so we talk about something else instead."

We decided to focus on an implicit conflict in Tempe, rather than an explicit one like the conflict between churches and the council in Houston. Here we worked with the local homeless population and with Downtown Tempe Community director Nancy Hormann, whose career included working for a business improvement district in San Francisco prior to arriving in Arizona.

At this point, Gammage wisely asked us to work with two local artists who could keep the process moving forward between our visits and come with a sense of the communities we were engaging with. Gammage had a history of long-term projects initiated by out-of-town artists and then carried forward locally after the initial work is done—for example, Pat Graney's *Keeping the Faith*, created with incarcerated women, became Journey Home, a program facilitated by local artist Fatimah Halim.[3] When we began working with Gammage, they expressed interest in that possibility. Elizabeth Johnson, who'd been a guest artist at ASU for several years and who had worked with groundbreaking choreographer Liz Lerman, joined the project, as did Gregory Sale, a visual and social practice artist who worked with many different populations on and off campus. They were both engaged in community-based projects and had worked together before, so were comfortable sharing responsibilities.

After meeting with Johnson, we decided pretty quickly that she would make a great city secretary for the meeting portion of the production. This was a special role—this person was the only one onstage with a full script and was sort of deputized to be able to take over the meeting and make changes if necessary during the performance, so her kind, communicative, and personable demeanor was just what the job required. Johnson was also instrumental in helping us find local people of mixed age, race, and experience to be our staffers.

In our first meeting with Sale, we outlined how the process was going in New York and Houston, and he said something revelatory to us about the difference between a theatrical process and one in visual arts–based performance. He said visual artists tend to focus more on the conceptual gesture of a piece, honing it over time and then throwing it out into the world to see how it lands, whereas theatre artists have this wild thing they do called rehearsal.[4] To include him deeper in our process, we asked Sale to play the role of Pete Colt in the meeting, a very conceptual performance that also required rehearsal.

As we began assembling staffers from both on and off ASU's campus, we did more research. Mallory found a nervous but articulate parks department worker who would only talk to us about the trees if we didn't use his name or anything that could identify him. In his interview he said the environment of Mill Avenue was hard on the trees—in the summer the sun reflected off the windows of buildings and glared on them; the exhaust from cars was hard on their leaves; young partiers sometimes tried to uproot a tree as a gag or peed on them late at night. He could have been describing the effects on the human body of being in a desert city downtown. We looked again at the young people taking shelter and wondered why most of them—seemingly able-bodied and relatively sane—would stay in such a difficult climate.

The trees, they really can suffer in the heat. June, July, August, when it gets up around 116 degrees, and the tree is out there in front of the bank building with the mirrored glass. That's when you start to see the signs of distress.

Through Gammage, we found a couple of great liaisons to the homeless population there, which led us to an organization called Tumbleweed. Providing services to anyone on the street, on the clients' own terms, made them both generous and a little controversial, and that was perfect for us. They didn't prescribe what kinds of things a person could take advantage of there or the order in which they drew goods and services. If you wanted to just come in and use a computer to try to expunge a criminal record or work toward a GED, that was fine; it was also OK to seek housing and employment or pick up some Pampers for your kid. Some just came for a meal.

Tumbleweed let us spend time at their facility, a block off of Mill Avenue, over three afternoons. While we loved their generosity and their nonjudgmental approach, their connection to community art was different from how we wanted to work. On our first day there, a staff member introduced us: "Mallory and Aaron are making a play about the homeless in Tempe and they want to listen to your stories and then take them for their play."

This was exactly what we didn't want to do. We explained that we were just gathering information and educating ourselves, and we hoped to find collaborators to work with on the project. The worker who'd introduced us looked at us like we were a little bit crazy but also like we were doing something unique.

For the next three days, we sat in Tumbleweed's back room for two to three hours a day and listened to the stories of the people there. What was immediately clear was that what is often stigmatized as laziness or even nihilism among young able-bodied white homeless people was a logical choice for many individuals we met there. The community, the sense of belonging, and the protection they gave each other from violence were far more comforting and welcoming than what many of them had experienced in their homes growing up. Fleeing abuse, neglect, and other horror stories, the people who came to talk to us at Tumbleweed had made sensible decisions, even if at first they looked like mere posturing or provocation. To be sure, the desert environment and the harsh political reality of being homeless in America were punishing, but what these young people had left behind was worse. They showed us that the notion of home was relative, that sleeping several to a tent was better than being constrained to abusive settings.

In three days, we met a lot of people: one guy who buried his money in different holes in the hills surrounding the city; another who planned to go to medical school; a couple who had walked all the way to Arizona from Texas; several people who hopped trains seasonally, from Tempe to Portland to San Diego over the course of the year. While the stories and characters were fascinating, it was pretty clear we weren't going to be able to rely on anyone being in town in a year, when the performance at Gammage was scheduled.

And then we met Smilez, aka Heather Hernandez. Smilez was an assertive, bright-eyed twenty-one-year-old woman. Originally from Phoenix, Hernandez had lived on the streets in Tempe and was a single mother of a son about Aaron's son's age. Ironically, though she introduced herself as "Heather, but my nickname is Smilez because I smile a lot," she didn't actually smile for the first hour or more of our interview. She was too busy recounting a very detailed story. Hernandez had spent five years on the streets, like many of the clients at Tumbleweed, after fleeing an unsafe home. She had since done some reconciling with her family, and at times they were able to take care of her son for her.

Hernandez demonstrated remarkable sophistication at manipulating Arizona's skeletal public health and services framework in order to get what she needed. For instance, though she suffered from several chronic health issues, for which she needed medication, her father was in worse shape. In order to get his treatment paid for by the state, she had to make her son a dependent of her father, because people with families got priority. To do this, she had to give up her own treatments, because as a single person, rather than a single parent, she was deemed less entitled to services. While some people might call what Hernandez described gaming the system, to us it made perfect sense. Hernandez's choices were indicative of what anyone really poor in this country must go through, and she made pragmatic choices based on her love for her family.

She talked about her worry that, because of the custody switch, she wouldn't get to see her son enough, since he had to live with her folks. She talked about wanting to open a restaurant. She was both incredibly sophisticated and wildly naive, perhaps like many twenty-one-year-olds. We sat in the back of Tumbleweed, both Mallory and Aaron asking questions. We realized that Hernandez had talked to us longer than anyone, and since she was rooted by her family in the Phoenix area and in the process of trying to get off the street and into an apartment, we might be able to find her when we next came to visit.

We also noticed that the story she was recounting for us was one she knew well—she had rehearsed it. She was performing the version of herself that the situation required, the story you'd give to any caseworker you needed something from. Maybe all of us have done versions of this subtle manipulation when we wanted a grade raised, or a job, or a day off, or a reason to go do something we knew we had to fight for.

Eventually her recitation of strategies and difficulties began to become a little boring, even as it was instructive and interesting on a factual or observational level. She had told this story so many times. We wondered: Would she want to work with us? What art would come from our interaction? That somewhat cool, detached question of dramaturgy and craft prompted us to ask Smilez a simple and unplanned question: *So, do you want to work on this theatre project with us?*

Hernandez stopped and asked what we meant, and we explained: we were interested in having her work with us as a paid member of our theatre project, to make a performance around the kinds of stories she was telling us right now. She stumbled a little, clearly not expecting this to come out of our talk. She broke into a huge grin, the first of the afternoon. Its brightness explained her nickname, finally.

When we visited again, we found out Hernandez was still on the street but closer to getting an apartment. We exchanged emails—a kind of placeholder to make sure she was still on board. Between that visit and the next one, her father, not yet forty, died of the heart disease she was gaming the system to get him treated for. On the flip side, she was in her apartment, was doing some kind of job training, and had custody of her son. We started doing interviews with her and worked out a fee of twenty dollars per hour.

Our first visit with her was at her new apartment, a little one-bedroom in a nondescript complex northeast of downtown Phoenix. We got there to find several people hanging out, cigarette smoke in the rooms, trash—but we didn't say anything. It was a huge deal to be invited into her place. All her friends were polite, if a little nervous about us and putting up a bit of a front; after a quick hello with her son Quintin, they took the boy out so we could talk. Quintin seemed cheerful and bright and well loved.

Hernandez was very proud of having a place to live and custody of her son. She said getting used to sleeping alone, in a bed, indoors, was one of the hardest things. She had spent five years in tents with at least four other people, sleeping on the ground; the shift in environment gave her insomnia, sometimes panic attacks. She said she often put the phone next to her bed and kept her boyfriend on the line, so it was like they were putting each other to bed. She was enrolled in a program to train for her food handler's license, which would allow her to work at a fast-food restaurant; she said she loved cooking and wanted to open a few places of her own. Her affect was manically positive.

A bus pass costs $55 a month. My son Quintin's birthday is February 28, 2009. Rent is $512 a month. My dad's birthday was yesterday, February 15. He is my number one supporter. He passed away a year ago in January.

She talked about how long it could take to get to a food pantry that gave her food, or to her training sessions—sometimes a trip that would be fifteen minutes by car would take ninety by bus. If she had to go downtown and take a urine test, then go to training, and then pick up Quintin, she'd end up spending five or more hours in transit.

At one point, Aaron was interviewing her in her apartment courtyard and her boyfriend popped by to ask her for money. The exchange was tense and gave Aaron an inkling of the conflicted feelings that would dog the rest of the process. We were paying her in cash because she didn't have a bank account. We assumed she'd be putting it to good use and felt that telling her how to spend her money was paternalistic.

The interviews themselves with Hernandez were great, and it was clear she took her work with us seriously. She was on time, forthcoming, articulate, funny, and clear. It felt like life was breathing down her neck but that she could rise above it—the same narrative she had told us and herself her whole life.

At the same time, we did not necessarily ask for support from our local artist collaborators, though we did talk to them. It might have been better if we had said, "We want to continue, but we are in over our heads. What should we do?"

Soon after the exchange with her boyfriend, Hernandez called Aaron in a panic. Child Protective Services (CPS) had taken Quintin from her, she was pregnant, and she was behind on rent. Still, she never asked for an advance on her fee, or an increase. She was just distraught and needed a sympathetic ear.

One staff member at Gammage wondered if we should cut off Hernandez because we were out of our depth working with someone in the midst of such a struggle. We talked about it but felt like Hernandez was being responsible to us, as far as our work together went, so how could we fire her? It seemed a worse thing to cut ties now, when everything else was falling apart. It felt like we'd be saying to her that because her life was spiraling, the good work she was doing with us didn't matter.

As we sorted through the situation with Johnson and Sale, we decided not to focus Hernandez's interview material on her current problems, which might exploit her misery; instead, we would ask both her and Nancy Hormann to speak more generally on homelessness in Tempe and the issues that arose among the different groups on Mill Avenue. We also decided that we would put them both on video. This ensured formally that they were presented in the performance on equal footing and practically that we could more easily accommodate their lives and schedules.

Audience members would walk through a small forest of potted nine-foot ficus trees, encounter video of Hormann and Hernandez, and hear a recorded description of how the climate was hard on the ficus trees, as described by the parks employee we met. Finally, they'd hear from Darci Niva, who did homeless services for the city and who appeared live in the show. Everything seemed to be moving along nicely.

Less than ten days before the show, Aaron got a call he had not anticipated in his life as an experimental theatre artist. Phoenix CPS had come to take Quintin from Hernandez a few days before, and they wanted to talk to Aaron about his experiences as her employer.

By this point in the process, we had assumed Hernandez might drop out, as her life was increasingly difficult for her to manage, and we'd have to come up with a plan B. She also said she was experiencing intense morning sickness, which took her to the emergency room more than once, sometimes to get an IV drip since she couldn't hold down food. At the same time, Smilez really wanted to be part of the show and, miraculously, kept showing up for our work sessions and filming.

CPS needed Aaron's input about Quintin's living conditions and Hernandez's parenting, so he was included in a conference call with Hernandez, her sister, and Quintin's father (who, according to Hernandez, had not been on the scene much at all). As Hernandez's employer, Aaron was asked about his experience when he visited Hernandez for work at her home, as well as his experience of Quintin. Aaron was conflicted—on one hand, he said, the house was a mess, people were definitely smoking inside, and it was not always clear who was in charge of the boy. On the other hand, Quintin himself seemed happy with his mother, she seemed relatively calm with him even when he broke rules, and he appeared well fed and cared for. The friends hanging out all seemed to treat Quintin beautifully. It was not what he would have wanted for his own son, but it did not seem abusive or neglectful. He worried that had he arrived on a different day his impression might have been different. And in some way, he worried that expressing that fear would endanger the working relationship. At this point we began to keep all our collaborators in the loop rigorously.

Aaron said all of this on the call. Quintin's father was belligerent, as was Hernandez's sister. Hernandez was in tears, and the CPS social worker was amazing at keeping everyone on track. Aaron was only asked to talk about his direct experience, which was a relief.

Later, Darci Niva told him that if CPS was involved, there was likely more than one complaint on file and the situation might have been more serious than it appeared. Meaning that perhaps it was a good thing they came for Quintin. Over the next week and change, Quintin stayed with a foster family, then was transferred to Hernandez's mother's house—a mixed blessing, as Hernandez had described leaving there on purpose as a teenager due to safety concerns. She began to have visitation rights with Quintin, which was both welcome and distressing to her.

We did not focus on any of this in our video interviews with her. We focused on her childhood, her time on the street, and her views on homelessness, the Phoenix metro area, and other peoples' attitudes toward her. Pregnant and sick, she often had to stop the taping to vomit; she'd then clean up, come back, and pick up where we left off. We mention this last detail to say that throughout all of the incredibly difficult circumstances Hernandez faced while working with us, she continued to be a solid working partner.

I think that these people, who are here by choice, even though it's difficult to

The final moments of the ASU Gammage performance, when the curtain rose
to reveal the stage lighting and full space of the theatre. Photo by David A. Brown
Photography / Houston, Texas.

*deal with them, and I understand the business owners' concerns, they represent
something larger that is falling apart for us, as a nation. And there should be a
place for that.* (Darci Niva)

Due to the massive size of the Gammage theatre, normally used for touring
Broadway musicals, we set the audience and the performance on the stage,
with the auditorium seating behind making it feel both small and expansive
at once. For the local ending, we brought the audience back onto the stage but
closed the main curtain so the auditorium was no longer visible. This gave the
space a sense of enclosure that felt radically different from the meeting.

At the start of the local ending, we gave the audience a link to a sound file
of the starlings on Mill Avenue that Gregory Sale had recorded early in the
process. It's early in the morning and we hear a sense of wonder in his voice
when describing the birds as they flock above the ficus. In the final moments
of the ending, the staffers cued each viewer to play this audio track on their
phones on speaker. Hearing each recording at a slightly different time created
a kind of madrigal of birds—a digital murmuration—that grew as each person
played it, an informal chorus that let us hear something beautiful and see how

we all had a hand in making it. As the sound of the birds swelled, we slowly opened the main curtain to reveal theatrical lights pointed onto the stage, where we all stood under the canopy of trees. It was an expansively theatrical moment listening to the last recording play out on a final lone cell phone.

Thankfully, Hernandez made it to the show. While her interview played on video, she was with us in the audience, revealing herself as part of the very last gesture of the piece. *City Council Meeting* was provocative to the Tempe audience, and after the show we ended up having some fairly heated conversations with audience members, one of whom asked if it "was art or was some kind of weird social experiment." (Her teenaged son popped his head in and said, "That was the coolest thing I've ever seen!") Still, the reception felt great to us because we were all able to be there—Hernandez, Mallory, Aaron, Sale, Johnson, Niva, and the Gammage staff.

What we found out later was that after we went back to the theatre to strike, Hernandez had asked Johnson to help her with her custody battle. She told Johnson she had cancer as well as being pregnant, and that she wasn't sure how she'd make ends meet; she was about to be evicted for back rent. The next morning, we flew home, and Johnson remained in Tempe, feeling somewhat abandoned by us and responsible for Hernandez. She said, "I was alone with Heather when she was asking for help the most. She asked me and my partner to take her to prenatal appointments. I was used to coming into communities outside my own. Because I was local, there was a different kind of partnership."[5]

Given this new information, we wondered whether we should have done something differently. This question remains open to us. Certainly, within the rush to production, though we were able to take care of Hernandez's needs and did not make a spectacle of her difficulties, perhaps we could have taken care of our local collaborators better and included them more in the ethical decisions we made, so that they could have been better prepared.

In general, we found that people who participated in this process benefited from it—working group members ran for public office, other members were able to have creative input in the work. We are proud of our ability to welcome a diverse group of colleagues into each city's production. But there are always going to be gaps, missteps, and blind spots. In Tempe we didn't really grapple with what it would be like to be an artist who was still there the next day.

This problem with the Tempe process has influenced our own process as artists. When Aaron teaches community-engaged artmaking at various colleges and universities, he uses a set of questions and protocols that allows students and collaborators to think through power relationships, individual and collective impact, and how to leave a place and a person in ways that are constructive. Aaron's process is broken into phases: invitation, agreement, collaboration, sharing, exiting. As so many of us in the arts, the academy, and community organizing work with shoestring budgets and constrained timelines, we are hopeful that thinking through the possibilities of the whole process from the outset can mitigate some of the possible risks.

Colleen Jennings-Roggensack, Gregory Sale, and Elizabeth Johnson

Colleen Jennings-Roggensack is the executive director of Arizona State University Gammage. Since we made *City Council Meeting*, she has become ASU's Vice President for Cultural Affairs, with artistic, fiscal, and administrative responsibility for two cultural facilities and additional responsibility for Sun Devil Stadium and Wells Fargo Arena for non-athletic activities including concerts and commencement and convocation exercises. Jennings-Roggensack is also a member of the Broadway League's board and leads that organization's diversity initiative.

Of all the presenters we spoke to, Jennings-Roggensack was most positive about the experience, perhaps because of the size and financial stability of Gammage, the already strong relationship with the Tempe City Council, and the fact that the stakes of presenting our project were lower for the organization. Her memory of *City Council Meeting* was that it expanded upon what Gammage had done in the past, strengthened prior community relations, and added organizational capacity that allowed them to take on more ambitious projects with community members after that, including a groundbreaking engagement with Native American populations through playwright Larissa FastHorse's *Native Nation* project.[6]

Gregory Sale has continued to do long-term artistic engagements with incarcerated individuals, most recently the multi-year work *Future IDs at Alcatraz*, in which he and many collaborators repurposed the storied island in San Francisco Bay as a space of art and learning. He is a professor at ASU in visual art and intermedia. In his own projects he often puts himself in direct debate with individuals with whom he disagrees, most notably the infamous

Maricopa County Sheriff Joe Arpaio for his *It's not just black and white* exhibition.

Sale talked with us about questions common to all of our work: "You're getting in the middle of someone's life, [someone] who is dealing with all these institutional structures. What does it mean to work with communities and individuals who are at this level of grappling with how to move forward in life? How do we have the grounding and the maturity and support to navigate and negotiate those structures with them, without having them negatively impact the project?"[7]

Sale again reflected on the ways *City Council Meeting* draws from both performance art strategies more common to the visual arts, in which "you are often there as yourself, even if as an explicit performance of self," and those from theatre, where "you may be interpreting another person." He related it, in part, to the roles we play as artist facilitators and as teachers, finding different modes of relating to participants, collaborators, and students depending on their needs and a project's needs.

Elizabeth Johnson now works as an associate artist and partnerships director at Dance Exchange, a company founded by MacArthur-winner Liz Lerman, where Johnson worked prior to being in Arizona. In Johnson's current work, she has created a series of ethical questions that exist on a spectrum from one's relationship to a community to who is paying whom for what work.

As Johnson said in retrospect, "There is a great value in being a catalyst and convener in another community. And there's a value in something with a beginning, middle, and end. Because some people need to experience a good ending." At the same time, it's such an important lesson, if you are exiting a community when a project is done, to envision how that community resides with themselves on the other end.[8]

Tempe and Homelessness

Since performing *City Council Meeting* in Tempe, the rate of homelessness has vastly increased there. The city has adopted a more comprehensive program for "ending homelessness," for which the council has increased the budget in each of the last two years. Tempe is "considered an innovator in creating successful strategies for assisting people out of homelessness." Their new allocations include more rapid responses to get homeless individuals into shelters, additional mental health specialists to help homeless people navigate the court system, and a full-time homeless outreach coordinator.[9] While some of this new approach does what many cities do, which is to mask policing the homeless as a more compassionate service provision, Tempe is making a much more explicit attempt to address the problem systematically than they were in 2012–2013, when a council staffer told us simply that "no one wants to talk about the homeless because no one knows what to do about the problem."[10]

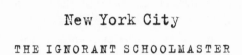

New York City

THE IGNORANT SCHOOLMASTER

Some of us take college classes but still dress hard. We like messing with teachers, making them think we are ignorant, and then turning in something great. The payoff is when one of them says, "I didn't expect such good work from you, based on how you sit in the back of the room and glare at me from under that baseball cap."

The whole time we were developing *City Council Meeting* in Houston and Tempe, with separate working groups and local endings, New York City was our home base. We worked out structural issues in the meeting and the three of us had regular creative work sessions. We did two fully produced work-in-progress performances at HERE Arts Center and another at the American Repertory Theater's Emerging America festival.

We also had to make a New York City–specific local ending, one that would work in three performance venues in two boroughs and still be specific and galvanizing. Because it is our hometown, it was difficult to stick to our rule of letting something that came up at an actual meeting we attended guide us to a possible solution for the ending. In other cities it was easier not to feel beholden to a comprehensive story or artistic gesture that defined that place; we felt that limiting ourselves to what we saw acknowledged our insider-outsider status. In New York, all three of us felt it was *our* city. We had all been there for twenty years or more and had been engaged with local politics in different ways—through protest, by attending community board meetings, and by lobbying for arts funding at the city and state level.

After debating several ideas, we decided to deal with the public schools, beginning specifically with the contentious issue of standardized testing and corporate charter schools. Aaron and Jim are both public school parents, and that created a vehicle for looking at larger issues through a single lens. In a way, we were honoring how personal New York City politics felt in order to avoid pretending to be objective, an inverse approach to what we did in the other cities. Our local connection would show its depth if we got more specific. We were also interested in the fact that New York's political workings often feel too big and ungainly for one person or group to impact, in contrast to the smaller cities we visited, where access seemed more available. Mallory had always been interested in the public school next to HERE Arts Center, since she'd been a HERE artist in residence for several years, so that school became our first performance site.

In the 2000s, then mayor Michael Bloomberg consolidated his power over a school system that would not easily fall in line with his neoliberal plan to prioritize the public-private partnership of charter schools and diminish union power.[1] One of his strategies was to replace the democratically elected school board with a body called the Panel for Educational Policy (PEP) board, for which he appointed the majority of members—the others were appointed by borough presidents, most of whom did what the mayor wanted. He also implemented a new standardized testing regimen[2] that penalized entire schools for low test scores, part of a city effort to close what they called failing schools.[3] Once a school was deemed to fail, the Bloomberg administration created a policy of "colocation," which meant private, for-profit charters were invited to move into the building where the "failing" public school had been. Often, under this policy, more than one school would occupy a single building.[4]

It didn't seem to matter to Bloomberg that testing companies like Pearson, which administered the New York City tests, were already under fire over racial and class biases embedded in the tests themselves, or that the same companies benefited financially from both the testing industry and for-profit charters.[5] Bloomberg had already garnered an illegal third term by fiat and seemed not to care about the public's opinion since he wouldn't be able to run again, so he used his considerable power to push the colocation policy through.[6]

Bloomberg did this because it was the most expedient way to give privatization a foothold in public education; once a charter was allowed into a building, it was hard to get them out. Like much of New York City politics, it was a matter of real estate. And with a majority on the PEP board appointed by the mayor and borough presidents, students, parents, and teachers had very little say in the expansion of charters and standardized testing as a metric of success.

Mallory's friend Paul Thompson, who is a principal at the Urban Assembly

High School of Music and Art in Brooklyn, told her that if she wanted to know what was going on in NYC schools, she had to go to PEP meetings. Thankfully they were all recorded and viewable online. Mallory found that these meetings had been devolving into shouting matches for some time. Like many aspects of government and planning, the meetings presented a Goffmanesque performance of inclusion and listening, usually followed by a predetermined outcome through votes that ignored public comment and did exactly what the mayor wanted them to do. So parents and teachers simply began showing up with bullhorns to shut down the meetings they knew were shams.

After watching quite a few meetings, Mallory noticed that a lone member of the PEP board was standing up to the predominating approval of Bloomberg's plan. The board member's name was Patrick Sullivan; he worked for an insurance company, his kids had attended public schools, and he'd been appointed by Manhattan Borough President Scott Stringer. Bloomberg's relationship with Stringer was adversarial, and Stringer himself was seen as a possible future mayoral contender. When Stringer appointed Sullivan to the PEP board, he gave full permission for Sullivan to vote with his conscience and go head-to-head with Bloomberg's appointees.[7]

If it had not been for Sullivan, Mallory might not have understood what was really going on. At a critical meeting when the test results were badly handled, it was Sullivan who made the motion for a public hearing. In response to the board's justification for denying the audience a chance to speak, he said, "Frankly, what I heard was an attempt at spin to protect the reputation of the people who are responsible for the school system. I could talk at length about my concerns, but I won't, because as a policy maker what's important for me is to hear from parents and the public about what their concerns are about what I think is about one of the worst debacles in the history of the public school system in the city."[8] His insistence on getting public comments from the crowd of parents openly applauding him eventually led to the mayor's contingent of the PEP board walking out of the meeting. This video would eventually become part of our local ending.

Mallory got in touch with Sullivan through the PEP board website and found that he was simply a citizen activist who'd decided to take on the challenge of speaking truth to power. In a way, from a very different position, Sullivan reminded Aaron of Steven Costello in Houston; both were citizens who decided to do the right thing just because they felt it was right.

In part because of our experience with secondary school students in Houston, we decided to create a paid working group of high school kids from several public schools and to perform *City Council Meeting* in their buildings. It was important to us to make the group geographically and culturally diverse; while the school system here remains notoriously segregated,[9] one of the things that makes New York unique is its ongoing and fluid mix of people. By working with a range of students and neighborhoods, we had a chance to show both sides of the city.

Through our own connections and those of HERE Arts Center, we asked principals for recommendations and ended up with thirteen kids from four different schools across the city; we met with the students for work sessions every other week over a six-month period. We talked about testing and city council meetings and read excerpts from Rancière's book *The Ignorant Schoolmaster* about the intricacies of the teacher/student relationship. Rancière's thesis, often boiled down to the phrase "Any idiot can teach any idiot anything," was a good starting point for us, because it allowed us to consider the working group as experts in their experience of education. It put us on more equal footing in our meetings. And it was true, we had a lot to learn.

Our discussions were exciting in a lot of ways, even if they were awkward at times. Our cohort of students included kids who might never have met, who came from very different backgrounds—well-to-do white kids in Brooklyn, working-class Latinx immigrant kids from Queens, Harlem-based African American kids from a performing arts high school. There were kids with lots of theatre training and kids with none. Gavin Kroeber, who describes himself as a social dramaturg, an artist who works within community-engaged settings to help move projects forward, helped structure our sessions with the group, reminding us that we were often pitching ideas to them they hadn't considered, to leave enough time for them to respond without us filling the gaps and silences, and to get to know each other. We met after class hours at their schools, most often in classrooms or conference rooms at LaGuardia Community College in Queens, where two of the schools were located.

While the students' opinions on testing diverged, they were always nuanced, their thinking rigorous and complex. For some, the tests were just something to get through, a doorway to the next level of access or achievement; for others, they were a source of deep anxiety, even illness, because for them the pressure to achieve and grow beyond their family circumstances was immense.

Some of us think creating competition in the room is a pain in the ass and doesn't teach you anything. Some of us know we're always going to be competing, so this is just practice. The game is walking in and just concentrating on the game, not the what-if. The what-if is somewhere else.

Some of us came here speaking another language, but we had to take the same test everyone else did.

And we got really nervous.

We threw up. In our second language.

These conversations allowed us to start thinking about our New York City local ending, which included several components. As a kind of preview, we had two members of our high school working group—Alannah Bilal and Xavier Pacheco—record the orientation video. This meant high school students who came to the piece felt included from moment one and were perhaps more likely to participate actively. We also worked a couple of the young people into the meeting; some volunteered to be on the council table or were given the Audience Participation testimony, again allowing the ending to seep into the meeting in interesting ways. Aaron wrote down notes after each working group meeting and did one-on-one interviews with the students.

At first it was difficult to figure out how to use these interview notes to represent the multiplicity of voices in the room with any kind of cohesion or inclusivity. Gradually, with group members' consent, we worked their individual voices into a monologue that pointed to their differences rather than trying to hide them. The voice of the students as a whole contained disagreements, a continuing nod to Rancière's irreducible distances.[10] Each of these individual "narrators and translators" helped make up a whole that didn't need a constructed or imposed unity to function.[11]

We initially tried to change the space for the local ending in a big way, as we'd done in Houston and Tempe, but it kept feeling forced. As a designer committed to not having ideas just for the sake of having them, Jim refused to let us make something dramatic just because we felt we should, or because we felt the pressure of expectation that comes with a hometown gig. What we arrived at ultimately was a simple repositioning of tables, adding yellow tablecloths to replicate a particular PEP board meeting video that was integrated into the performance.

From our student discussions we created our own version of a standardized test that we printed in blue book form, made to look exactly like the New York

PEP board member Patrick Sullivan stands to address the audience, with the student
working group members Max Cabra, John Catala, Alannah Bilal, Alan Saenz,
Ella Geismar, and Emmet Dotan on the stage behind him assuming the position
of the PEP board. Photo by David A. Brown Photography / Houston, Texas.

Regents Exams, and passed it out to the audience as they reentered the space
for the ending. In our standardized test, all the questions were philosophical,
and all the answers were correct.

*14. What is the relationship between intellectual emancipation and the insti-
tution that is providing it?*

a. There is none

b. The Student is the Relationship

c. They might be at odds

*d. The institution provides the information and the student provides the
emancipation*

After we'd passed out the booklets, we reconstructed a PEP board meeting, with the students on bullhorns yelling at each other as the parents in the
actual meeting had done. Jim's video design started with the PEP meeting
video and devolved into a chaotic scene from the movie *Gremlins*, which was
a way to add a layer of adolescent playfulness to the proceedings. Two students then read the monologue Aaron generated through one-on-one student
interviews. Because the kids' schedules and circumstances were all so varied,
this monologue was something that any student who wanted could pick up

and read in one of our performances. Like the text we gave on the spot to councilors in the meeting, this piece of text did not demand special acting skills to perform effectively. Finally, students sat at or on the PEP board table to question a different person each night, including Councilors Brad Lander, Melissa Mark-Viverito, Gale Brewer, Jimmy Van Bramer, and Helen Rosenthal; PEP board member Patrick Sullivan; education expert Julie Landsman; and public school parent Bruce Allardice, whom we invited as special guests.

Hello. Please introduce yourself.

COUNCIL MEMBER ANSWERS.

Here are questions for you: What did you learn in school?

COUNCIL MEMBER ANSWERS.

What did you learn in spite of school?

COUNCIL MEMBER ANSWERS.

What did you learn outside of school but because of it?

COUNCIL MEMBER ANSWERS.

As in the other cities, *City Council Meeting* came with its specific set of production and promotion challenges in New York. We presented the work at a high school "gymnatorium" in the Chelsea Technical School building across the street from HERE, at LaGuardia Community College in Queens, and at El Museo del Barrio in Upper Manhattan.

HERE was coproducing the event with us; their marketing staff was fluent in more traditional strategies and accustomed to promoting typical performance runs at their home theatre in SoHo. Like most small- to mid-sized nonprofit theatre venues, they were also underfunded and overcommitted, with a busy season of performances in two theatre spaces. From our presentations in Houston and Tempe we knew we needed to do different work to get a more diverse audience into the room with us and have them feel welcomed, especially given the difficult-to-describe nature of the piece.

When we treated our hometown as a city we didn't know as well as we thought, especially for the presentations at El Barrio and LaGuardia, our promotional efforts started to pay off. Kroeber had us canvas the students in our working group to find out what would get their peers in the room, and we tailored our marketing imagery around their suggestions. They were insightful about what size image to use in school hallways, what colors worked best, and how to capitalize on the fact that their peers were involved in the work. We arranged visits to several classrooms and community centers. We engaged Manhattan Neighborhood Network, an East Harlem–based community broadcast training program and TV station, to run a story about us. We also worked with The Foundry's Audience Ambassadors program.

Thanks to Kroeber, we also used a community organizing spreadsheet that allowed several people—working group members, HERE staff and interns, and us—to work on the same series of activities. This simple tool let us make progress on an overall strategy for each venue, with labor shared among many people over time.

The spreadsheet started with the names of individuals, institutions, and associations (community groups, business associations, business improvement districts, and the like) and let users leave a record of whom we'd spoken to, the last interaction we'd had, and how to follow up. That way, if you were a HERE intern who only came in on Tuesdays, you could do a couple hours of calls and emails, leave notes for the next person, and keep momentum going. This simple spreadsheet let us reach out beyond our usual constituencies and bring in audiences that were neighborhood specific as well as issue oriented and demographically diverse.

We often started with people we knew and worked outward. Sheila Lewandowski, who codirects the Chocolate Factory Theater in Long Island City, Queens, where both Mallory and Aaron have presented work, is deeply connected to the community. Lewandowski gave us the names of specific business owners, business improvement districts, senior centers, and adult education programs. Often when we reached the people on our list they were happy to hear about the project and would bring people with them to the show. Simply taking the time to reach out in this way made for more community buy-in than an email, poster, or social media post ever could.

City Council Meeting was resonant in New York City even though the reception was mixed. Visual art makers and viewers, already deep in a conversation around the value of antagonism and social engagement in art, tended to like it more than theatre people, who wanted it to be less boring or have more polished performances and shiny design elements. Our New York staff became well-versed in handling the diverse audience that we built on some nights.

For the students, the challenge of reliability and the commitment we made to working with a diverse group at their own levels of engagement meant that it was anyone's guess whether it would hold together each night, even as the whole experience felt worthwhile. Some students who originally wanted only to contribute to the development process of the piece later saw their working group counterparts participating in the performances and decided last minute to do the same, which left us scrambling to bring them up to speed. But it was satisfying to have the piece remind them of the simple principle of the democratic process, which makes it possible for a lot of different kinds of people to assume positions of power, even if it doesn't always shake out that way in the actual cities where we live, work, and protest. We wanted to create a forum in which we could show that even if this is a messy way to go about governing ourselves, most of the other forms or criteria for giving power that humans have tried (religion, gender, money, property, family) at a large scale are more flawed and less equal. The students belonged on the power-bearing side of the table. Their participation was a vital part of the picture.

At best, our New York performances involved multiple overlapping publics who saw people like them and very different from them in the room, all trying to help make the same thing happen—white hipster art audiences alongside school-age people of color, elected officials and candidates alongside restaurant owners and artists. When this happened, viewers got to see that their reactions to the piece derived in part from their identities and communities. If the audience in the room represented some of the city's diversity, it became clear that whether a moment was funny or boring or engaging depended in part on your own subjectivity, rather than a neutral idea of good or bad, democratic or autocratic. And presenting the piece in schools meant that we could implicitly question the aesthetics of public institutions like schools, even as we embrace the people who work and study there.

Kim Whitener, Alannah Bilal, and Tory Vazquez

Kim Whitener was the executive director of HERE, and she cocurated and coproduced the programs that made *City Council Meeting* in NYC possible. She has now returned to her work as an independent creative producer and consultant with her company KiWi Productions. In our conversation, Whitener's interest and focus was on the fact that now, more than five years on, organizations are much more likely to want to be deeply engaged in building and growing the community around a project. "Everybody talks about wanting to do that in depth, and nobody really has the template for it."

Because Whitener was involved with *City Council Meeting* from early in our development of the work, and because she saw the piece in Houston, she had perspective on how New York City differed from the other places where we presented the work. "New York is just different from other cities. . . . In a smaller town, the council holds so much more sway. Council members have a lot more personal connection with their constituents."

While at HERE, Whitener had developed a partnership with Chelsea Technical School, where three of our performances took place. "I was very excited about the relationship with the school, made contact with the principal, was hopeful to continue a relationship post–*City Council Meeting*. Then the principal retired and they just had no interest."[12] This echoes some of Sixto Wagan's concerns and reflections in Houston about the institutional capacity to maintain relationships as individuals move on.

When we worked with her, Alannah Bilal was a sophomore who took several years of high stakes testing in stride. She is currently working her way through John Jay College, studying forensic psychology and nursing, and working as a surgical coordinator at Columbia Hospital. She was involved in other theatrical productions at her school through their work with EPIC Theatre Company, which was in residence there: "Even though my school did a lot of theatre, it was different because you all were from outside." She said the piece was "not prominent but impactful" in her memory. "Even though people came with different views, we could still come together in the same room." She also appreciated the value of having us come to the various school sites from HERE to work with students. When we asked her about whether the piece made an impression on students as a whole, she admitted that most of it might have gone over their heads. "There was a lot going on," she said.[13]

Victoria Vazquez played the city secretary in our New York shows and was key in holding together those performances. She is a longtime performer, writer, and director with whom Aaron worked in Elevator Repair Service and on separate performance projects each of them authored in the past. Vazquez has more recently become a full-time public school teacher at Liberty High School in Manhattan, working with immigrant high schoolers and young adults on curricula that includes writing, theatre, and Common Core. When we went back and spoke with her, we were curious about whether her experience in *City Council Meeting* had informed her teaching and her experience as a public educator having gone through our process of artmaking.

Vazquez recalled that the process with the high school cohort made her aware of some of her own biases: "One day I said something about how standardized tests weren't that hard, and one of the kids kind of schooled me about that—how biases, learning styles, and opportunities to prepare and learn were not taken into consideration when making the tests."[14]

What we learned through our process about how New York City's PEP board worked had also been new to Vazquez. We talked about the fact that while New York City's subsequent mayor, Bill de Blasio, came in with an agenda and mandate to scale back some of Bloomberg's pro-charter reforms (like colocation) and achieved a measure of success in making pre-K accessible to more of the city, he did not dismantle the PEP board in favor of a more democratic structure. This perhaps speaks to how, across the political spectrum, once a certain level of power is gained, whoever is in charge is loath to give it up.

As an educator and thinker, Vazquez saw our working group sessions and the ending we made with the students as combining "controlled chaos and creative agency. There was an open question posed [that] everyone could respond to on their own; there was logistical flexibility that allowed people to come and go on their own schedules," which doesn't happen as much in a typical school setting. In the performance itself, she found it powerful to watch the students work and take control of the room.

Vazquez is now deeply involved in building culturally relevant classrooms as a way to make the Common Core State Standards work for immigrant students. She is also cocreating a school setting diverse enough to accommodate a broad range of learning styles, ages, and life circumstances—from fourteen-year-olds recently arrived from Senegal who speak more than one language fluently to young adults who need reading skills in order to enter the job market. For Vazquez, testing is clearly a means to an end, which the school system defines as college readiness. This means she and the other teachers at Liberty often have to find creative ways to make Common Core relevant to students who have little cultural frame of reference for skills like argumentative essay writing.

She talked about how the issues of for-profit charter schools and high stakes testing remain complicated. "There are some Black and brown parents who feel the charters can offer their kids more opportunities than public schools. And the charter teachers can sometimes be more creative with what they do." She's also encountered parents who chose charters and then felt they were not meeting their kids' emotional needs, so went back to public schools.[15]

PEP and Testing

In response to high stakes testing, New York has had the largest test refusal /
opt-out movement by far, with approximately one in five students refusing to
participate each year since 2015 (when they started keeping records).[16] While
the city does have a high opt-out rate in some schools, the district has found
ways to punish those schools—like the Earth School, where Aaron's son attended elementary—for opting out, withholding a portion of their funding or
designating them as failing simply because a large number of students refuse
the tests.[17]

While de Blasio and former superintendent Richard Carranza worked to
make certain aspects of NYC schools more equitable, the de Blasio administration's retention of the PEP board established by Bloomberg remains a
problem. In the words of Patrick Sullivan, "for us not to have the same role
in our kids' education as people who live in the suburbs or Middle America
is patronizing."[18]

The PEP board recently approved a recommendation to transfer responsibility for the 5,100-member police force that governs the schools from the
NYPD to the city's education department, a policy that was eventually taken
up in the controversial 2020 NYC budget—instead of defunding the police,
the policy simply changed who was paying them.[19] While former mayor de
Blasio's priorities shifted from Bloomberg's to a degree, the PEP board remained in his consolidated power, as it did in the prior administration. As of
this writing, there is no indication that the new mayor, Eric Adams, will alter
the arrangement.

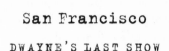

San Francisco

DWAYNE'S LAST SHOW

What are pathways we make that don't look possible? What does it cost to pave them over?

After the first three sites—Houston, Tempe, and New York City—San Francisco was the first city where we presented *City Council Meeting* more like a tour than an extra-long-term development process. Mallory had figured out a basic structure for teaching the meeting to the staff, and we knew we'd draw on our outsider-insider status when making the ending. We spent fewer weeks in San Francisco (roughly six, between 2011 and 2014) and relied heavily on local dance-theatre artist Erika Chong Shuch to cocreate the ending, drawing on her own approach and her collaborators in conversation with us. Both Mallory and Aaron have long-standing connections to the Bay Area. Aaron had been visiting for study and work since 1992, when he took workshops with the iconic dance-theatre ensemble Contraband and later taught workshops for local artists through the Creative Capital Foundation. Mallory knew collaborators in the local dance community including Knee Jerk Dance and the theatre companies Banana Bag & Bodice and Shotgun Players. It wasn't as if we were coming in cold, but we weren't as embedded as with the first three cities.

Shuch is a prominent Bay Area performance maker whom Aaron had known from a workshop he'd taught. Like us, she makes work using a range of approaches and styles, from devised dance-theatre to more socially engaged performance installations to long-term collaborations with people working in social justice and mental health fields.[1] In return for sharing partial authorship credit for the local production, we could be newcomers with a kind of stamp of approval, which in turn gave us access to people we wouldn't have otherwise gotten to know and an aesthetic that was steeped in the Bay Area's tradition of multidisciplinary performance. While the structure of the piece, with a local cohort of staffers and a local ending, ensured we'd never be able to operate like a typical touring production, Shuch and her company took on a lot of the heavy lifting, including casting our San Francisco staff, codirecting the ending, and doing some promotion and production work at Z Space. San Francisco's experimental performance community is close knit, and Shuch's involvement also garnered us social credibility.

Our approach was influenced in part by budgetary considerations. Operating inside a legendary Mission District space called Project Artaud, a big former tooling factory that's now part of an artist housing collective, Z Space is primarily a presenter and developer of new plays by local artists rather than a site for incoming productions from out of town. Thanks to David Szlasa, who was Z Space's producing director at the time, they had signed onto our successful NEFA National Theater Project and NPN applications; this meant there was money in place for us to do one or two site visits and a final production residency, but not much more. Shuch and her collaborators, with their twenty-plus years making experimental work in the Bay Area and their understanding of our venue, became incredibly important to us throughout the process.

Like New York City, where Jim, Mallory, and Aaron had so much history that it had been hard to identify a single approach or an issue for the local ending, San Francisco proved initially challenging for Shuch. We recognized some of the same forces at play in both places, like rampant gentrification, real estate overdevelopment, and corruption within city government, so it was hard to zero in on a single issue or moment at a government meeting that could encapsulate and drive our local ending.

Over the course of two or three visits, we did start to piece together possibilities. First, the meeting we saw of the San Francisco Board of Advisors (their version of a city council) took place the day after a beloved community member named Stuart Smith died. Smith had been a stalwart of the SF gay community. People spoke of his generosity, his mentorship, and his deep impact on the city's cultural and economic life.

One of the tragedies of his death was that, because of a temporary block on same-sex marriages in the city, he had not been able to marry his long-term partner, Dave Earl. The marriage ban had been lifted a day before, just as Smith's health took a sharp downward turn. In the supervisors' meeting, we learned that a justice of the peace had been trying to get to the couple's house so they could be married before Smith passed, but he'd gotten there just hours too late. Everyone gave tribute to Smith and to his and Earl's partnership. Something about the way people described him gave us the sense that he represented a bygone era in San Francisco's gay life. The bureaucratic dryness cracked and gave way to a moment of pathos. At least one supervisor choked up.

About that time, Shuch's two-year-old son, who was with us at the advisors' meeting, was getting restless, so she took him out for a walk through the old city hall building. On her way out of the chambers, she saw a number of young same-sex couples getting married by justices of the peace, a celebration of the fact that the ban had just been lifted.

We wondered if these couples had weighed the right to equality with a desire to reject a norm like marriage and all its attendant baggage. We wondered whether marriage made them reconcile their own mortality and its legal element, survivorship, which Earl wouldn't be able to have over Smith's legacy. We saw the city reclaim its place as a haven for progressive rights; or was it conformity, or was it both? We had walked out of a memorial for one chapter in the city's life and into the start of another. Even as San Francisco was being taken over by new, oblivious tech company money and people, another generation of LGBTQIA+ people were asserting themselves at city hall. Like many cities, San Francisco is in a constant state of flux. The notion of a eulogy for the city became key to how we imagined the ending.

In addition to visiting the board of advisors' meeting, Aaron and Mallory visited the Occupy encampment on the steps of city hall on one of our visits. Like many similar sites around the country in those years, Occupy Oakland had become a kind of model alternative civic space, filled with possibility while remaining fragile.

The idea for our ending in San Francisco was that all the local staffers except Secretary Sarah Curran would perform. This would be the "reveal": the people serving in a support role in the meeting became the focus of the local ending. Shuch handled the challenge well, picking people who she felt could both work with her to create the ending and fit our needs for staffers who were not trained actors. They were diverse in age and race, and many had dual backgrounds as artists and activists.

The departure point for our local ending in San Francisco was Dwayne Calizo. If Pete Colt in Portland provided the prompt that started the whole project, Calizo became its bookend in a wholly different way. Calizo had

worked with Shuch throughout her career, and he was a fixture in a part of
the local queer community that was very different from the one Stu Smith
occupied. A trained opera singer, Calizo had also run a space and a performance series in the Mission District that had been central to the city's overlapping punk and queer communities. Calizo was one of those people who is
so certain of himself that it's a little intimidating. He was a little wary of us
at first, so we met once or twice just to see if working together was something
he wanted to do. Gradually we found moments of connection, decided to
make him a staffer on the piece, and then worked to build an ending around
his history and voice. We also made material with Shuch's company members,
drawn from interviews about their history in the city and neighborhoods,
along with choreography created collaboratively.

To start making material with Calizo, Aaron met with him near the MLK
Fountain in downtown SF on a sunny July afternoon, about ten days before
we presented the piece at Z Space. Shuch was also working with the staffers
and other performers to generate material for the ending. Our timeline was
often this way—a week before the show opened, we were still zeroing in on an
ending figure or gesture. Because the meeting part of the piece familiarized
viewers with the notion of reading as performance, rather than a typical memorized play, we felt we were better off refining the material up to the last minute rather than trying to arrive at an idea or script to memorize too soon. This
let us build some energy around the immediate connections we were making
as we worked in a city—especially in the Bay Area, where we had less time;
this proved fruitful, if stressful.

Both Aaron and Calizo came to the park assuming they'd speak for a half
hour, maybe forty-five minutes. Their conversation ended up going on for a
couple of hours: about Calizo's childhood in Hawai'i, his days singing backup
for Don Ho, his time on the streets, and his current struggles living in a single
room occupancy. The two men ended up sharing a lot, and when he left, Aaron
was pretty sure he'd forgotten most of it, since he'd been so caught up in the
talk and lost any pretense of objectivity; as with most interviews, he didn't
record anything. He made some notes and hoped for the best.

When he got up to write the next morning, he was surprised that he could
recall quite a bit, and also that he had the desire to write in the third person. Both he and Mallory thought it would be interesting if a boy read the
third-person text while Calizo was sitting onstage, a kind of eulogy for the city

through the eyes of one of its longtime, marginal dwellers, told by a very new resident. Calizo's presence and his work in the world—artist, caregiver, radical queer icon—embodied a tension San Francisco's alternative communities were losing. We also hadn't heard back from Dave Earl, Stu Smith's partner, about whether we could integrate their story into our production, so this felt like a logical and powerful alternative.

Calizo liked the idea of this younger self narrating his life, and so did Shuch. From our earliest meetings, Shuch said she wanted Calizo to sing Purcell's "Dido's Lament" aria as part of the ending, with its refrain of "remember me, but ah! forget my fate." He had sung it previously in something they had worked on, and she wanted it to be revived in this ending; so like many things in the process, we now had a reason. It was the best way to eulogize the city as the version of it he'd known was dying.

He puts three fingers of one hand over the center of his chest and then points them to the sky and then places them on the ground, in the same measured rhythm. This is how he describes what singing feels like. At the same time he is talking about the possibility of not singing any more, that this is the end of performing.

When we were starting our production residency, we reached out to Smith's partner Earl again, through mutual friends of Shuch's, but didn't hear back. We heard that he was having a hard time, as we could imagine, so we let it go. We hadn't planned to mention his or Smith's name in our piece. On the Monday before we opened, we got an email from Earl. Smith's ashes had been spread in places he loved, in the water around the city. He said Smith had been a huge supporter of the arts and that we were free to mention him and Smith. He said he might even make it to the show one night.

When we brought the different elements together, we found we were able to stage the San Francisco ending through a relatively straightforward reversal. The audience reentered the space and stood onstage. Like us, Shuch had been experimenting in her own work with audience participation and a porous boundary between performer and viewer, and her insights here were invaluable. Onstage, individual viewers were invited to sit across from members of Shuch's ensemble, who'd previously been staffers in the meeting, and listen to recordings of them telling the story of their city and their identities while they looked each other in the eyes. For those recordings we asked the ensemble members to talk about things that were disappearing from what

Dwayne Calizo sits at the head of the table surrounded by audience
members filling out the Remember/Forget cards at Z Space in
San Francisco, California. Photo by Aaron Landsman.

they considered to be *their* San Francisco. Throughout this first scene, Calizo
sat at a table in the center of the space and wrote furiously on index cards
printed with the lines

*Remember*_____

*Forget*_____

We invited viewers to contribute responses to these prompts as well. As
notecards accumulated and Calizo wrote more furiously, the sound of the
recorded interviews flooded the space through the theatre's speakers. At a
certain point the cacophony of voices stopped as a young boy stepped up to a
microphone and began reading the text Aaron had made from Calizo's interview. To keep things spontaneous, Calizo was told he could ring a hotel bell
on his table anytime he got uncomfortable with something in the boy's text.
This was the cue for the young man to move on to the next paragraph, and it
accommodated Calizo's ambivalence about being the center of attention and
revealing so much about himself.

At the end of the monologue, the lights faded on Calizo, and the ensemble began moving in pools of their own light, singing a choral round of fugue-like text drawn from musical figures in "Dido's Lament." As the round built, Calizo appeared at the top of the risers with a giant spotlight behind him, like a ghost or an angel. There, he sung the aria, building to a torturous, punk crescendo punctuated by an abrupt blackout, capturing the swift disappearance of the former city.

POSTSCRIPT

A little less than a year after our shows in San Francisco, we got a message from Shuch letting us know that Calizo had died. Singing "Dido's Lament" at *City Council Meeting*, his eulogy for the city, had been his last public performance. It felt wrenchingly, ironically fitting to the work we'd all done together, a reminder that for some people, ideas like gentrification, queerness, and the power of a community of artists do have life or death implications. We sent Shuch a handheld video Aaron had taken of Calizo singing "Dido's Lament," along with a few pictures we'd taken of him during our process, which she played at his memorial. Calizo scowling and smiling at the same time; Calizo handing a piece of text to a council member; Calizo making all of us laugh in the middle of a tense rehearsal.

David Szlasa and Erika Chong Shuch

David Szlasa, the former programming director at Z Space who originally brought *City Council Meeting* to San Francisco, now lives in the Hudson Valley in upstate New York, where he teaches part time, is raising two kids with his partner, and helps to design art spaces. His mobile studio project, which Aaron participated in in 2015, is now installed permanently at Stanford. Though he continues to design projections and lights for artists in the Bay Area including Mark Bamuthi Joseph, Joanna Haigood, and Sara Shelton Mann, he has mostly given up what he called "the gig life" of being an itinerant designer and said he and his family have allowed "the life changes to change us."

It was because of Szlasa's enthusiasm for *City Council Meeting* that Z Space signed on to become one of our commissioning and presenting partners: "You all were using Project Artaud in a specific, responsive way, and that was appealing as a designer." Although he'd left Z Space's administrative staff by the time we started working there, he felt a loyalty to our project, so he helped us with production issues during our culminating residency there, securing equipment we needed and ensuring the project ran smoothly, even though Z Space was having a hard time keeping up with our needs, as they were not used to being a tour presenter.

Szlasa recalled San Francisco at that time as being in a state of transition, with our project situating itself right in the middle of it: "I'd known Dwayne for twenty years. He was intimidating, a powerhouse, and also a deep lover. He was really indicative of a time and place in the Bay Area." As a marker of how things had changed, Szlasa said, "They now teach LGBTQ curriculum in middle school." He said he was happy the project is being memorialized in this book: "It's hard to see in the moment what you can see looking backward."[2]

We spoke with Shuch, whose current work has moved toward reexamining the performer-audience relationship with *For You*, a series of performance works created through extended encounters with and for selected audiences of twelve people. With *For You*, Shuch's ensemble creates personalized performances for each audience member and brings together the group of twelve to experience each other's performances. Her collaborators include artists and theorists, as well as people with expertise in brain development, dementia, and psychology. When the Covid-19 pandemic forced some of her company's plans to be put on hold, the *For You* project began creating a series of one-to-one gifts made by artists for an elder in quarantine called *Artists & Elders*.[3]

For Shuch, the project proved a kind of record of the ways Calizo's vibrancy paralleled that of the city during a distinct period of time. The fact that Calizo had been a hospice nurse for AIDS patients in the 1980s, when many people were afraid to even acknowledge or go near those same people and when the disease had barely been spoken about in the mainstream, was resonant with a whole generation of artists in New York and other cities whose stories had been lost in that earlier pandemic.

Shuch talked about how our work with Calizo brought him (and us) up against our ideas about what acting is—Calizo was larger than life, a drama queen, and we were used to a more stripped-down aesthetic. Shuch recalled Calizo once asking, "How do you treat a story as a loaded gun?" She said too that "Dwayne's story was a powerful bullet."

She also said the artistic gesture of *City Council Meeting* offered a sense of freedom. "It's hard to remember we can do anything we want. We are not bound by any kind of rules. And then the question is how to insert a sense of rigor into that total freedom." She specifically spoke to Mallory's sense of rigor within this wild framework we'd made, her ability to "find the simple gesture that deepens that freedom."

Finally, as Shuch develops *For You* in different cities—and has received some of the same grants we did for *City Council Meeting*, including from the NEFA National Theater Project, which focuses on touring ensemble projects—she's thinking about "how touring is an act of engagement rather than an act of display."[4]

Gentrification in the Tenderloin

The Tenderloin neighborhood, where Calizo lived, has resisted the gentrification that has remade much of San Francisco. In the 1980s the community organized to save affordable housing, bringing about policies that have protected the neighborhood, including nonprofit land acquisition, zoning policies to prevent high-rise buildings, protections for SROs, and historic district protections. According to Randy Shaw, who has worked in the neighborhood since founding the Tenderloin Housing Clinic in 1980, "the Tenderloin is really a model for how communities across the country can stop gentrification." But as the city around it changes, the pressure on this neighborhood grows and excluded elements from other neighborhoods filter in. At the same time as the residents' demands for quality-of-life improvements are made, there is skepticism about whether this may eventually force current residents out. There are ways in which the challenges faced by this neighborhood, as a place for displaced people, mirror the challenges faced by the culture Calizo represented.[5]

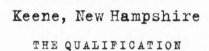

Keene, New Hampshire

THE QUALIFICATION

Most of the time you don't make a decision about how to see where you are. It's just where you are. You see somebody own their style, and it makes you want to learn what they do. They go hard at a trick, and land it, and it inspires you. You give it a try, you get outside yourself.

Keene, New Hampshire, was the last stop on our five-city production itinerary for *City Council Meeting*. It was the smallest city in which we presented the work (with a population of about thirty thousand, including Keene State College, which hosted the work[1]), and the presentation in some ways fit more closely than any other to a more traditional touring model for experimental theatre. We met Redfern Arts Center's Shannon Mayers and Sharon Fantl at a booking conference in New York in early 2012; we negotiated a contract for three short site visits and a production residency, and we started to work. For our local ending we worked with skateboarders who were trying to get city funding and approval for a languishing skate park and with council members who, though personally sympathetic, represented the authoritative body that stood between the skaters and their plans.

The production in Keene brought us full circle, back to where we began in two ways. First, we were fortunate to work with photographer Paul Shambroom as our local Pete Colt; Shambroom's photo and book series *Meetings* had originally inspired us when we were conceiving the piece. We'd been in conversation about the joys and sorrows of civically engaged art throughout our process and working together came out of our exchange. Second, we encountered the only real resistance in our five-city run from a council member we'd asked to be a part of the work—Plato's principle of democracy, "the qualification of no qualification," was too challenging for him to get behind. The promise and provocation of democracy itself was the starting point for the work and remained resonant up until the end.

Keene is on the New Hampshire-Vermont border, about a four-hour drive from New York City. It's a college town located in the Monadnock Valley that once had a thriving canning and mill industry. Keene State College houses the Redfern Arts Center, and while the college is a local economic engine, providing many of the town's jobs, it was also the source of a town-gown tension common to small, deindustrialized cities. A shortage of good jobs and the availability of fentanyl and meth have impacted the local young adult population, further amplifying the gulf between college students and local residents. At the same time, because of the college, it's fared better than other neighboring towns. The worst effects of urban renewal planning bypassed it, and it's a gateway to a well-touristed region.[2]

Keene was also a good spot to end the piece because the town itself hosts the quadrennial theatre of presidential primary season. There's an iconic old-school diner called Lindy's, owned by the same family since 1961, with Formica counters and friendly locals; it's here that candidates often have photo ops and interviews every four years in which they talk about the real America.[3]

I'm looking at some people hanging out in front of Scores in the middle of the day. They are playing with their kids in the leaves like any other parents would. It looks like they are good parents—they just look kind of young. They're chatting with a friend who has a handgun in a holster, and he's showing how he puts it under his arm, because it's easier to draw. It's pretty easy to focus on one or the other. The kids in the leaves. The guy with the gun. It's pretty easy to make a judgment call.

Until 2014, Keene was the site of an annual pumpkin festival, the self-proclaimed world's largest, in which residents and guests carved and decorated thousands of pumpkins and lined the streets of downtown with them.[4] This seemingly innocuous event, which took place a few weeks before our show, played into some of the aforementioned tensions we unearthed while we were finishing the piece.

Keene already had a skate park, located downtown in an underused parking lot, but it had languished for years and was not used seriously by local skaters. Instead, it had become a spot for drug deals and petty turf battles between rival groups of BMX bikers.[5] What the local skaters were proposing to council was that an additional skate park become part of a larger park planned just outside of town.

We know each other when we see each other, and we have something to talk about. The shoes, the board, a cap, a brand, a trick. Ollie. Nollie. Nose flip. 50-50 grind. 360 flip. You have something to connect to, instantly.

On our first site visit, Mallory and Aaron attended a council meeting at which the skate park was to be discussed. We noticed that, like in many small towns, the council skewed older, and of eleven councilors there was only one female member (there are now five[6]). All the councilors were white, though to be fair, so is the town. Councilors in Keene receive an annual stipend of $2,000 (now $2,500, marking the first increase in seventeen years),[7] so they must be able to commit the time without real pay. We had met previously with Andy Bohannon, who worked for the New Hampshire Parks and Recreation Department and who explained that the allocation of public funds for what was sometimes seen as a deviant activity had been controversial in Keene.

At the council meeting, we noticed that a somewhat similar drama played out here as in other cities: an expert, often speaking on behalf of a group, testified to the council with informed passion, breaking down the reasons why the proposal was sound. Then the council took it up, debated it, and seemed to do what they wanted. Here the expert was Brian Quigley, a Keene State College administrator and avid skater who said "skateboarding saved [his] life" by keeping him away from drugs and other illegal activities. Quigley described how the subculture offered a community to people like him, who didn't have ready access to supportive communities through the usual avenues of home, family, or more traditional sports. He talked about how what had once been associated with deviant behavior was now a $3 billion industry.

A little bit like Pete Colt in Portland, Quigley's articulate passion and willingness to push things with the council seemed to be at least somewhat considered; he dressed the part of responsible adult (gray sport coat and slacks, tie) as a way to indicate how skateboarding could lead to a comfortable, conforming life, but he challenged the council to think past its usual associations with a behavior and a group of people many of them didn't understand. *Look, if a buttoned-down guy like me can be a skateboarder, maybe you need to rethink what you believe.*

While the skaters had the support of one or two council members, including Emily Hague, who would later be part of our ending, their cause was hampered by a lack of turnout at the meeting. How do you motivate people whose subculture is in part about defying authority over public space to show up at that authority's chambers and ask to be included in a more acceptable way? It's not an easy sell, and perhaps one or two skaters, neither of whom were particularly articulate, came to the meeting. The councilors' arguments for and against tended to be about whether public funds should support the skaters' endeavor, and a lot of references were made to a contentious dog park in town that had needed to resort to raising private money a few years earlier. In general, the council liked the *idea* of a skate park but didn't feel like it was the right thing on which to spend public funds. The decision was postponed until the following month.

On our next visit we met with as many of the players involved in both the council and the skate park as we could. Everyone pointed us toward Carl Jacobs, a longtime council member with a generations-long history in the region; Jacobs helped us understand some of the ways Keene had escaped the more dire poverty and disenfranchisement of nearby towns and how the local government tried to walk a line between helping people in need and encouraging self-reliance. Though he didn't seem to know exactly what to make of us, Jacobs was interested enough by our project to agree to shoot our orientation video during our production residency the following year.

Jacobs also pointed us toward two council members as possible ending collaborators: Terry Clark, who people told us had a reputation for being a sort of "bad boy" on the council, and Emily Hague. Along with Quigley, Jacobs was the kind of local or community advocate who influenced our work heavily and proved invaluable to our process without actually making a physical appearance in the work. Quigley, who ultimately did not perform because he felt it would potentially compromise his integrity with the council or the school, did put us in touch with two local skaters, Colin Trombley and Greg Burroughs, who performed the work.

Trombley worked for FedEx and was the more avid skater of the two; Burroughs worked at the local shoe store called Ted's.

I'm Greg. I work at Ted's. I might have sold you your shoes.

Both were thoughtful, a little reserved, and perfect for the piece because they embodied the tensions in Keene; they were both from town but went to Keene State, and they both saw the shadow side of skating even as they participated in the culture. During one site visit and the production residency, Aaron did three or four interviews total with them, in bars or restaurants and sometimes at the college. Councilors Clark and Hague agreed to work with us too, and since both of them played music in local coffee shops, a rough outline of our ending started to take shape. We would do one performance at the local

Masonic Hall: skaters would take over the space, and between their tricks and the monologues they created with Aaron, the council members would play a few songs. Quite a few of the Keene council members, including Jacobs, played in local bands.

Redfern was strategic in using our production to fulfill a goal they had for the organization. Instead of having their programming remain somewhat insulated from the town, they wanted to make more connections to local social and civic life. The relationship with Carl Jacobs and the council was a part of that: we built connections with the library that oversaw the Masonic Hall and with the local Waldorf school, where we did a workshop and then assembled part of our staff for the production. Redfern did a great job of building audience interest throughout our visits, as with Project Row Houses in Houston, so the community came knowing a bit about what they were in for. Instead of a usual presenting model where a venue has to use press quotes and catchy photos to sell a piece to their audience—a kind of "trust us, we know art" model—our process built interest because everyone who had participated in the work would talk it up and bring folks. So the production coalesced a growing energy rather than having to generate it from scratch.

The working group included Keene State students and an administrator, high school students from the local Waldorf school, and a woman who worked at city hall. They gave us a window onto the college, town, and city government. The skate park issue felt like a subtle one that wasn't widely discussed, so it was helpful to see it from these differing perspectives, to understand how it intersected with their lives.

Keene was a good place to think about sunsetting the project too, because we realized that while we loved working on the piece, it was a huge time commitment for us, for presenters, and even for paid ending collaborators. We also saw that we were getting into a bit of a formula. We knew the piece a little too well. We all had other projects we were starting to build, separately and together.

A couple of factors did stir up the productive kind of trouble during our production residency. First was the Keene Pumpkin Festival 2014. If you Google *Keene pumpkin festival riot*, you will be treated to imagery and commentary that is, depending on your take, hilarious, harrowing, or both. You will see wild bunches of young people throwing bottles and starting fires; you'll see videos of paramilitary vehicles rolling down a campus street and hear helicopters overhead; you'll see people in tears being interviewed and the detritus of many, many smashed pumpkins (no band reference intended). Inaugurated in 1991 as a way to get more tourists to town in the fall, Keene Pumpkin Festival had, in recent years, turned into an excuse for kids to party after the more family-friendly celebrations had ended. The year we were there was the final year for the festival—the rioting was so intense that Keene decided to cancel it.

The drama of the pumpkin festival and its aftermath was a way for the city to air out its tensions and for characters and themes that had plagued Keene to emerge. The tendency of all the parties to pass off blame was profound: Keene State students claimed it was either a few bad actors or a crowd from the University of New Hampshire that provoked the destruction; some students said it was people from town using the college as cover; and the town said it was the students because they didn't feel a responsibility to the town. Local churches humbly and piously sponsored people to clean up and spread the word that "this is not who we are." And lots of people said it was just some kids blowing off steam.[8]

At the same time that the town was fretting over how to frame what had happened and what to do with itself, uprisings around police violence toward African Americans were playing out in Ferguson, Missouri, and other cities. Those actions were being framed much differently in the media and by authorities. These protestors were Black, but in Keene it was almost all white folks. When we mentioned this to a couple people in town, even just as a point of comparison, they said it was "too sensitive a time to talk about this." But we couldn't help but feel that when people in Keene said, "this is not who we are," what they meant was that *we* were not like *those* people over near St. Louis or New York. It was, for us, a healthy shake-up of Keene's identity, even as it was clearly painful for some members of the community.

On a much more subtle level, the shake-up around the pumpkin festival made people a little more cautious about what they said to us when we were making the piece. Trombley and Burroughs, our two skaters, were happy to deal with the destruction in town and talk about what it might mean, but the council members we were working with preferred to keep away from the subject.

We also ran into an issue with Jacobs, Keene's elder statesman on the council, who'd agreed to shoot our orientation video. This was the first time a council member had objected to our content. Specifically, Jacobs wanted to change the wording, derived from Plato, about how democracy was a framework in which equals agreed to rule and be ruled, and that no one was more qualified than anyone else. Jacobs couldn't abide by that. He indicated that he felt more qualified because he knew more than most people in town about how things worked and that's why people had elected him.

On the day we'd planned to film, we set up our equipment, understanding that we'd have to clear up this disagreement before we went ahead. Jacobs was firm in his belief, very literally stating that he couldn't abide by the idea that someone else was equally qualified to govern Keene, and asking us to please change the text to reflect that. We were firm as well—that this had worked in four cities, that this actually celebrates democracy as a governing of equals, that these ideas had been espoused from everyone from Plato to Rancière, and that if it was good enough for them, we wanted to keep it. Though the conversation was respectful, Jacobs refused to record the orientation with us, and we had to scramble for a replacement. We ended up shooting it with Hague and Clark at the last minute.

We couldn't help but think that the Keene Pumpkin Festival riot, which had happened not two weeks before our show, was part of what made Jacobs a little cautious. Regardless of the reasoning, we were in some way gratified that the piece itself could still be provocative to a figure who seemed otherwise entirely comfortable with the principle of democracy. It also allowed us to see how we could use our unorthodox production model to be flexible in the face of a small crisis.

Keene's Masonic Temple was built in 1858 and is now known as Heberton Hall, an annex of the public library.[9] We had never performed in such a bucolic meeting hall space, with a small, raised stage and colonial color scheme. For the ending, we repurposed the council tables as makeshift ramps so the skaters could jump off the small stage after the intermission. Mallory worked with the skaters the day before the show to find something that felt like a violation of the space without putting anyone in danger. We reorganized the seating into groups so that the skaters could ride through and around the audience during the performance. This gesture replicated the tension we felt between the skaters and council members. We wanted a space where they could coexist on their own terms, where everyone had an equal opportunity to express themselves but there was still a sense of unease. There was always going to be something not right about skateboarding inside a Masonic Hall.

Skating is falling and getting back up. People tell you to get back up. They encourage you. You see someone get back up and you do too. It's like, that fall doesn't define me. That grade doesn't define me. That job. The way you see me. You just get back up.

Keene allowed us to come full circle by including Paul Shambroom, the Minnesota-based photographer who had inspired aspects of the piece with his *Meetings* photos, in the role of Pete Colt. Shambroom had a colleague in the Photography Department at Keene State, and we used that connection so that he could come work with us: the department covered Shambroom's travel. We were able to do a joint artist talk, and we rehearsed him into our final show at the Masonic Hall. He was the right age and had the right affect—neighborly, slightly edgy with a dry sense of humor.

Sharon Fantl

We spoke with the assistant director of Redfern, Sharon Fantl, who worked with us and continued her work at Redfern until 2020 with a focus on interdisciplinary programming and strategic initiatives. Fantl managed the Creative Connections program and spoke about how *City Council Meeting* was an opportunity for the Redfern Arts Center to forge new relationships with the college and the town. Our partnership with Professor Brian Kanouse from Keene's Philosophy Department on a classroom presentation and long table discussion gave the project a certain weight for the Redfern. Fantl described the project as a "catalyst for us with a lot of engagement elements connecting to different departments. There was a lot that really was new for us. We knew we didn't necessarily have all the answers. In years to come it would be a defining moment for us."

Among the challenges Fantl described were an interdepartmental suspicion of interdisciplinary projects that don't fit a particular mold and an uncertainty about how theatre and civic engagement fit together. There was a hope that Keene State would look at this project as a vehicle to build relationships that would help us both, but that didn't really pan out.

"What is the training we could have had to make stronger impressions on the powers that be, that could have helped us with the project?" As with other presenters, the impact of the work was not immediate or direct. "Doing *City Council Meeting* helped us flex our muscle, and that was useful for later projects."[10]

The Skate Park: Brain Quigley and Colin Trombley

We were able to get an update from Brian Quigley, who is still an administrator and supporter of the ongoing skate park rebuilding initiative in Keene, on the current plans for the skate park. After lying fallow for some time, the old park has had a bit of a renaissance. According to Colin Trombley, one of the skaters who performed in the local ending, the "skate scene is really good in Keene, best it's been in years, a whole new generation." This is evidenced by the skate park's Facebook page and a three-hundred-thousand-dollar fundraising campaign, almost complete. The plan for a new 9,800-square-foot skate park is part of the Monadnock Economic Development Corporation's proposed arts corridor.[11] Quigley noted, "When I think about all the pieces and layers and levels and story line—your time and investment was a part of that story. Gave it a legitimacy that helped it make it possible."[12]

For Trombley, who is currently and ironically a risk mitigation consultant, the impact was more personal—"It was a pretty accomplishing event. We worked a bit. You gave us advice. Then we did the show. It was like working toward a new trick."[13]

Afterword

When we decided to wrap up *City Council Meeting* as a theatre production, it was largely for reasons of time and money. The months it took to build relationships, form a working group, teach the meeting, and create a local ending with local collaborators had become difficult to sustain. Our commitment to equitable pay for ourselves and everyone on the project meant that after we had drawn down funding from NEFA, MAP, and NPN, venues that wanted to present the work couldn't afford to. But something about the project felt unrealized.

Since 2015, we have made educational curricula for students in high school and college, from single-session workshops to semester-long courses, as a way to continue *City Council Meeting*'s inquiries. We are continuing to partner with several institutions on flexible models for schools to participate, including deep dives into our research materials and process with Mallory and Aaron as hands-on guides, as well as simpler ways for a school to take on versions of the piece on their own.

Our work with school kids began in Houston, thanks to Assata Richards and Project Row Houses, where we saw how well middle schoolers took to *City Council Meeting* as structure, lesson, and play. There was something simple and disarming about helping a sixth grader navigate the procedural language of our Bismarck section, which spoke to how civic engagement is at once alienating and teachable. Invite her to sit in the mayor's chair and she may develop a new sense of possibility for herself.

In addition to the Third Ward middle school kids, we did our classroom presentation with private high school students at the Kinkaid School in a Houston suburb thanks to staffer Christa Forster, who taught there. Students were at least as excited as adult audience members to discuss not only

Student working group members Alannah Bilal, Max Cabra, and John Catala before
a performance at the Chelsea Career and Technical Education High School,
New York City. Photo by David A. Brown Photography / Houston, Texas.

the political issues and intellectual framing of the piece but also their own
emotional responses to participating. They wanted to talk about the choices
they made, a primary departure point for us.

By the time we left Houston, Mallory had put together a folder with testimonies from San Antonio, our Audience Participation plan, and an excerpt
of a councilor's opening speech. The version we did in schools began with
our orientation video, plunged participants into the choice-making that was
key to the work, and gave them a sense of the main concerns and themes in
twenty-five minutes. From there, we guided discussion about what the piece
brought up for them as young people. We were inevitably helped by their excellent teachers, who could keep us on a track that was comprehensible and
interesting to the students based on their grade and aptitude levels. As we
developed the piece in subsequent cities, we often used this classroom demo
during our residencies.

Our experiences with students in Houston helped us commit to a long-
term process with the high school cohort in New York for both the local

ending and the meeting. In Tempe we used our classroom demo at schools throughout the Phoenix metro area. In Keene we worked with a group of Waldorf students as staffers and presented the classroom version of the work with Brian Kanouse's American studies course, as well as a long table conversation Kanouse and the Redfern organized.

Because university venues were often part of our presenting teams in different cities, building curriculum at that level felt like a natural outgrowth of our process. Aaron has since adapted *City Council Meeting* for one-time engagements at NYU's Tisch School of the Arts, George Mason University's Fall for the Book, and Bennington College's Center for the Advancement of Public Action, for groups ranging from fifteen to two hundred people.

We have found that these sessions are easy to run with a single staffer (often the faculty member bringing us in), can be staged multiple times in a day, and can lead to both robust discussion and written responses. At Bennington the project was part of a short seminar alongside several other community-engaged artworks for a course called Ethical Community Collaboration. For NYU we presented the classroom demo three times in two days, for one hundred and fifty students each session, and then the students were asked by their instructors to write critical essays about it. At Fall for the Book, we held a panel discussion afterward with professors in literature, political science, and history.

At NYU in particular, our matter-of-fact approach to *City Council Meeting* allowed us to transcend some of the current fears in academia around how we engage with students about identity and difference. Prior to our presentation for the writing program at Tisch, Aaron was told by an administrator that the school was a powder keg, that students would surely freak out if a white instructor asked them to take on voices or text different from their own backgrounds. Given the demographics of the Tisch students and the range of testimonies in the session, this difference in backgrounds was likely.

In introducing the work, Aaron told students that those who took testimonies and became speakers had choices: they could speak the text as written, decide not to voice a person different from them and hand it to someone else, acknowledge before reading a testimony that they were appropriating another person's words and that they felt uncomfortable (or comfortable), or raise their voice in protest against what the piece was asking them to do. Before even beginning the classroom performance, we talked for a few minutes about choice-making as a departure point for the conversations we wanted to have.

Giving students options and trusting their ability to process their responses seemed to work. They were excited to talk about their fears, anger, enjoyment, and discomfort. For the classroom, then, it has felt important to not only ask participants to speak the words of another person but also invite them to give voice to their experience of that role-play within the sessions.

In 2020, Aaron began offering a freshman seminar at Princeton called Is Politics a Performance?, which takes students through our research and development process, using local government meetings in Princeton and Trenton as source material and culminating with a presentation using our structure for the university and local communities.

Building a freshman seminar gave us the chance to make our work more explicitly resonant for students beyond the live performing arts. Within a college semester, we can deepen the research we came to through our own curiosity and intuition, turn it into a lens through which to view a familiar arena and event, and teach on ancient and contemporary philosophy, sociology, activism, civic engagement, and theatre.

Aaron's course takes students from Plato's *Laws* to Erving Goffman's *Presentation of Self in Everyday Life* to Rancière, Paulo Freire, and other philosophers. We also look at the Design Studio for Social Intervention's book *Ideas-Arrangements-Effects* to question the physical setup of a council chamber and its rules and procedures.

This course asks students to populate Mallory's structural framework for participation and choice-making with excerpts from meetings the students attend, either together or separately. The interdisciplinary approach of the project itself is integrated from day one, bringing together classes in government, theatre, and sociology to make iterations of the work that embody civic learning and possibility. We will have course plans available for teachers to download and adapt on our website (http://www.citycouncilmeeting.org) for both secondary and college students, including key readings, discussion prompts, and an outline of the mechanics of the piece.

Appendix

City Council Meeting Script

About the Script

What follows is the script for *City Council Meeting* as presented in Tempe, Arizona, in February 2013. *City Council Meeting* took the form of a local government meeting and used found and original text, live and recorded video, and excerpts from a half-dozen real meeting transcripts. It was performed by the audience without rehearsal. In each city we created a local ending with people on different sides of specific local issues; in Tempe we combined homeless youth and ficus tree care. The piece was performed in many spaces in the five cities where we presented it. In Tempe the audience sat onstage at ASU Gammage, a 3,000-seat auditorium with multiple balconies. For the meeting we allowed the open, empty auditorium to dwarf the proceedings on the stage. In the local ending, we closed the stage curtains until the very end, when we opened them to allow for a sense of renewed, expansive possibility.

We intend for this script to help you find your way through *The City We Make Together*, to show you how we accommodated multiple simultaneous conversations within a single performance and how we put together the piece's three sections: orientation, meeting, and local ending. We do not intend for this script to be directly reproduced or performed as it appears here, as your technology and intentions may differ from ours. We invite you to use our project as inspiration for making your own version of *City Council Meeting* or another task-based performance work.

In our performance, all participants and staffers read from scripts that took a variety of forms, including orientation instructions read from clipboards, messages on video monitors, fragments of transcript dialogue, testimonies on a single sheet of paper, and instructions read aloud off index cards or whispered into the ears of audience members in the councilors group. The performance text was purposely cut up this way to create an interdependence among facilitators and participants.

The script was created for the reader of this book to show the variety of ways the words were spoken and instructions were communicated. To account for the gap between what you're reading and the totality of the performance text, here are some helpful notes:

- The stage directions demarcate each city section of the script and show when the transcripts change. This is how the script is structured and organized. By shifting seamlessly from city to city, without interruption, the intention is to make the meeting feel like one city made up of transcripts from many cities.
- Anything set in italics is a stage direction and includes the actions of staffers.
- Any text in **bold** and **ALL CAPS** is an action that participants do rather than say. This is included to show how individual scripts instruct the reader (audience and staffers) in the performance of the text. These actions are always contained within the participants' spoken text, unlike the stage directions that appear between passages of dialogue.
- Anything set in regular sentence case is spoken.
- As the councilors' names shift from city to city, we list them as "COUNCILOR #," followed by a name that changes.
- Councilor and speaker testimony is transcribed verbatim from video and audio, so apparent errors or typos reflect the way people spoke.
- Names placed within brackets are placeholders for where the actual audience member names would be spoken, which change from performance to performance.

About the Video

We used four live-feed cameras (two of which were operated live by camera people) and two video monitors downstage of the council table. The councilors and staffers cannot see what is on the monitors. Most of the video that the audience sees is live feed of the council table and the testimony lectern with chyrons to designate the city we are in at any given point.

Disclaimers are interruptions to the meeting shown on the video monitors. This is where the meeting talks directly to the participants seated in the audience.

About the Set and Props

In the front of a large room (often on a stage, if available) there is a long table made from two standard eight-foot tables. Behind the table there is a U.S. flag and a state or city flag of the place where the meeting is happening. There are six chairs for the staffers and the city attorney along the wall behind the table and six chairs at the table for the five councilors and the secretary, who sits at one end. On the table are six tabletop mic stands and mics, one in front of each chair. There are five nameplates in front of the mics, five copies of the meeting agenda, pencils for taking notes, and a gavel at the center seat. There is a vase of flowers. Near the secretary's seat there is a Bible, a bell, and two awards. The audience seating is also part of the set and should be set up with a central aisle, if possible, that leads to a lectern with a mic. On the lectern is a sign-up sheet for the speakers, a box of golf pencils, and index cards. This is where the speakers give their testimony. On the left and right side of the room, just downstage of the table, there are two video monitors, which project the *City Council Meeting* logo. All referenced and handled documents too numerous to list here, are copies of the actual documents from the original meeting from which the transcript is pulled.

Additional local ending scripts, as well as further examples of testimonies and instructions, are on the project's website, citycouncilmeeting.org.

Cast of Participants

STAFFERS

These are people who facilitate the meeting for the audience. They are cast from the local working group we assembled in each city and they rehearse prior to the performance, unlike the audience.

SECRETARY: Sits at the end of the meeting table and runs the meeting.
STAFFER 1: Assigned to facilitate the performance of COUNCILOR 1.
STAFFER 2: Assigned to facilitate the performance of COUNCILOR 2.
STAFFER 3: Assigned to facilitate the performance of COUNCILOR 3.
STAFFER 4: Assigned to facilitate the performance of COUNCILOR 4.
    This staffer also reads for SPRITZOMATIC, a Bismarck councilor who
    retires and is replaced early in the meeting.
STAFFER 5: Assigned to facilitate the performance of COUNCILOR 5.

COUNCILORS

This self-selecting group of audience participants includes five councilors and a city attorney. Each councilor has several names to reflect the changes in transcripts from city to city (Bismarck, San Antonio, Houston, Tempe, Oakland, Portland). These changes are demarcated by the changing nameplates on the council table.

COUNCILOR 1: Grossman, Medina, Costello, Ellis, Salzman
COUNCILOR 2: Smith, Taylor, Bradford, Shekerjian, Reid, Fritz
COUNCILOR 3: Mayors Warford, Castro, Parker, Hallman, Quan, Adams
COUNCILOR 4: Aspic, Chan, Hoang, Navarro, Nadel, Leonard
COUNCILOR 5: Seminary, Lopez, Noriega, Woods, Kaplan, Fish
CITY ATTORNEY: Represents the city attorneys from Bismarck and
    Houston.

SPEAKERS

This self-selecting group of participants signs up to receive a unique testimony from among the many we collected from the public record in the meetings we visited. The following thirteen testimonies are used in the performance:

CHAPLAIN: Bismarck's city chaplain
TEQUONDRIA TAYLOR: San Antonio Urban Leadership Council youth
    participant

TALIQ PRYOR: San Antonio Urban Leadership Council youth participant
TIARA HARRIS: San Antonio Urban Leadership Council youth participant
VIVIENNE HARRIS: Houston neighborhood activist
STEVE RIGGLE: Houston pastor of Grace Community Church
CLYDE BRYAN: Houston representative for the U.S. Pastor Council
AUDIENCE PARTICIPATION: A fictional testimony written by Aaron
    Landsman
BOBBY VALENTINE: Oakland Occupy activist
SADIYAH: Oakland Occupy activist
MAX ALSTEAD: Oakland Occupy activist
NANCY HORMANN: Downtown Tempe Community board chair
PETE COLT: Portland neighborhood activist, played by an actor who has
    rehearsed prior to the performance

SUPPORTERS

These self-selecting participants remain anonymous and only perform instructions throughout the meeting from an index card they pick up. We don't take their names or count how many choose this role.

BYSTANDERS

These self-selecting participants remain anonymous, and we don't count their numbers. They receive a program at the start of the meeting while waiting in the lobby.

Start of Script

After the audience enters and is seated, the orientation video plays on the two monitors at the front of the room. The video includes content recorded with local participants in each city speaking directly to the camera, as well as footage accompanied by a voice-over (V/O) that is the same in each city, overlaid with archival images from local government meetings or written text.

LOCAL PARTICIPANTS (on video): In the *Book of Laws*, Greek philosopher Plato lists seven qualifications required for governing, and for being ruled. Four are based on what he calls "a natural difference"—the difference of birth. Parents over children, the old over the young, masters over slaves, nobles over serfs, and so on. The fifth, Plato calls "the principle of principles," or the power of those with a superior nature, the strong over the weak. But for Plato, the only one really worth discussing is the sixth one: the power of "those who know over those who do not." So you have four categories based on hard facts (I was born before you, I was born richer than you, I own you), but these aren't as good as the two more theoretical pairs: natural superiority and the rule of science (I'm better than you, or I know more than you). You'd think that was enough. But here's the thing: Plato lists a seventh category. This is the form of government only a god could save: democracy. He says democracy is "the drawing of lots," or "the qualification of no qualification." So welcome to *City Council Meeting*, where no one is qualified to be in charge. Or everyone is. God help us.

V/O: By joining us tonight, you'll be stepping into the shoes of someone who was actually part of a local government meeting somewhere in the United States in the last three years. You can be as involved as you'd like.

Text and images appear on the screen to match the V/O description of roles.

V/O: Question: I've never been to a city council meeting before. Is that a problem? No. You do not need special qualifications. There are several ways to participate.

1. You can be a councilor. Councilors sit at the council table and conduct the meeting. We have room for six councilors.
2. You can be a speaker. Speakers receive a piece of testimony that was given by someone at an actual city council meeting somewhere in the

United States in the past three years. Speakers sit at the testimony table and speak directly to the councilors. If you want to be a speaker, we'll need your name so we can call you up to give your testimony.

3. You can be a supporter. Supporters don't have to speak, but get simple instructions like stand up, applaud, answer your phone, or get up and leave the room for a few minutes, the kinds of activities that take place at any local government meeting.

4. You can be a bystander. Bystanders are people who just want to observe. If you're a bystander, we'll need you to exit the room until the meeting begins.

Throughout the meeting, there will be staff on hand to guide you or in case you have a problem. If you've got a smartphone, you can have a Twitter conversation with the meeting using the hashtag #citycouncilmtg.

Question: Once I make my decision, can I go back and change it? No.

LOCAL PARTICIPANTS: Sometimes *City Council Meeting* can seem like just a bunch of procedures and paperwork. Sometimes there's no way to know if you're doing it right. People want so many different things! Sometimes *City Council Meeting* can seem like, *is anyone driving this boat?* The answer, most of the time, is no. Right now, if you look around you, you'll see you're part of a group that has never done this before. Some people get to *City Council Meeting* and go, "Wait a minute, I thought I'd get to speak my mind. I thought I'd be engaging in dialogue." Well, you do get to engage in dialogue, but it's a dialogue that has already happened, among other people, somewhere else. You're just filling their shoes for a little while. Why? Because we think it's more interesting to have you put your mouths around other people's words than to have you speak your own minds. You might feel like, "Hey, didn't you just say I was in charge?" The fact is, you *are* in charge. You're deciding at every moment how to participate. That's a kind of power, isn't it?

Text appears asking bystanders to please leave the room. The orientation video ends and monitors show live feed of the room we are in. The SECRETARY stands in front of the table.

SECRETARY: If you want to be a bystander, please leave now, and we'll call you in when the meeting starts. I need six volunteers to be councilors. *(She counts out the six volunteers and hands them over to STAFFER 4, who gives them a name card and hands them off to individual staffers for their one-on-one orientations).*

Now, who would like to be a speaker? Please go get your testimony at the table there and sign up. Supporters, please take an instruction card at the supporter table. If you have questions or need a little refresher on what each of the jobs is, let me know. *(After answering questions, she orients* CITY ATTORNEY *and* COUNCILOR 4, *who are sitting in the front row.)*

The following is one variation of a supporter card:

Actions to do during the meeting:

1. Stand in solidarity when video monitors change to Oakland.
2. If anyone smiles, smile with them.
3. What small thing do you do when you are having trouble concentrating or find something boring? Do that. At least once.

If you have a cell phone:

- Please leave your cell phone on. If it rings during the meeting, please go to the back of the room to take the call. Answer it by saying, "I'm in a meeting." Quietly finish the call, then return to your seat.
- If you have a smartphone, you can have a Twitter conversation with the meeting: #citycouncilmtg or @citycouncil.mtg

The following is the SECRETARY's *orientation script that she reads to* COUNCILOR 4 *and the* CITY ATTORNEY, *while the other staffers are orienting their individual councilors:*

SECRETARY: *(To* COUNCILOR 4*)* You are playing Aspic. *(To* CITY ATTORNEY*)* You're the city attorney. After the first few minutes of the meeting, a councilor will leave and you two will have a short scene together where the city attorney swears in Aspic. POINT OUT WHERE EACH OF THEM WILL STAND IN THE SPACE. I'll be there holding a Bible for you to swear on. SHOW THEM WHERE THEY WILL BE AT THE TABLE. After that, Aspic will sit here for the meeting, and city attorney, you'll sit back behind me, and I'll let you know when we need you again. I will call you up several times and give you your text to say. For both of you: During the meeting, you'll get text to say and instructions for things to do. Anything in plain text is something you say—anything in bold and all caps is an action you do. HAVE THE CITY ATTORNEY TAKE A SEAT IN THE FRONT ROW. CONTINUE ORIENTING ASPIC. The meeting agenda is on the council table, and you're welcome to take a look at that if you want, before the meeting starts. The first thing that happens at the table will be a roll call. When you hear the name Aspic, say, "here." Any time after that, you just vote yes. If you're confused about something at any point during the meeting, just raise your hand or make eye contact and a staffer will come over and help you figure it out. **HAVE ASPIC SIT IN THE FRONT ROW.**

The SECRETARY *collects the names of the speakers from the sign-up sheet. She then introduces herself to all the councilors seated in the front row of the audience. She hands them their opening speech cards and models what the councilors are asked to do next. The* SECRETARY *stands on the X that is on the floor in the center of the room, downstage of the council table facing the audience. She scans the room, clears her throat, and nods four times.*

After she sits, each councilor follows by standing on the X and reading off a set of speech and action cards.

STAFFER 4 / SPRITZOMATIC: **LOOK AT THE AUDIENCE.** You remember when you said yes to something someone asked of you, just because they asked? Because they asked, you wanted to say yes? **LOOK AT COUNCIL TABLE.** Anybody can do this. Anybody can do this. I don't know what I am doing. **CLEAR YOUR THROAT.** Would you like to make a difference? Would you like to be an instrument of the city? OK, me too. I did too. **NOD SEVEN TIMES.** So I'm on that side of the table. For now. **TAKE YOUR SEAT AT THE COUNCIL TABLE.**

COUNCILOR 5 / SEMINARY: **LOOK AT THE AUDIENCE.** People ask me how we're going to bring more people into the process. And every time I say the same thing. "You can't push a rope." **CLEAR YOUR THROAT.** You have to demonstrate that you really care. You have to get down and really listen to what causes pain for people. And then try to do something. **NOD SEVEN TIMES.** We don't have to agree to get something done. **SMILE. LOOK AT COUNCIL TABLE.** If I can't see you, I don't have to think about you. There's nothing to see here. Get out of the way. **TAKE YOUR SEAT AT THE COUNCIL TABLE.**

COUNCILOR 2 / SMITH: **LOOK AT THE AUDIENCE.** Here comes the guy who always shows up and has something to say. Because he feels like someone should always have something to say. He's worried no one else will show up. Sometimes there's nothing to complain about in this town. **NOD THREE**

TIMES. CLEAR YOUR THROAT. Here comes the woman who said the secret police had put lasers in her dentures. Here's the guy who doesn't like the fact that I'm queer. **LOOK BEHIND YOU AT THE COUNCIL TABLE.** I wish people would come to a meeting because they were happy. I wish they would tell us what was going right. **SMILE. TAKE YOUR SEAT AT THE COUNCIL TABLE.**

COUNCILOR 3 / WARFORD: **LOOK AT THE AUDIENCE.** Many things are coming apart right now. I don't know what to do about that. **LOOK AT THE COUNCIL TABLE.** Can we just talk to each other? Can you just answer my question? **CLEAR YOUR THROAT.** There are so many rules. And we're on that side of the table now. And this is never about you. It's about the people who aren't here. **NOD SEVEN TIMES.** My name is Mayor William Warford. I'm supposed to be in charge. Someone please tell me how to rule. **SMILE.** Do, uh, call the roll, please call the roll.

The staffers enter. The Bismarck section begins. STAFFER 3 meets COUNCILOR 3 / WARFORD and helps them find their seat, hands them a script of this portion of the meeting, and points out their first line. The rest of the staffers explain to their councilors that in this part of the meeting, everything has been decided, so when they hear their name called they will answer "here" and vote yes. All staffers take their seats behind their respective councilors. The SECRETARY calls the roll.

SECRETARY: Spritzomatic.

STAFFER 4 / SPRITZOMATIC: Here.

SECRETARY: Seminary.

COUNCILOR 5 / SEMINARY: Here.

SECRETARY: Grossman.

COUNCILOR 1 / GROSSMAN: Here.

SECRETARY: Smith.

COUNCILOR 2 / SMITH: Here.

SECRETARY: Warford.

SECRETARY hands STAFFER 3 the name of the speaker who is reading the CHAPLAIN, who gives it to COUNCILOR 3 / WARFORD.

COUNCILOR 3 / WARFORD: *(Reading from the script)* Here. I'd like to have, uh, Reverend [CHAPLAIN], who's our chief chaplain, please bring our invocation. Chaplain?

CHAPLAIN: *(Reading off a set of cards)* **WHEN THE MAYOR CALLS YOU, STAND UP, GO TO THE LECTERN WHERE THE COMMISSIONERS JUST GAVE THEIR OPENING SPEECHES, AND SAY THE TEXT ON THE NEXT CARD.** Thank you, Mr. Mayor. Father God, we're sorry to see, uh, a commissioner leave us tonight. **YOU ARE REFERRING TO COMMISSIONER SPRITZOMATIC.** We pray that you'll be with her as other doors of opportunity open for her. We thank you for the new commissioner coming on tonight. We pray that you'll be with them as they serve our city in this way. We pray for tonight's meeting that you'll be with the commissioners as they listen to the people who've come out tonight; give them wisdom in the decisions that they make. In your name. Amen. **SIT BACK DOWN.**

COUNCILOR 3 / WARFORD: Thank you very much. We have, uh, some business here, which is to consider the approval of the minutes of the meeting of [DATE OF LAST PERFORMANCE]. Motion and second to approve those minutes. Please call the roll.

SECRETARY: Commissioner Spritzomatic.

STAFFER 4 / SPRITZOMATIC: Yes.

SECRETARY: Seminary.

COUNCILOR 5 / SEMINARY: Yes.

SECRETARY: Grossman.

COUNCILOR 1 / GROSSMAN: Yes.

SECRETARY: Smith.

COUNCILOR 2 / SMITH: Yes.

SECRETARY: Warford.

COUNCILOR 3 / WARFORD: Yes. Motion carries. We have now completed the business of this commission. This meeting is adjourned. **BANG GAVEL ON THE TABLE.** However, we have, uh, some awards that, uh, we would like to give, uh, tonight. And then I will ask, uh, the retiring commissioner to make a speech. I'd like to go out front, uh . . . two awards.

COUNCILOR 3 / WARFORD goes down in front of the table, as explained in the orientation.

STAFFER 4 / SPRITZOMATIC: *(Reading from a script)* Uh, Mr. Mayor, I always wanted to be Miss America, but that, uh, wasn't in the cards. I was kinda OK being Queen of the City. But am I finally gonna get that crown?

COUNCILOR 3 / WARFORD: *(Reading off the award)* Commissioner, this is pretty close, uh, this is pretty close. The first, uh, is, uh, a congratulations award from the League of Cities. Uh, for thirty-two years of service to the city. Signed by Keith Hunky, our assistant city administrator, uhhm. He is the League of Cities president. So Connie, please come forward; let's get a round of applause for thirty-two years of service.

Applause. STAFFER 4 / SPRITZOMATIC goes to accept the award and goes back to her seat.

COUNCILOR 3 / WARFORD: *(Reading off the award)* Second award, uh, I have this, uh, beautiful plaque for Connie Spritzomatic for invaluable service to the city. A commissioner from 1989 to 2009. "Thank you for twenty years of outstanding service to the citizens of this city. Dated [TODAY'S DATE]." So. Please come forward, Connie.

Applause. STAFFER 4 / SPRITZOMATIC comes back down to accept the award and goes to the testimony table.

STAFFER 4 / SPRITZOMATIC: Can I address the commission from here? In twenty years I haven't been able to be at this side of the lectern. *(She goes to the lectern.)*

STAFFER 5 gives COUNCILOR 5 / SEMINARY a card with the following line on it.

COUNCILOR 5 / SEMINARY: *(Reading from the card)* Can you state your name for the record?

Staffers laugh.

STAFFER 4 / SPRITZOMATIC: Y'know, I'm gonna miss you. I'm gonna miss the Mutt and Jeff team over there.

Staffers laugh.

STAFFER 4 / SPRITZOMATIC: I'll let you decide who's who. You know I've been called a lot of things today. I started out my day with the question: So how does it feel to be almost a has-been? Uh, someone else asked me, so how's it going to be to go back to being someone who's completely unimportant? But since, uh, since we're elected to these positions, and since we don't have any, uh, power and glory except as we act as a body, the—those questions are jokes. I was given a lovely, uh, award, from a coworker as I left to come to my last commission meeting. It was a Life Savers candy. He said, "Thanks for being a lifesaver for the city." And I felt pretty good about that. Y'know, when I ran for my first office back in 1978, I can assure you that I never intended to be, uh, it wasn't about leaving a legacy, it was about being part of the legacy of leadership in this community. And it has been a privilege. I have worked with wonderful people. Look at all these—to the new commissioner—look at these staff people who are here to help.

Staffers wave to the audience.

STAFFER 4 / SPRITZOMATIC: They keep us smarter than we are, they answer, I'm pretty sure, a thousand questions on my behalf. They're the ones that keep us out of trouble; they keep the city going, so kudos to you. To the citizens who elected me over and over and over again. I'm not sure if that's 'cause I didn't get it right the first time, ha ha, and I had to keep learning the lessons, but it's been a privilege to work on so many different issues. I really will miss all of you, but since I'm not going anywhere in my day job with the League of Cities, I have everybody on speed dial. Expect to be hearing from me. To the new kid on the block, you're going to love it. Enjoy the ride.

Staffers laugh. Applause.

COUNCILOR 3 / WARFORD: *(Reading from a script)* Thank you very much for those words, Connie. I'd just very much like to, uh, state, that, it has been a, uh—pretty nice flowers by the way—that's, that's, that's cool—

STAFFER 4 / SPRITZOMATIC: My family did that.

COUNCILOR 3 / WARFORD: Yeah.

STAFFER 4 / SPRITZOMATIC: Isn't that great?

COUNCILOR 3 / WARFORD: Yeah, flowers, uh, it has been my distinct privilege to, uh, to have served with you for eight years. PAUSE. You know, looking back I think that one of the most important things when I asked you was the Growth Management Plan. For those of you who aren't up to speed on that, it's our visionary plan to offer our community as a community that is orderly and organized. **PAUSE.** Some of the more mundane things, she did the first solid waste task force. I think she was the, uh, self-proclaimed Sultana of Solid Waste. So let's be sure and get that down in the record, the uh Sultana of—

STAFFER 4 / SPRITZOMATIC: Mr. President, you forget the Debutante of Debris.

COUNCILOR 3 / WARFORD: Uh, excuse me, I'm sorry.

STAFFER 4 / SPRITZOMATIC: The Guru of Garbage.

COUNCILOR 3 / WARFORD: Ha ha, yeah.

STAFFER 4 / SPRITZOMATIC: You know, the former mayor used to say, "If it smells, it's in Connie's portfolio." (*To* COUNCILOR 4 / ASPIC *seated in the audience*) Y'know, you have to inherit my chair.... Did they tell you that? (*She leaves the stage, taking the flowers and awards with her.*)

COUNCILOR 3 / WARFORD: We are now at the point where—before we can call the next city commission to order—we have to have the oath of office administered by the city attorney to the new commissioner. So we'll have the city attorney come up and administer the oath of office and then we'll be seated.

The SECRETARY *signals to the* CITY ATTORNEY *for the swearing in and gives them the stack of swearing-in cards. The* SECRETARY *brings the Bible and holds it while the* CITY ATTORNEY *gives the oath of office.*

CITY ATTORNEY: I'll read you the official oath. Raise your right hand and repeat after me. I do solemnly swear

COUNCILOR 4 / ASPIC: I do solemnly swear

CITY ATTORNEY: that I will support the Constitution of the United States

COUNCILOR 4 / ASPIC: that I will support the Constitution of the United States

CITY ATTORNEY: and the constitution of the state

COUNCILOR 4 / ASPIC: and the constitution of the state

CITY ATTORNEY: and that I will faithfully discharge the duties

COUNCILOR 4 / ASPIC: and that I will faithfully discharge the duties

CITY ATTORNEY: of the office of commissioner, board of city commissioners for the city

COUNCILOR 4 / ASPIC: of the office of commissioner, board of city commissioners for the city

CITY ATTORNEY: in the county and the state

COUNCILOR 4 / ASPIC: in the county and the state

CITY ATTORNEY: according to the best of my abilities, so help me God.

COUNCILOR 4 / ASPIC: according to the best of my abilities, so help me God.

CITY ATTORNEY: I further swear

COUNCILOR 4 / ASPIC: I further swear

CITY ATTORNEY: that I am under no direct or indirect obligation

COUNCILOR 4 / ASPIC: that I am under no direct or indirect obligation

CITY ATTORNEY: to elect or appoint any person, to any office position or employment

COUNCILOR 4 / ASPIC: to elect or appoint any person, to any office position or employment

CITY ATTORNEY: under the city government.

COUNCILOR 4 / ASPIC: under the city government.

CITY ATTORNEY: Congratulations.

Audience and staffers applaud. SECRETARY, COUNCILOR 4 / ASPIC, *and* CITY ATTORNEY *return to the council table.*

A disclaimer video plays with the Emergency Broadcast System sound and color bars. Only the audience can see these instructions on the screens: **PLEASE STAND. ALL BUT THREE OF YOU PLEASE GO TO THE BACK OF THE ROOM.** *There were only three people in the audience at the beginning of this meeting. Who are those three?* **YOU THREE, PLEASE SIT DOWN.** *The disclaimer ends and video returns to live feed of the room.*

During the disclaimer, STAFFER 3 *takes the* SPRITZOMATIC *nameplate away and tells* COUNCILOR 3 / WARFORD *to hold it. Then staffers instruct the council members and hand out the consent agenda paperwork.*

STAFFERS: (*Whispering to their councilors*) This section is just the procedural part of the meeting. Nothing gets decided here. This stuff has already been decided. This packet of information is the stuff you've decided on. You really need to read this script as quickly as possible, because we have a lot to get through tonight, and because everyone has to stand up back there until you're done with this part. The first thing that happens is a roll call, and you say "here." Then the secretary will call votes and everyone should just vote yes on everything. The person you're reading may be referred to as [_____]. The meeting will start shortly. In the meantime, look at the people out there and think about what they might want from you.

Once the audience has chosen three people and everyone else is at the back of the room, STAFFER 3 *tells* COUNCILOR 3 / WARFORD *to continue.*

COUNCILOR 3 / WARFORD: Now I will call this meeting of the city commission to order. Secretary, please call the roll.

SECRETARY: Aspic.

COUNCILOR 4 / ASPIC: Here.

SECRETARY: Seminary.

COUNCILOR 5 / SEMINARY: Here.

SECRETARY: Grossman.

COUNCILOR 1 / GROSSMAN: Here.

SECRETARY: Smith.

COUNCILOR 2 / SMITH: Here.

SECRETARY: Warford.

COUNCILOR 3 / WARFORD: Here. OK, commissioners, we are moving to our public agenda. The first item is item 5773-5775 on the agenda.

A disclaimer video plays on the monitors but does not interrupt the action at the council table. The text on the screen reads, Be ready to be bored. Be ready to watch a kind of irrelevant, antsy unfolding around you that wonders if it's even worth it. This room breathes and thinks of itself as it goes. **THE MEET-ING ITSELF WONDERS.** Are you even here? Or are you just represented? *The disclaimer ends and video returns to live feed of the room.*

COUNCILOR 3 / WARFORD: These are ordinances relating to water and sewer trunk line repair. Does anyone in the audience wish to appear? Does anyone wish to appear? I see no one in the audience wishing to appear on these, uh, charges. Your wishes, commissioners?

STAFFER 3 gives COUNCILOR 4 / ASPIC a card that says "Motion" and sits down.

COUNCILOR 4 / ASPIC: Motion.

STAFFER 5 gives COUNCILOR 5 / SEMINARY a card that says "Second" and sits down.

COUNCILOR 5 / SEMINARY: Second.

COUNCILOR 3 / WARFORD: Motion and second to approve these charges, ordinance 5773-5775. Any further discussion? Seeing and hearing none, please call the roll.

SECRETARY: Commissioner Seminary.

COUNCILOR 5 / SEMINARY: Yes.

SECRETARY: Smith.

COUNCILOR 2 / SMITH: Yes.

SECRETARY: Aspic.

COUNCILOR 4 / ASPIC: Yes.

SECRETARY: Grossman.

COUNCILOR 1 / GROSSMAN: Yes.

SECRETARY: Warford.

COUNCILOR 3 / WARFORD: Yes, motion carries. **BANG GAVEL.** Item number four, this is a public hearing. A second reading on item 5776 relating to sick leave. **PAUSE FOR FOUR SECONDS.**

STAFFER 3 helps COUNCILOR 4 / ASPIC find where they are in the paperwork.

COUNCILOR 3 / WARFORD: Any, uh, questions of staff, co-commissioners?

Staffers look up.

COUNCILOR 3 / WARFORD: OK, as this is a public hearing, anyone wish to appear on item 5776 relating to sick leave? Anyone in the audience wishing to appear? **PAUSE AND LOOK AT AUDIENCE.**

Staffers look out at the audience.

COUNCILOR 3 / WARFORD: Anyone wishing to appear. **PAUSE AND LOOK AT AUDIENCE.** As this is a public hearing—

STAFFER 3 shows COUNCILOR 4 / ASPIC a "Move to Approve" card.

COUNCILOR 4 / ASPIC: Move to approve.

STAFFER 1 shows COUNCILOR 1 / GROSSMAN a "Second" card.

COUNCILOR 1 / GROSSMAN: Second.

COUNCILOR 3 / WARFORD: Motion and second to approve the sick leave. Please call the roll.

SECRETARY: Commissioner Seminary.

COUNCILOR 5 / SEMINARY: Yes.

SECRETARY: Smith.

COUNCILOR 2 / SMITH: Yes.

SECRETARY: Aspic.

COUNCILOR 4 / ASPIC: Yes.

SECRETARY: Grossman.

COUNCILOR 1 / GROSSMAN: Yes.

SECRETARY: Warford.

COUNCILOR 3 / WARFORD: Yes, motion carries. **BANG GAVEL.** Item number five, this is a public hearing and second reading on item 5778 relating to rules for operation of all-terrain vehicles.

STAFFER 3 helps COUNCILOR 4 / ASPIC find the sheet in the packet.

COUNCILOR 3 / WARFORD: Does anyone in the audience wish to appear on this item? **PAUSE.** Is anyone wishing to appear? **PAUSE.** Anyone wish to appear?

STAFFER 3 turns to the COUNCILOR 3 / WARFORD and tells them to just keep reading until they read the word housekeeping *in their script.*

COUNCILOR 3 / WARFORD: Just might add that there was a, uh, an incorrect reference in the ordinance, not really a typo but an incorrect reference, and so, it just referred to the wrong sections, and that's kind of a housekeeping thing. Final call on the public hearing. Close the public hearing.

STAFFER 3 shows COUNCILOR 4 / ASPIC a "Move to Approve" card.

COUNCILOR 4 / ASPIC: Move to approve.

STAFFER 1 shows COUNCILOR 1 / GROSSMAN a "Second" card.

COUNCILOR 1 / GROSSMAN: Second.

COUNCILOR 3 / WARFORD: Motion and second to approve, please call the roll.

SECRETARY: Commissioner Seminary.

COUNCILOR 5 / SEMINARY: Yes.

SECRETARY: Smith.

COUNCILOR 2 / SMITH: Yes.

SECRETARY: Aspic.

COUNCILOR 4 / ASPIC: Yes.

SECRETARY: Grossman.

COUNCILOR 1 / GROSSMAN: Yes.

SECRETARY: Warford.

COUNCILOR 3 / WARFORD: Yes, motion carries. **BANG GAVEL.**

Transition to San Antonio.

A disclaimer video plays, with the Emergency Broadcast System sound and color bars. The text on the screen reads, PLEASE TAKE A SEAT. You've just sat through a two-hour presentation on the city's annual budget. *The disclaimer ends and video returns to live feed of the room.*

During the disclaimer, STAFFER 4 *rejoins the table. All the staffers change the nameplates to the San Antonio names and give the following instructions to councilors:* In this section you're [_____]. These next testimonies are from kids who just finished the Urban Leadership Council's summer training program. They were considered "at-risk" youth, and this is their first time doing anything like this publicly. You just need to listen to them. You don't have to respond.

STAFFER 3 hands the mayor, COUNCILOR 3 / CASTRO, *a script and tells them to begin speaking.* STAFFER 2 *goes to get the budget packets.*

COUNCILOR 3 / CASTRO: Well, Sheryl, thank you very much. That was 120 pages of a presentation, and a fantastic one.

STAFFER 2 passes out the budget packets.

COUNCILOR 3 / CASTRO: You've done an excellent job of shepherding the staff through this process. And I also wanted to thank Maria and her entire staff. I know that her, uh. This is an ongoing process, and in some sense, for the council, this is just the beginning. Uh, but a year ago, we were predicting, uh, $67 or $68 million deficit. Y'all have worked hard to close that. When you compare us to other cities, we see that we truly are blessed, in the sense that we're in much better shape. It's been a challenge, I know, but y'all have done a great job of meeting that challenge. I think it's a testament to the fine work that y'all have done that, generally, what we see today will look a lot like what we pass. Now, we have several citizens signed up to speak from the Urban Leadership Council and I know they've been waiting for a while, and we'd like to call them up.

SECRETARY: Our first speaker is [AUDIENCE MEMBER reading TALIQ PRYOR]. To be followed by [AUDIENCE MEMBER reading TEQUONDRIA TAYLOR].

COUNCILOR 3 / CASTRO: You just have to give us your name and then you have two minutes for testimony.

TALIQ PRYOR approaches the podium.

TALIQ PRYOR: *(Reading off a page of testimony)* Thank you, city commission and mayor, for your time. Uh, my name is Taliq Pryor, and I attend East Central High School. Thank you for the opportunity to—you gave us to be a part of this summer youth program. I enjoy going to the universities and seeing the college atmosphere. Although I'm thankful to have had this experience, I'm not satisfied with the state of the East Side. You all were elected by the people, for the people, yet little progress has been made. There are plenty of positive things going on in—in the East Side, yet it is portrayed as a poor and unsafe community. The school system needs to be reevaluated. There needs to be more productive programs for the youth throughout the summer and during the year also. This would decrease crime in the community because it would provide something to look forward to besides being in the streets. We are just as capable to achieve bigger and better things if given a chance, but it seems as if you have, um, I'm, excuse me, we have been, I'm sorry, oh, there's been a bad label unfairly placed upon us. Get used to seeing the faces of ULC, and this is just the beginning of a huge movement to help and rebuild the East Side community. **PLEASE RETURN TO YOUR SEAT, THANK YOU.**

STAFFER 2 goes to COUNCILOR 2 / TAYLOR and tells them that these kids are from their district.

SECRETARY: Next is [AUDIENCE MEMBER reading TEQUONDRIA TAYLOR], followed by [AUDIENCE MEMBER reading TIARA HARRIS].

TEQUONDRIA TAYLOR approaches the podium.

TEQUONDRIA TAYLOR: *(Reading off a page of testimony)* Ee, OK, I'm ready. Um, good morning, Mayor and city council. My name is Tequondria Taylor and I'm seventeen years old. Thank you for allowing me to speak to you in regard to my concerns in my community, the East Side. Most kids on the East Side have been caught up in crimes and gangs and has no way out. I come here today to present to you that I have lived on the East Side most of my life and there have been many blessings from these streets. I don't want to be classified as a bad, Black child from the East Side. Here today, my voice may be—may be one of the many you will remember. I'm not leaving here today without a positive outlook on what we have presented to you. I ask you today to create more opportunities for my youth—for my youth community, save my brothers and sisters from these crimes and gangs. Hear me out. These in—these individuals here with me today mean business and ask for change. We are honored and symbolize unity for our community. Thank you. PLEASE RETURN TO YOUR SEAT, THANK YOU.

COUNCILOR 3 / CASTRO: Thank you.

SECRETARY: Next is [AUDIENCE MEMBER reading TIARA HARRIS].

Staffers come up behind their councilors and ask them to stand, to look out at the audience and think about what they want from the councilors. A disclaimer video plays. A sound cue of a lone harmonica interrupts the action. The lights shift and the video monitors alternate between recorded closeups of a cowboy showdown from the film The Good, the Bad, and the Ugly *and live closeups of councilors, who stand behind the council table.*

After the second harmonica in the music, STAFFER 1 *hands* COUNCILOR 1 / MEDINA *the following text.*

COUNCILOR 1 / MEDINA: I frickin' love my job, dude. We don't have to say anything because we rule, you know. CLEAR YOUR THROAT. We put up a couple tables, put a few of us on one side, and the rest of us on the other, and boom! Power.

TIARA HARRIS: *(Reading off a page of testimony)* Good morning, Mr. Mayor and city council members. My name is Tiara Harris. I am sixteen years old, and I attend Highlands High School, which is in Ms. Ivy Taylor's district. These past three weeks we visited several colleges, cleaned up our community, and was taught job readiness skills. I have learned that although I am young, I can make a difference in my community, so I would like to first off thank you for this opportunity, but say our work here is not yet done. I want to start off by saying that you guys pay too much attention to the other sides of town in leaving the East Side out. I mean, we're all a people so we need to be given the same treatment, regardless of what side of town we live on. Instead of spending millions of dollars on AT&T and saving farm animals, why not invest in our youth and give us some activities like jobs, bowling alleys, and movie theatres? Y'all are also quick to criticize the education system and put our—shut down our schools for low performance, when y'all aren't doing anything to help us pass and do good. Here at ULC, we have big dreams, and we plan to make it happen, but we need your help. Thank you. **PLEASE RETURN TO YOUR SEAT, THANK YOU.**

COUNCILOR 3 / CASTRO: Thank you, uh, Ms. Harris.

Transition to Houston.

A disclaimer video plays. Images and sounds from local news footage of Houston flooding play. Then: text on the screen reads, This city houses our total lack of originality. It cherishes it because it makes the machine run. *The disclaimer ends and video returns to live feed of the room with the Houston chyron.*

During the disclaimer, staffers change the nameplates to the Houston names and give instructions to their councilors. Each staffer in this section has something different to tell their councilor depending on their district and their relationship to the issues at hand. Here is an example of what STAFFER 2 tells COUNCILOR 2 / BRADFORD.

STAFFER 2: You are now Council Member Bradford, the former police chief. This part is all about the new drainage fee the city is trying to levy on property owners. It's 3.2 cents per square foot of "impervious cover." Like parking lots. The city budget is $2 billion. Councilor Costello is an engineer. He's a little controversial. You get a lot of votes from the churches, so you're going to be supportive of the churches when they come up to talk about why they shouldn't have to pay the drainage fee. They're doing an investigation to try to make Costello look bad, because he wants the churches to pay. You're going to do everything you can, when Clyde Bryan comes up, to help them make him look bad.

The SECRETARY calls the CITY ATTORNEY to sit in the extra chair at the table and gives them a microphone to use. When the disclaimer is complete, STAFFER 3 signals to COUNCILOR 3 / PARKER to continue.

COUNCILOR 3 / PARKER: The next item on your agenda is a public hearing regarding proposed rates and exemptions to the newly established Municipal Drainage Utilities System.

CITY ATTORNEY: This public hearing is conducted in accordance with Section 552.045(c) of the Local Government Code, uh, regarding proposed rates and exemptions to establish and levy a schedule of drainage charges for property subject to implementation of a Municipal Drainage Utility System.

COUNCILOR 3 / PARKER: Call the first speaker, please.

SECRETARY: [AUDIENCE MEMBER reading VIVIAN HARRIS]. To be followed by [AUDIENCE MEMBER reading CLYDE BRYAN].

VIVIAN HARRIS: Good morning.

Staffers and councilors respond, "Good morning." At various points during the following testimony, STAFFER 3 and STAFFER 5 feed their councilors information about VIVIAN HARRIS and what her point is, specific to their points of view.

VIVIAN HARRIS: *(Reading from pages of testimony)* Mayor Parker, um, I'm Vivian Harris. I am here before you again, asking you to take a real close look at what some of you council members are asking and expecting voters and nonvoters alike to do. Please believe me when I tell you, I'm a voice of experience on churches and their operations. And I promise you, with my experiences, some of the churches you are fighting for are not what they are pretending to be. Before I go any further, please do not judge me, nor my relationship with God. This is not about God, nor my relationship with God, and I dare any of you to question that, because if I do not have anything else that I'm sure of, I know my relationship with God is secure and personal. For the ones of you who think you are sitting here supporting the churches wanting to be exempt from the drainage fees, because of election time? Beware. Gone are the days when ministers had the abilities to sway voters. In the Gospel of St. Luke, chapter 20, verses 24 and 25 reads, "'Show me a penny. Whose image and superscription have it?' They answered and said, 'Caesar's.' And he said unto them, 'Render therefore unto Caesar the things which be Caesar's, and to God the things which be God's.'" I believe the same money that you and I use are the same monies that we contribute to the churches, and I do not see where there is a difference in the obligations the churches have and the obligations that we the people have.

SECRETARY rings a bell, signifying time is up. STAFFER 1 tells COUNCILOR 1 / COSTELLO to raise his hand.

SECRETARY: Thank you, ma'am. Your time has expired.

VIVIAN HARRIS: I need to finish.

SECRETARY: Thank you.

COUNCILOR 3 / PARKER: Council Member Costello?

STAFFER 1 tells COUNCILOR 1 / COSTELLO to give VIVIAN HARRIS a few minutes to finish up.

COUNCILOR 1 / COSTELLO: Ms. Harris, I'll give you a few minutes to finish up.

VIVIAN HARRIS: Please. There are but approximately twenty or more churches in about a two-square-mile area in my community doing absolutely nothing that I can determine is beneficial to our community. I have dedicated thirty-five years of my life to trying to do the right thing for my community. I'm not taking monies under the table.

STAFFER 2 and STAFFER 4 lean in and tell COUNCILOR 2 / BRADFORD and COUNCILOR 4 / HOANG more information.

VIVIAN HARRIS: No kickbacks. Have not gone along to get along. What consideration are you all giving to persons such as myself that has a limited income each month and has not had an increase in income in more than two years, with everything continually increasing in cost? When will the churches ever feel their need to pay for anything?

STAFFER 1 tells COUNCILOR 1 / COSTELLO to ask VIVIAN HARRIS to wrap it up.

VIVIAN HARRIS: Churches are billion-dollar businesses—

COUNCILOR 1 / COSTELLO: Please wrap it up.

VIVIAN HARRIS: OK, just a minute.

STAFFER 1 tells COUNCILOR 1 / COSTELLO to say, "Thank you."

COUNCILOR 1 / COSTELLO: Thank you.

VIVIAN HARRIS: I'm a—minute.

Staffers laugh.

VIVIAN HARRIS: Churches are billion-dollar businesses. I thank you all for your time and your consideration, but I can promise you, you will not get the votes out of the churches.

STAFFER 1 tells COUNCILOR 1 / COSTELLO to say, "Thank you."

COUNCILOR 1 / COSTELLO: Thank you.

SECRETARY: Thank you.

COUNCILOR 3 / PARKER: Ms. Harris, thank you for coming down. And thank you for being a civic leader for a very long time. We've all worked with you down here and we appreciate it.

VIVIAN HARRIS: Thank you.

SECRETARY: OK, [AUDIENCE MEMBER reading CLYDE BRYAN]. To be followed by [AUDIENCE MEMBER reading STEVE RIGGLE].

The SECRETARY distributes a City of Houston contract. As CLYDE BRYAN talks, staffers feed their councilors information about him and what his point is.

CLYDE BRYAN: *(Reading from pages of testimony)* Good morning, Mayor, members of council. My name is Clyde Bryan. Um, I brought with me this morning a, a contract by, from, uh, Costello Inc. And they're distributing that now. **CHECK WHETHER THEY ARE PASSING OUT THE CONTRACT.** And I'm just trying to understand the timeline, uh, of this contract and how it relates to, uh, Council Member Costello's appointment to the, uh, chair of the Drainage Committee. Uh, this contract, uh, was evidently executed in October of 2009, and, uh, that was prior to, uh, Council Member Costello's election. Uh, but he did receive the contract. It's $1.7 million. Uh, he was then appointed to chair of the, uh, Drainage Committee. And I'd like to ask you, Mayor, was that appointment made by you, or was that, uh—

Staffers look at the mayor.

COUNCILOR 3 / PARKER: By me.

CLYDE BRYAN: OK. Uh, were the other members of council aware at that— at that time of the appointment that, that he had a $1.7 million contract?

COUNCILOR 3 / PARKER: Since it was my appointment, uh, I didn't ask them, but I was not aware of it.

CLYDE BRYAN: Well, I know you, as controller, you probably signed millions of, I mean hundreds of contracts, thousands probably. But it did pass through your office as evidenced on page two of the handout.

STAFFER 3 points out the signature on the contract to COUNCILOR 3 / PARKER.

CLYDE BRYAN: Again, you signed many of them, so you probably could not have been aware of it. But the point still stands. Uh, he signed a $1.7 million contract for infrastructure improvements. Uh, he was appointed to chair of the Drainage Committee. He was instrumental in the charter amendment action that the city went with on Prop 1. And I just, I just wanted to throw this out to some of the other council members. Council Member Bradford, did you, uh, did you have knowledge of this?

CITY ATTORNEY: Mayor?

COUNCILOR 3 / PARKER: Mr. Feldman.

CITY ATTORNEY: The purpose of this public hearing is to discuss, uh, rates and exemptions.

COUNCILOR 3 / PARKER: And uh, there is an active OIG investigation going on of this incident, is there not?

STAFFER 2 tells COUNCILOR 2 / BRADFORD *to raise a hand.*

CITY ATTORNEY: In fact, it's, uh, Mayor, it's being completed and a report will be on your desk today.

COUNCILOR 3 / PARKER: I would ask then that, uh, we not engage further in this discussion until the OIG report is presented to council. Council Member Bradford.

STAFFER 2 tells COUNCILOR 2 / BRADFORD *to ask whether* CLYDE BRYAN *has filed a complaint.*

COUNCILOR 2 / BRADFORD: Have you filed a complaint?

CLYDE BRYAN: Uh, Chief, I've made a request, a public information request, uh, for all the, all the contracts and purchase orders of all the sitting council members, and that was done over three weeks ago, and I'm still waiting for that. And I don't think it, I don't think the, uh, council should vote on this until we have that information. Because we need to know if there's a conflict of interest here.

STAFFER 2 tells COUNCILOR 2 / BRADFORD *to ask if* BRYAN *has received any response at all.*

COUNCILOR 2 / BRADFORD: Mr. Bryan, have you received any response at all?

CLYDE BRYAN: Well, uh, Chief, they, they sent me an email that said they were checking into it. But I also want to point out that David Welch, through his secretary Stephanie, made another request, and that was over three weeks ago.

COUNCILOR 3 / PARKER: Who responded to you about the, uh, your TPIA request? Who did you submit it to and who responded to you—do you know?

CLYDE BRYAN: It was someone, it was someone, uh, I can't remember her name, but I can send you the email—

COUNCILOR 3 / PARKER: Thank you.

The SECRETARY tells the CITY ATTORNEY to go back to his original chair. BRYAN leaves.

SECRETARY: OK, [AUDIENCE MEMBER reading STEVE RIGGLE].

As RIGGLE approaches and begins, the staffers feed their councilors information about him and what his point is.

STEVE RIGGLE: *(Reading from pages of testimony)* Uh, I'm Steve Riggle, and I'm not sure I want to admit that I'm the pastor of Grace Community Church after what I've heard here. Um. **CLEAR YOUR THROAT.** We as a church are opposed on principle, in terms of we view this as a tax, and a tax against the church, and an open door, uh, to things that have not taken place before in our culture, as a nation. And so, uh, I want to go on record as stating that. Another point I want to make, is that when you ask the people to vote on something, do they clearly understand, uh, what they're voting on. I just saw a video of, um, of Councilman Costello in the last public hearing, uh, in my judgment rebuking one of the speakers, and saying that he was insulted that the people, that the idea would be brought, that people didn't understand. Well I just read it, sitting right back there. And I've gone to college. And I'm sixty years old. And I pastor a church with thousands of people. And frankly, if what's happening, now, that's proposed, is what that said, I didn't get it.

STAFFERS 1, 2, and 4 tell COUNCILORS COSTELLO, BRADFORD, and HOANG to raise their hands.

COUNCILOR 3 / PARKER: Council Member Bradford.

STAFFER 2 gives COUNCILOR 2 / BRADFORD the following speech.

COUNCILOR 2 / BRADFORD: Why thank you, Mayor. Um, Pastor, thanks for, uh, coming down, and for your supporters as well. You know some previous speakers have said some things that, uh, reasonable minds, uh, can differ. But we know at the end of the day, when it's all said and done, that we don't differ when it comes to one aim, one destiny, OK? I think we can connect on that. Pastor, I thank, I want to say thanks for your comments, because, uh, when we talk about a drainage fee or tax, whatever you want to call it, openness and real transparency is important. You and the thousands of people that attend your congregation, you pay a fee through you, your residences—through your homes, where you live—you pay that fee. Now because you choose to worship, because you choose to praise and uplift God, why should you pay twice? And someone who does not choose to worship, any place, they don't pay that second time around. That's just wrong in my view. Thank you.

RIGGLE begins to leave.

COUNCILOR 3 / PARKER: Council Member Noriega. There's three more in the queue. Don't go away.

RIGGLE returns. STAFFER 5 gives COUNCILOR 5 / NORIEGA the following speech.

COUNCILOR 5 / NORIEGA: Thank you, Mayor. Uh, I just wanted a chance to say thank you to you. Um, I've been very blessed in your church at funerals for our first responders. And I, I'm the daughter of pastors, and the granddaughter and the great-granddaughter of pastors, and I know a lot goes in to putting, uh, those kinds of services on, so I just wanted to say thank you.

STEVE RIGGLE: Thank you very much.

COUNCILOR 3 / PARKER: Thank you. Council Member Hoang.

STAFFER 4 gives COUNCILOR 4 / HOANG the following speech.

COUNCILOR 4 / HOANG: Thank you, Mayor. Thank you, Pastor, for coming down here. I just wanted to echo my concurrence with Council Member Bradford. I know, as you just said, that if we are going to impose the fee on your church, on the church, the church will have to cut some of the activities, some of the programs, like after-school programs, and, uh, uh, junior programs, and, uh, crime will rise. And it will cost the city more. So I concur with Council Member Bradford, and I will do within my, my duty and my power to make sure that, uh, churches are going to be exempt.

STEVE RIGGLE: I think what's important for everyone here is that, whatever final resolution is, that we get to where it removes the cloud. There's definitely a cloud that exists. That cloud affects all of you and affects our city. Because we want the issues before us, agree or disagree, to be resolved in a way that everything was done properly and right.

STAFFER 1 gives COUNCILOR 1 / COSTELLO the following speech. During the speech, STAFFER 5 tells COUNCILOR 5 / NORIEGA that they support COUN-CILOR 1 / COSTELLO.

COUNCILOR 1 / COSTELLO: Pastor, pastor, I think it's my turn to talk.

STEVE RIGGLE: OK, it is.

COUNCILOR 3 / PARKER: Council Member Costello.

COUNCILOR 1 / COSTELLO: And uh, I think it's, uh, it's interesting how, uh, my reputation is now become political fodder for people who don't want to discuss the merits of the program. This is not a debate about Steve Costello and Costello Inc. This is a debate about the long-term future of our city. And as an engineer, when I campaigned in 2009, I campaigned on a long-term source and solution for streets and drainage. And I also was interviewed by a number of the local stations and radio stations, questioning my firm. And I told them: we have ongoing contracts with the city. Less than two percent of my business was with the city over a twenty-year period. I will not do any work for the city as a council member. And when it comes to the churches, this is my view: You pay for utilities. Drainage is a utility. You pay for water, you pay for sewer, you pay for electric. You should pay for drainage services. And that's why, for years, I've advocated for everyone to contribute to the program. Uh, as relative to the conflict of interest, I don't have a conflict of interest. Am I going to abstain from voting? No. I'm going to sit here and I'm going to advocate for the program. And Pastor, I do appreciate everything that Grace has done for our community, and I know you will continue to do that. And whatever this program comes out in the long run, I think we'll all benefit in the future. But thank you, sir.

STEVE RIGGLE: Yes, well, with all due respect, I think we can disagree agreeably. And, um, I certainly respect your opinion.

STAFFER 5 tells COUNCILOR 5 / NORIEGA to raise a hand.

STEVE RIGGLE: I disagree with that. I think it is a tax. I think it is, uh, it is the opening of—it is cracking the door open to tax the church.

COUNCILOR 1 / COSTELLO: Thank you.

COUNCILOR 3 / PARKER: Council Member Noriega.

STAFFER 5 gives COUNCILOR 5 / NORIEGA the following speech.

COUNCILOR 5 / NORIEGA: Thank you, Madam Mayor. One of the things we talk about is, you know, how do you walk that line? Because everybody works for somebody. You know, do lawyers vote on laws? Yes, they do. And, and I have found my colleagues' expertise helpful. And when I had the opportunity to talk to a group of engineers, they told me that they weren't concerned about the future, they said they were really scared that we were all gonna be under water, in no time. And their expertise combined with their real concern got my attention. I think there's a real belief on their part this is a desperate situation and not just a, a money issue or a tax issue. That, that we have a very serious, serious, um, concern here. And I listened to them. Because they know what they're talking about.

The SECRETARY brings the CITY ATTORNEY back to the table.

STEVE RIGGLE: Again, I don't question that. That's not my question. I think my question is that, uh, this is the people's house, and if it's the people's house, the people ought to know exactly what they agree to, and if they agree to it, fine, but uh, I think that that's my only issue.

The SECRETARY calls over STAFFER 3 to tell COUNCILOR 3 / PARKER that there is an answer to CLYDE BRYAN's request.

COUNCILOR 3 / PARKER: I understand that there's an answer to the, uh, Mr. Bryan's request, the TPIA request.

CITY ATTORNEY: Yes ma'am. The, uh, the record shows that a request was made by, uh, one Stephanie Welch, for all contracts that Costello Inc. had with the city of Houston. The record also shows that those documents were timely provided, uh in CD form, uh, approximately three and a half weeks ago. That's what I have to report, Mayor.

STEVE RIGGLE leaves. If he doesn't leave, the SECRETARY speaks.

SECRETARY: Thank you, Mr. Riggle. *(Sends the CITY ATTORNEY away)*

COUNCILOR 3 / PARKER: I'm glad to know that we did respond to the TPIA request, and through the controller's office. **BANGS GAVEL.** This concludes our public agenda, and we are now onto our open agenda items. For the open agenda, everyone who signed up has three minutes.

Transition to Tempe.

A disclaimer video plays. Loud Emergency Broadcast System sound and color bars on video interrupt the action. Text on the screens reads, This is the city we make together every night. Who are you in it? You live here. What's your problem? *The disclaimer ends and the video returns to live feed of the room with a Tempe chyron.*

During the disclaimer the staffers change the nameplates and tidy up the council table, removing paperwork from the Houston section.

SECRETARY: Our first speaker is [AUDIENCE MEMBER reading NANCY HORMANN], speaking on ficus trees downtown.

NANCY HORMANN: *(Reading from a page of testimony)* I am Nancy Hormann. I am not a resident, but my heart belongs to downtown. And I am here representing the Board of Directors of the Downtown Community. And I wanted to talk about the Mill Avenue landscape. And today I wanted to make sure that the council knows that the DTC voted unanimously to support keeping ficus trees on Mill Avenue. Um, over three years ago we presented a report showing if ficus trees had been maintained properly, that they a good alternative for down here. And we feel that, like the Mill, like the bridge, our ficus trees are a brand of downtown. And we would like to continue that brand and see if there's a way that we can work with all of you to complete the "leafiness" of downtown with our ficus trees. So, it's just a very simple request, is that you listen to the stakeholders of downtown and take into consideration what they would like for their trees downtown. **PLEASE RETURN TO YOUR SEAT, THANK YOU.**

COUNCILOR 3 / HALLMAN: Thank you, Ms. Hormann.

SECRETARY: Our next speaker is [AUDIENCE MEMBER reading AUDIENCE PARTICIPATION] speaking on audience participation in live performance.

AUDIENCE PARTICIPATION: *(Reading from a page of testimony)* WHEN YOUR NAME IS CALLED, WALK UP BEHIND THE MAYOR'S CHAIR, PUT YOUR HAND ON HIS/HER SHOULDER, AND SAY THE FOLLOWING QUIETLY. I am the new mayor. This is not me saying this. EXPLAIN TO THE CURRENT MAYOR THAT YOU'LL BE TAKING OVER. THANK THEM FOR THEIR TIME AND ASK THEM TO TAKE A SEAT IN THE AUDIENCE. TAKE THEIR CHAIR. Thank you. LOOK AT AUDIENCE, SMILE. I am on this side of the table now. NOD SEVEN TIMES. OK. EXPLAIN TO THE AUDIENCE IN YOUR OWN WORDS THAT YOU DON'T KNOW WHERE TO START. PAUSE. Are we working together? Are we capable of it? Is that why this structure is here? Or is that what the structure prevents? PAUSE. Maybe I don't like you. Maybe when your opinions come up in conversation with other people, I disparage them. I don't enjoy honoring your feelings or beliefs. My tolerance of you is tested daily. Most of the time, I dismiss you in my thoughts. Let me get a show of hands. Who thinks we can all agree on something? PAUSE. Who thinks it doesn't matter? PAUSE. Who doesn't know? PAUSE. I don't know either. But listen. You made it to this room; I made it to this room. I think this is the only room we could find ourselves in together. No, that's not true. We could go to that same coffee shop. You could date my cousin. You could fight for our country. Or chain yourself to a polluter's fence. I've thought of doing that. STAND AND STAY WHERE YOU ARE. There are little cards and pencils on the lectern. ASK THE AUDIENCE FOR HELP. DIRECT THEM TO HELP PASS OUT THE CARDS AND PENCILS. DO THIS IN YOUR OWN WORDS. YOU CANNOT CONTINUE UNTIL PEOPLE FROM THE AUDIENCE HELP YOU. ONCE THEY ARE PASSING OUT CARDS AND PENCILS, SIT DOWN AND CONTINUE. PLEASE SPEAK THIS NEXT SECTION OF INSTRUCTIONS SLOWLY AND CLEARLY INTO THE MIC. This is an invitation. We're passing out little cards and pencils. Please write a resolution. Something you want in the public record. Something you think no one here will agree with. Or that you care so much about you can't stand it. About yourself, or about God, or about drainage, or ficus trees. Or something more important. Write down the opinion you think no one will think is OK. For instance, I might say: [_____]. I wrote that line myself. Write the big concern that the small worries have eclipsed. Free yourself of the thing you think you can't say. Don't put your name on it. Make sure it's readable. And someone will say it for the record. That's how we're a community. **PLEASE COUNT TO SIXTY WHILE THEY WRITE.** We'll be around in a minute to pick up the cards.

A disclaimer video plays during this speech and the writing process. Text on the screen reads, This is not a seizure of power. It is just the next tiny infraction that isn't on the books yet. It is like the tiny law we break when we walk down the street, unmediated, absorbed. *The disclaimer ends and the video returns to live feed of the room with an Oakland chyron.*

STAFFER 2 takes the gavel from COUNCILOR 3, bangs the gavel for COUNCILOR 2 / REID, and hands them the following speech. STAFFER 3 tells AUDIENCE PARTICIPATION to exit, as the mayor was not present for the following meeting.

Transition to Oakland.

COUNCILOR 2 / REID: Excuse me. Excuse me. We wanna get on with the meeting?

STAFFER 2 bangs gavel again.

COUNCILOR 2 / REID: Can we start the meeting so we can hear the speakers that have signed up? So Madam City Clerk, if you can call the speakers?

STAFFER 3 changes nameplates to Oakland names. All other staffers exit and go into the audience to gather audience members into a line at the back of the room. As they do this, they are also collecting index cards that the audience has written on. STAFFER 2 stands at the front of the line to make sure the right three speakers are in front.

SECRETARY: As I call your name, please come to the podium in any order and state your name for the record.

COUNCILOR 2 / REID: Those of you who are standing in the back of the room, can you leave and shut the door, please? Thank you, so we can hear the public speakers.

SECRETARY: As I call your name, please come to the podium in any order and state your name for the record. Again, we understand that there will be some people coming from upstairs and from downstairs, so we will allow a little time for that. [AUDIENCE MEMBER reading BOBBY VALENTINE], [AUDIENCE MEMBER reading SADIYAH], [AUDIENCE MEMBER reading MAX ALSTEAD].

STAFFER 2 helps the following three speakers to the lectern one after the other. Other staffers continue to collect index cards discretely during the Oakland section.

BOBBY VALENTINE: *(Reading from a page of testimony)* Hello, my name is Bobby Valentine. **PAUSE. LOOK AT CAMERA.** We, and by we, I mean the humanity on this earth right now, are mired in an infinitude of deeply seated illusions about the nature of reality. And these illusions are based on fear. **PAUSE. LOOK AT CAMERA.** We have been asleep for thousands of years, although, of course, there have been glimpses of the truth, people wakening up over time, that have been brutally crushed by the forces of oppression, or had their message co-opted by those same forces. **INTERRUPT APPLAUSE.** I'm not done. I'm not done. **PAUSE. LOOK AT CAMERA.** There is a wave of love and peace and understanding and compassion that is raging, sweeping through our souls. You can act in fear. You can think in fear. You can speak in fear. Or you can act and think and speak in love and compassion. **PAUSE. LOOK AT CAMERA.** I ask all of you—I know that many of you standing up here have very many moral dilemmas about what is going on in your potential place in the scheme of things. I just urge you to act in peace. Think in peace. Speak in peace and love and understanding and compassion. It's very important that you do this. **PAUSE. LOOK AT CAMERA.** Think deeply—I know that you have many moral dilemmas going through your head. But this is really a time of celebration. So please, join us and celebrate life and help us create a world in which we can all thrive. Thank you. **PLEASE RETURN TO YOUR SEAT, THANK YOU.**

SADIYAH: *(Reading from a page of testimony)* My name is Sadiyah. I'm a resident of District 2, East 18th and 6th. Good evening, Council Member Kernighan. I work in downtown, 19th and Franklin. My favorite restaurant is, uh, Rico's. I go to Aroma all the time. Shoutout to Brother Maurice, at Café Madrid, who suffered some loss. So please accept all of this street cred. I'm a resident. The entire city, community, workers, youth, and you all as our leaders need to come together and lead this city. I support—I ask that you support Council Member Nadel's resolution in support of free speech and its support-ers. That you return and become accountable to east and west foreclosures. Remember that while broken glass, graffiti, trash, and displaced families—it's just ugly all over the city, not just downtown. Um, lastly, I appreciate your taking the time to show a few things that were wrong with yesterday and the last two weeks while taking no time to lift up the things that were wonderful about the march. Where were the pictures of the baby brigades? Where were the pictures of the community and the family that got started at eight o'clock in the morning and went 'til dusk? Where were those pictures? Where are the pictures of the families that are foreclosed by the banks that you took so much of your city—so much of your PowerPoint to show us? Where are the pictures, lastly, of you all? Many of you who know and need to get on the correct side of all of this. Many of you were out there yesterday. Where were your pictures standing with us? Thank you. **PLEASE RETURN TO YOUR SEAT, THANK YOU.**

MAX ALSTEAD: *(Reading from a page of testimony)* **PLEASE READ THIS QUICKLY. DON'T SIT. LEAN OVER CHAIR TO REACH THE MIC.** I'm gonna start off with a—my name is Max Alstead—I just got out of jail a couple hours ago. I'm gonna start off with a slight tangent and ask Mayor Quan—**LOOK TO SEE IF MAYOR QUAN IS THERE. SHE ISN'T.**—and City Administrator Santana to immediately contact the police department, and to return, uh, the necessary belongings. They're still being held, there was a bit of a snafu in terms of moving personal effects that were confiscated. There are people without their house keys. I'm one of them. There were people with-out their wallets and cell phones. I'm among them, and I would like you to get somebody down at OPD to immediately take action on that.

STAFFER 1 enters from the audience, looks at MAX ALSTEAD, and then goes back behind the council table.

MAX ALSTEAD: Now on to the actual topic at hand. I can support maintain-ing a dialogue with Occupy and I can support maintaining a dialogue that keeps it safe. What I cannot support is the idea that we can use conversation to deal with the violence that we saw last night. There were people there, there were people there waving claw hammers at people who tried to put out fires.

And there are people there among the movement who are saying that vandalism is not violence, and those people are wrong. People who vandalize our city? Those people ought to be prosecuted because those people are preventing what any reasonable and right-minded people from exercising their free speech by endangering us, by potentially provoking serious police action. You cannot have a conversation about a giant fire in the street, it's not possible. But the people who started need to be held accountable, thank you. **PLEASE RETURN TO YOUR SEAT, THANK YOU.**

STAFFER 1 takes the gavel, hands the Portland script to COUNCILOR 1, and bangs gavel. The video chyrons change to Portland.

Transition to Portland.

COUNCILOR 1 / SALZMAN: Carla, please read item 396.

STAFFER 1 bangs gavel again.

COUNCILOR 1 / SALZMAN: And as the audience knows, we don't allow audible demonstrations, so if you'd just wave your hands in support of what someone says, that would be appropriate.

The SECRETARY waits for the audience to sit and quiet before continuing.

SECRETARY: Item 396 is, uh, Sheila Harton, testifying about the "illegal secret testing on citizens." Ms. Harton? Ms. Harton? **PAUSE.** Does anyone have a piece of paper with the name Sheila Harton written on it? Testifying on "the illegal secret testing of citizens"?

Staffers stand and look out at the audience, searching for Ms. Harton. STAFFER 1 feeds COUNCILOR 1 / SALZMAN the following line.

COUNCILOR 1 / SALZMAN: Apparently not here today.

STAFFER 3 changes nameplates to Portland.

SECRETARY: Item 397. We have Mr. Pete Colt, who wants to thank the city civil servants.

COUNCILOR 1 / SALZMAN: Here comes Mr. Colt. Mr. Colt, it's always a pleasure to have you with us. Uh, you know the rules, but for the record, please state your name, and you have two minutes.

PETE COLT: Thank you. My name is Pete Colt. Uhm. I'm happy to see you up there, Commissioner Fish. And Commissioner Salzman, I want to apologize to you. Because I had lost faith in you, when you were running the parks department and you were worried about the dogs that were infesting the park on 11th and 19th, and the feces. You said something that struck a chord with me, and it made me say, "Oh my god, he really is who he says he is," and I'm gonna go to all the people I talk to and say, "I was wrong, Commissioner Salzman really does care about our kids," because you're right, we care more about our puppies and ponies than we do about our kids. So thank you and I'm sorry. Now, I'm here to talk to you today because I live in the Kids Zone. The Kids Zone is everything within a quarter-mile walk of the Northwest Cultural District, and that includes Con-Edison Park on the river there. The Kids Zone is a zone where infants, toddlers, and youth come to play, work, learn, entertain, and entertain and live. I'd like to invite Mr. Paulson to come and move in there. Shirley Riley here is selling her home and I'd like to invite him to move in. It's a huge historic home. He'd have neighbors like little Carson, three years old. The reason he wouldn't want to live in our neighborhood is this, and I'm sorry to say.

He gets his bag and opens it, pouring a pile of refuse on the lectern. At the same time, the video shifts from live feed to the actual Portland City Council meeting video with the actual Pete Colt. The actor begins to sync his movements with the video.

PETE COLT: These are from the McDonald's on 18th Street, the Episcopal Learning Center, the Catholic girls' school right across the street from the children's symphonic choir? Those of you who know me from the neighborhood know that I pick up this stuff every day. I do not clean up the vomit on Thirsty Thursdays. Although I do draw a line at bodily fluids.

SECRETARY: You're about at time—

The SECRETARY gives COUNCILOR 5 / FISH a script.

PETE COLT: Thank you—the rector at Trinity Seminary and I agree that it gets tiring to pick up used condoms.

The SECRETARY rings a bell, then instructs COUNCILOR 5 / FISH to point their left finger (as in the video) at PETE COLT during the following testimony.

COUNCILOR 5 / FISH: Mr. Colt. Your time's up, but I have a more fundamental concern. What you've just put on that table is actually just considered hazardous material. And I don't know what you put there, what drugs are involved, but we now have a public health issue.

PETE COLT: Thank you for agreeing with me. Thank you for making my point better than I ever could. Thank you for saying exactly what it is. The question is, how are we gonna help these kids?

COUNCILOR 1 / SALZMAN: You know, Pete, security just reminded me that we have other people come up to testify on that chair. So I think we're gonna take a recess until we can get someone to come up here with some alcohol, some Clorox, because it would be unfair to have another—

COUNCILOR 5 / FISH: We appreciate your passion, but this was not at all well thought out.

SECRETARY: We're going to take a recess for about ten minutes. We're really going to need everyone to leave right now, so we can disinfect.

COUNCILOR 1 / SALZMAN: That's it, folks. We're going to take a ten-minute recess.

SECRETARY: Please clear the room, everyone.

The SECRETARY and staffers clear the room.

End of meeting. Following the meeting, audience members leave the space so that the stage can be cleared away and rearranged for the local ending. The intermission lasts approximately fifteen minutes.

Local Ending: Tempe

NANCY HORMANN: chairperson of the Downtown Tempe Community organization

SMILEZ: aka Heather Hernandez, formerly unhoused young adult from Tempe

SHANE: arborist for the City of Tempe

DARCI NIVA: employee of the City of Tempe and church director

The audience reenters the stage space. The council meeting setup has been cleared, and there are thirty ficus trees spaced evenly around the stage. Four video monitors are spaced around the stage as well. The curtains to the auditorium are closed, so we are enclosed in this small forest of ficus. Two previously homeless young people who participated in the meeting are reading the index cards that the audience filled out in the meeting into the microphone.

Live video feed of the ficus plays as the audience enters. NANCY HORMANN and SMILEZ appear on video. SHANE's voice-over is spoken by Aaron, with images of ficus trees on video. DARCI NIVA is live onstage at a microphone, surrounded by signs made by homeless people asking for change.

NANCY HORMANN: My name is Nancy Hormann. I work for the Downtown Tempe Community or DTC. I'm not here today, although I'd like to be, because it's a holiday weekend and we had long-standing plans to be out of town.

SMILEZ: I am Heather Hernandez. I live on Thomas Avenue, just across the line in Phoenix, but spent time on the streets in Tempe. My family is from this area and I've lived here my whole life. I may be here with you tonight, but illness and other circumstances may prevent that.

SHANE: My name is Shane Mueller, and I work for the city. I'm just here to answer questions about the trees, especially along Mill Avenue.

DARCI NIVA: My name is Darci Niva. My job involves getting services to people who need them, whether it's job searches, job training, counseling, rehab, or a home. I work for the City of Tempe, and I also just finished my MA at ASU. My job is to interact with people and provide services. That's why I'm here in person.

NANCY HORMANN: I performed on Broadway forty-five years ago, in *You're a Good Man, Charlie Brown*. And then I got tired of rejection. I went back to graduate school, and I raised a family. I started the first BID in California, in downtown Sacramento, and then worked in San Francisco. I particularly enjoyed living in Sacramento because there are parks in the middle of almost every neighborhood.

SMILEZ: A bus pass costs $55 a month. My son Quintin's birthday is February 28, 2009. Rent is $512 a month. My dad's birthday was yesterday, February 15. He is my number one supporter. He passed away a year ago in January. In seventh grade I won the talent show for a portrayal of my mother, which she did not appreciate. I have not performed onstage since that time. Sometimes my boyfriend and I plug in our phones and put them next to each other all night. So it's like we sleep together on the phone.

NANCY HORMANN: There are the ones who are truly homeless, and the ones who are choosing to live this way. And with those people, it's part of a migratory route, from Seattle to Portland to Tempe. A while ago a group of us took part in a roundtable with some of the street population, a police representative, and a council member, and we had them in to try and talk about what we could do to coexist. Obviously there was a disconnect, as one guy brought a machete with him. And after we'd pressed them for about a half an hour, they finally said the reason that they come here to hang out is that with the abundance of pedestrian traffic, they make more money panhandling here than anywhere else in the Valley.

SHANE: Mill Avenue is stressful. The trees show their stress—the stress of being exposed to the direct sunlight, asphalt, heat, car exhaust, and sometimes drunk people grabbing branches and breaking them off. The business owners want them to be pruned higher than they should be and that's stressful for them. The trees get a canker, or they get this kind of black film you can see along them.

SMILEZ: We call those guys in the yellow shirts Bumblebees. Or the Yellow-Jackets. A person who hangs out on Mill Ave is called a Millrat. Some of them rub charcoal on their faces, or dirt or whatever, and then panhandle.

NANCY HORMANN: I'd say there are about thirty regular so-called Millrats. And about 90 percent of them are doing this by choice. The disabled, the older ones, or the military veteran in a wheelchair, they for the most part don't bother anyone. It's the guy who grabs food off a diner's plate at an outdoor café or the group of unkempt youth barking obscenities at passersby—conscious not to break any existing law. The Millrats make it harder for people who are truly homeless, as they harden people's perception of those who live on the streets.

DARCI NIVA: I used to do advocacy in the nonprofit world, through my church. But in my job now I am responsible to the points of view of everyone —the homeless, the government, the business owners, the downtown committee. My first impulse is to support the homeless, because I'm familiar with what they are going through. But then you hear from someone who runs a small business downtown, and they're like, "I poured everything into this, and when they sit outside I can't get people to come in."

SMILEZ: I've been in my apartment for almost five months. This is the longest I have lived in one place since eighth grade. I am twenty-three years old. The first night in my apartment, I couldn't sleep because I was used to, like, eighteen people crowded into a four-person tent. I needed more people near me. This didn't make any sense to sleep alone.

SHANE: This company comes in from California, West Coast Arbor, and once a year, in October, they bring their trucks and equipment and they trim and prune everything. They have a crew of six people and they are here for a week, working eight hours a day.

SMILEZ: I'm three months behind on rent.

SHANE: We do irrigation, so they get water, underground, three hours a day, four days a week, mixed with a little fertilizer. It's like an IV drip with little vitamins in it. And we do street cleaning, power washing, garbage, seven days a week from 3 AM to 6 AM or so.

DARCI NIVA: I think there are not enough resources here to handle the number of homeless people we have.

NANCY HORMANN: In Dallas the city decided to do four economic development zones, not all of them downtown, and they made those no-panhandling zones. When we brought that up to the city attorney, he informed us of a recent ruling that would make it extremely difficult to get through this circuit court, because of First Amendment issues. This circuit court has overturned many attempts by cities in the west, so there is little chance anything that might interfere with someone's right of expression is going to pass.

SHANE: We prune up from the inside, so you start in the center and you take out any excess and work your way to the end of a branch. You get rid of the density, because the density is what makes the starlings want to nest there.

SMILEZ: In eighth grade I was valedictorian of my class, and I gave a speech at the Marquis Theater. It made me really nervous, like this makes me really nervous. And also in eighth grade I was in the citywide spelling bee, and I placed seventh, because I messed up *peanut butter*. Because somebody told me that if you're nervous, you should try and imagine everyone around you naked. And that will make you less nervous. And so I did, and when *peanut butter* came up, I spelled *peanut balls* because that is what I was seeing all around me.

SHANE: The starlings give us a lot of trouble. They are here from about October, November through about April. They're gone when it gets too hot.

NANCY HORMANN: When I was in San Francisco, we put up a camera near this one guy—he was at the same place every day, day in and day out, in front of a store. And we put the camera on him so we could calculate how much money he was making. And we figured he was making about $60,000 a year from panhandling. And so why don't we tax that?

DARCI NIVA: There was this study about a guy in New York they called Million Dollar Murray. And they calculated that by the time he died, he'd cost the city over a million dollars in services. Meaning, when he didn't have health care, he had to go to the emergency room. And when he didn't have housing and got busted for vagrancy, he went to jail. And that costs more than just housing the guy. And, you know, people feel like, "Well, how come this guy gets a house for free, when I have to pay for my house?"

SMILEZ: I think the average person, the average woman, let's say 25 to 26 years old, you'd need about $4,000 a month to live. Because women, you need rent, food, clothes, you need to get around, and you need like your body wash and makeup. Women—you need like twenty different kinds of eye shadow, and you're expected to have that. For me and Q to get by for a month, I think we'd spend about $2,500 to $3,000. Oh, and I think I know who brought the machete to the meeting she talked about.

DARCI NIVA: My husband and I just closed down our church. And the city got really excited because we have this building over on Apache, and the city is looking for somewhere to provide basic services. And the city is hoping to do that in our building, and the downtown business owners are excited about it because it takes the homeless away from downtown. But that community is really organized. They just had that Gracie's Tower development, that was really contentious. They think this will attract crime and cut property values.

SMILEZ: If I had a place on Mill Avenue, I would let homeless people use the bathroom. Because otherwise let's say you're homeless there, Starbucks won't let you use the bathroom, and neither will McDonald's, and so you have to go to Tumbleweed. But Tumbleweed closes at 4 PM and then you have to go to the campsite. But you can't get into the campsite until 2 AM sometimes, or at least after 10 PM. So I would let people use the bathroom.

SHANE: The trees, they really can suffer in the heat. June, July, August, when it gets up around 116 degrees, and the tree is out there in front of the bank building with the mirrored glass. That's when you start to see the signs of distress.

DARCI NIVA: Just like you start to see the signs you talked about on the trees, from stresses of being in an environment that's not what they're used to, you start seeing that on people. Because now they can't speak, because of the panhandling ordinance, you don't hear it, but you see it. The way being without a home can affect you over time, in the wrong environment.

NANCY HORMANN: In three or four years, if there's not a real solution, the city will be a larger haven for people who choose to beg for a living. So we want to shorten the time frame. So that in ten years it's not a problem.

DARCI NIVA: I think that these people, who are here by choice, even though it's difficult to deal with them, and I understand the business owners' concerns, they represent something larger that is falling apart for us, as a nation. And there should be a place for that.

Images of ficus return to the screens. Audience members who have received a sound file during the intermission are instructed by the staffers to play the file on their phones. It is the sound of starlings, a murmuration, in the trees. As their individual phones build in volume and numbers, the same sound cue plays over the auditorium speakers from behind the curtain and grows louder. The curtain slowly opens, revealing the empty auditorium, stage lights streaming onstage until the last lone cell phone plays the end of the file.

End of performance, Tempe.

Notes

PROLOGUE

1. David Savran and Peter Sellars, *Breaking the Rules: The Wooster Group* (New York: Theatre Communications Group, 1993).
2. Pete Colt, citizen testimony, Portland (Oregon) City Council meeting, April 15, 2009.
3. Jacques Rancière, *Dissensus: On Politics and Aesthetics*, trans. Steven Corcoran (London: Continuum, 2010), 51–53.
4. Joseph Beuys, *Joseph Beuys in America: Energy Plan for the Western Man*, ed. Carin Kuoni (New York: Four Walls Eight Windows, 1993), 19.
5. Barack Obama, U.S. Democratic Convention Speech, July 27, 2016.
6. Greg Sargent, "Donald Trump Is Not Qualified to Be President. And the American People Know It," *Washington Post*, July 18, 2016.

HOW WE GOT HERE

1. Erving Goffman, *The Presentation of Self in Everyday Life* (Doubleday/Anchor Books, 1959).
2. Erving Goffman, "The Arts of Impression Management," in *The Presentation of Self in Everyday Life* (Doubleday/Anchor Books, 1959).
3. Beuys, *Joseph Beuys in America*.
4. Jacques Rancière, *The Emancipated Spectator*, trans. Gregory Elliot (Verso, 2009).
5. Rancière, *Emancipated Spectator*.
6. Rancière, *Emancipated Spectator*.

WHAT IS A CITY COUNCIL MEETING?

1. Bismarck, North Dakota, city commissioners meeting, June 22, 2010.
2. Mike Seminary, in conversation with Aaron Landsman, June 22, 2010.
3. Victor DeSantis and Tari Renner, "City Government Structures: An Attempt at Clarification," *State & Local Government Review* 34, no. 2 (Spring 2002).
4. David S. Yassky, "Learning from Washington: A New Approach to Analyzing the Structure of New York City's Government," *New York Law School Law Review* 58 (2014), http://digitalcommons.pace.edu/lawfaculty/929.

5. Liz Navratil, "Most of Minneapolis City Council Pledges to 'Begin the Process of Ending' Police Department," *Minneapolis Star Tribune*, June 8, 2020, https://www.startribune.com/mpls-council-majority-backs-dismantling-police-department/571088302/.

6. Dana Rubinstein and Jeffery C. Mays, "Nearly $1 Billion Is Shifted from Police in Budget That Pleases No One," *New York Times*, June 30, 2020, https://www.nytimes.com/2020/06/30/nyregion/nypd-budget.html.

7. Bernadette Hogan, "Less than 20% of NYC Voters Cast Ballots This Year," *New York Post*, November 6, 2019, https://nypost.com/2019/11/06/less-than-20-of-nyc-voters-cast-ballots-this-year.

THE ORIENTATION VIDEO

1. Rancière, *Dissensus*, 30–31.

2. Brian Kanouse, "Humanities Expert Report on City Council Meeting," prepared for a New Hampshire Humanities council grant final report.

THE ROOM AND US IN IT

1. Ken Gewertz, "Augusto Boal's 'Theatre of the Oppressed,'" *Harvard Gazette*, December 11, 2003, https://news.harvard.edu/gazette/story/2003/12/augusto-boals-theatre-of-the-oppressed/.

2. Dominique Morisseau, "Why I Almost Slapped a Fellow Theater Patron, and What That Says about Our Theaters," *American Theatre*, December 9, 2015.

MEET THE STAFF

1. Rancière, *Dissensus*, 29.

2. Assata Richards, email message to Aaron Landsman, February 13, 2013.

A NEW WAY TO ACT

1. John Avalos, in conversation with Aaron Landsman, July 2014.

2. Goffman, *Presentation of Self in Everyday Life*, 6.

3. Rachel Barnard, Rad Pereira, and Mierle Laderman Ukeles, "City as Partner: Three Artists on Collaborating with Government Agencies," *A Blade of Grass*, no. 2 (2017), https://www.abladeofgrass.org/articles/city-partner-three-artists-collaborating-government-agencies/; Pam Korza, "Inside Artist-Municipal Partnerships," *Americans for the Arts* (blog), December 3, 2018, https://www.americansforthearts.org/2019/05/15/inside-artist-municipal-partnerships.

THE ARRIVAL OF JIM FINDLAY

1. Rancière, *Emancipated Spectator*.
2. Jim Findlay, in conversation with Aaron Landsman and Mallory Catlett, July 2017.
3. Findlay, in conversation with the authors, July 2017.

ACT 3, HOUSTON

1. Goffman, *Presentation of Self in Everyday Life*.

ACT 4, OPEN TESTIMONY

1. Rancière, *Emancipated Spectator*, 17.
2. "US Occupy Protesters Clash with Police at Oakland Port," *BBC News*, November 3, 2011, https://www.bbc.com/news/world-us-canada-15568057.

ORGANIZING AT HOME AND ON THE ROAD

1. Tim Etchells, *Certain Fragments: Contemporary Performance and Forced Entertainment* (London: Taylor & Francis, 1999), 49.
2. David M. Brown, "Arts Help Incarcerated Women Unmask True Worth," *AZ Republic/Mountain Times*, April 15, 2014.

PAYING FOR TIME

1. Isaac Kaplan, "Can Artists Do Anything to Help Detroit?" *Artsy.net*, May 10, 2016, https://www.artsy.net/article/artsy-editorial-can-artists-actually-do-anything-to-help-detroit.

PARTICIPANT-OBSERVER INTERVIEWS

1. Gregory Snyder, *Graffiti Lives: Beyond the Tag in New York's Urban Underground* (NYU Press, 2008), 13–16.
2. Snyder, *Graffiti Lives*, 21–22.
3. Snyder, *Graffiti Lives*, 19–22.
4. According to Oregon State University's Human Research Protection Program and Institutional Review Board, "The Institutional Review Board (IRB) is an administrative body established to protect the rights and welfare of human research subjects recruited to participate in research activities conducted under the auspices of the institution with which it is affiliated." https://research.oregonstate.edu/irb/frequently-asked-questions/what-institutional-review-board-irb.
5. Aaron Landsman and Adam Davidson, personal email exchange, May 2012.

NARRATORS AND TRANSLATORS

1. Rancière, *Emancipated Spectator*, 22.

HOUSTON

1. Coco Fusco, "Elevator Repair Service," *BOMB Magazine*, April 1, 1999, https://bombmagazine.org/articles/elevator-repair-service/.
2. Hilton Als, "Real Gone Girl," *New Yorker*, October 27, 2014, https://www.newyorker.com/magazine/2014/11/03/real-gone-girl.
3. Kathryn McNeil, in conversation with Aaron Landsman, September–October 2011.
4. Stephen Costello, in conversation with Aaron Landsman, 2011.
5. Igor Volsky, "Anti-Gay Pastor Continues Crusade Against Houston Mayor Parker: 'We Are on the Side that God has Declared,'" *Think Progress*, March 5, 2012, https://archive.thinkprogress.org/anti-gay-pastor-continues-crusade-against-houston-mayor-parker-we-are-on-the-side-that-god-has-349f822ed33/.
6. Stephen Costello, in conversation with Aaron Landsman, winter 2012.
7. Costello, in conversation, winter 2012.
8. Leigh Cutler, "Eldorado Ballroom," *Houston Review* 4, no. 1 (Fall 2006).
9. *City Council Meeting* viewer, in conversation with the artists, November 2, 2012.
10. Assata Richards, in conversation with Mallory Catlett and Aaron Landsman, February 2020.
11. Richards, in conversation, February 2020.
12. Katie Watkins and Jen Rice, "Turner Leads Houston's Mayoral Race and Voters Support METRO Bond, HPM-KHOU 11 Poll Finds," *Houston Public Media*, September 25, 2019, https://www.houstonpublicmedia.org/articles/news/politics/2019/09/25/347042/turner-leads-houstons-mayoral-race-and-voters-support-metro-bond-hpm-khou-poll-finds.
13. Bob Rehak, "Background on Houston Proposition A," *Reduce Flooding—NOW!*, October 20, 2018, https://reduceflooding.com/2018/10/20/background-on-houston-proposition-a-drainage-fee-re-vote.
14. Jasper Scherer, "Houston Mayoral Foes Debate City Finances, Drainage Fee, Airport Intern," *Houston Chronicle*, October 9, 2019, https://www.houstonchronicle.com/news/houston-texas/houston/article/Houston-mayoral-foes-debate-city-finances-14501858.php.
15. "Texas 2019 Ballot Measures," *Ballotpedia*, https://ballotpedia.org/Texas_2019_ballot_measures.

TEMPE

1. The Downtown Tempe Community, sort of like the chamber of commerce.
2. "ASU Gammage, an Architectural Landmark, a Home for the Arts," https://www.asugammage.com/about/asu-gammage.
3. Brown, "Arts Help Incarcerated Women."
4. Gregory Sale, in conversation with Mallory Catlett and Aaron Landsman, fall 2011.
5. Elizabeth Johnson, in conversation with Aaron Landsman and Mallory Catlett, February 2020.
6. Laura Latzko, "*Native Nation*: Immersive New Play about Issues Facing Indigenous People," *Phoenix New Times*, April 24, 2019, https://www.phoenixnewtimes.com/arts/native-nation-theater-issues-facing-native-americans-asu-gammage-11270554.
7. Gregory Sale, in conversation with Mallory Catlett and Aaron Landsman, February 2020.
8. Johnson, in conversation with the authors, February 2020.
9. Susie Steckner, "Tempe Boosts Care for Homeless by $1 Million," *Wrangler News*, June 21, 2019, https://www.wranglernews.com/2019/06/21/tempe-boosts-care-for-homeless-by-1-million.
10. Tempe city hall staffer, in conversation with Mallory Catlett and Aaron Landsman, fall 2012.

NEW YORK CITY

1. Valerie Strauss, "Mike Bloomberg Was in Charge of the Country's Largest Public School District. Here Are 8 Key Questions for Him," *Washington Post*, February 25, 2020, https://www.washingtonpost.com/education/2020/02/25/mike-bloomberg-was-charge-countrys-largest-public-school-district-here-are-8-key-questions-him.
2. David M. Herszenhorn, "Bloomberg Wins on School Tests after Firing Foes," *New York Times*, March 16, 2004, https://www.nytimes.com/2004/03/16/nyregion/bloomberg-wins-on-school-tests-after-firing-foes.html.
3. "Seven Years of Mayoral Control," *Gotham Gazette*, https://www.gothamgazette.com/index.php/archives/377-seven-years-of-mayoral-control.
4. Nicole Davis, "Tracing the Roots of Co-Located Schools," *Brooklyn Based*, June 21, 2011, https://brooklynbased.com/2011/06/21/tracing-the-roots-of-co-located-schools.
5. Valerie Strauss, "The Case Against Pearson—and Its Response," *Washington Post*, April 21, 2016, https://www.washingtonpost.com/news/answer-sheet/wp/2016/04/21/the-case-against-pearson-and-its-response.
6. Clyde Haberman, "Bloomberg Got What He Wanted, But at What Price?" *New*

York Times, October 23, 2008, https://www.nytimes.com/2008/10/24/nyregion/24nyc.html.

7. Dan Rosenblum, "The Anti-chancellor," *Politico,* August 3, 2011, https://www.politico.com/states/new-york/city-hall/story/2011/08/the-anti-chancellor-scott-stringers-education-board-appointee-objects-to-dennis-walcott-again-and-again-067223.

8. Patrick Sullivan, Panel for Educational Policy meeting, August 16, 2010.

9. Eliza Shapiro, "Segregation Has Been the Story of New York City's Schools for 50 Years," *New York Times,* March 26, 2019, https://www.nytimes.com/2019/03/26/nyregion/school-segregation-new-york.html.

10. Rancière, *Emancipated Spectator,* 22.

11. Rancière, *Emancipated Spectator,* 22.

12. Kim Whitener, in conversation with Mallory Catlett and Aaron Landsman, January 2020.

13. Alannah Bilal, in conversation with Mallory Catlett and Aaron Landsman, June 2020.

14. Victoria Vazquez, in conversation with Mallory Catlett and Aaron Landsman, July 2020.

15. Vazquez, in conversation with the authors, July 2020.

16. New York State Education Department, "State Education Department Releases Spring 2018 Grades 3–8 ELA & Math Assessment Results," news release, September 26, 2018, http://www.nysed.gov/news/2018/state-education-department-releases-spring-2018-grades-3-8-ela-math-assessment-results.

17. Principal Claudia de Luna Castro, email to parent association of Earth School (PS 364), May 2020.

18. Patrick Sullivan, quoted in Liza Featherstone, "Report Card: Our Fake School Board," *Brooklyn Rail,* September 2011, https://brooklynrail.org/2011/09/local/report-card-our-fake-school-board.

19. Dana Rubinstein and Jeffery C. Mays, "De Blasio and Council, Facing Fiscal Crisis over Virus, Agree on Budget with Big Cuts," *New York Times,* June 29, 2020, https://www.nytimes.com/2020/06/29/nyregion/nyc-budget-police.html.

SAN FRANCISCO

1. "For You," http://www.foryou.productions/home.

2. David Szlasa, in conversation with Mallory Catlett and Aaron Landsman, July 2020.

3. "For You: Artists and Elders," http://www.foryou.productions/artistsandelders.

4. Erika Chong Shuch, in conversation with Mallory Catlett and Aaron Landsman, July 2020.

5. Kelly O'Mara, "In a Changing City, How Does the Tenderloin Stay the Same?"

KQED, February 27, 2020, https://www.kqed.org/news/11803642/in-a-changing -city-how-does-the-tenderloin-stay-the-same.

KEENE, NEW HAMPSHIRE

1. New Hampshire Employment Security, "Community Profiles: Keene, NH," https://www.nhes.nh.gov/elmi/products/cp/profiles-htm/keene.htm.
2. Brian Quigley, Carl Jacobs, and Sharon Fantl, in conversation with Mallory Catlett and Aaron Landsman, 2012–13.
3. Brad Mielke, "5 New Hampshire Diners Candidates Need to Visit to Win the State's Primary," *ABC News*, October 20, 2015, https://abcnews.go.com/Politics /hampshire-diners-presidential-candidates-visit-win-states-primary.
4. Trent Spiner, "Keene Pumpkin Fest Breaks World Record," *WMUR Radio*, October 20, 2013, https://www.wmur.com/article/keene-pumpkin-fest-breaks -world-record/5185389#.
5. Andy Bohannon, in conversation with Mallory Catlett and Aaron Landsman, November 2012.
6. Keene City Council, https://ci.keene.nh.us/my-city-government/city-council.
7. Meghan Foley, "City Council Approves Pay Raise, More Money for Social Service Agencies," *Keene Sentinel,* June 3, 2016, https://www.sentinelsource.com/news /local/city-council-approves-pay-raise-more-money-for-social-service-agencies.
8. Local residents, in conversation with Mallory Catlett and Aaron Landsman, October 2014.
9. "The History of Heberton Hall in Keene," *Keene Sentinel,* May 18, 2010, https:// www.sentinelsource.com/news/local/the-history-of-heberton-hall-in-keene.
10. Sharon Fantl, in conversation with Mallory Catlett and Aaron Landsman, February 2020.
11. Paul Cuno-Booth, "Changes to Downtown Pitched with New Keene Arts Corri- dor Plan," *Keene Sentinel,* June 28, 2019, https://www.sentinelsource.com/news /local/changes-to-downtown-pitched-with-new-keene-arts-corridor-plan.
12. Brian Quigley, in conversation with Mallory Catlett and Aaron Landsman, February 2020.
13. Colin Trombley, in conversation with Mallory Catlett and Aaron Landsman, February 2020.

HUMANITIES AND PUBLIC LIFE

Behind the Big House:
Reconciling Slavery, Race, and Heritage in the U.S. South
by Jodi Skipper

Call My Name, Clemson:
Documenting the Black Experience in
an American University Community
by Rhondda Robinson Thomas

The City We Make Together:
City Council Meeting's *Primer for Participation*
by Mallory Catlett and Aaron Landsman

Contested City:
Art and Public History as Mediation at New York's
Seward Park Urban Renewal Area
by Gabrielle Bendiner-Viani

Engaging the Age of Jane Austen:
Public Humanities in Practice
by Bridget Draxler and Danielle Spratt

The Penelope Project:
An Arts-Based Odyssey to Change Elder Care
edited by Anne Basting, Maureen Towey, and Ellie Rose

See You in the Streets:
Art, Action, and Remembering the
Triangle Shirtwaist Factory Fire
by Ruth Sergel